Hippolytus of Rome
Contra Noetum

Text introduced,
edited and translated by

Robert Butterworth, S.J.

HEYTHROP MONOGRAPHS
London, 1977

De licentia Superioris Ordinis

Composer set by
Margaret Helps, King's Lynn, Norfolk
Printed by
Tonbridge Printers Limited,
Peach Hall Works, Tonbridge,
Kent TN10 3HD, England

MATRIBUS

CONTENTS

		Page
Introduction		i
Abbreviations		iv
Chapter 1	The growth of the problem	1
Chapter 2	The text of the *Contra Noetum*	34
Chapter 3	The structure of the *Contra Noetum*	94
Chapter 4	The style of the *Contra Noetum*	118
Bibliography		142
Index of biblical quotations and allusions		147
Index of Greek words of general theological interest		149
Index of modern authors		154

INTRODUCTION

There cannot be many patristic writings which have suffered from the same mixture of constant use and basic neglect as the *Contra Noetum* (CN). CN has been known to scholars for almost four centuries; the text has been 'edited' no less than five times; there can hardly be either a history of Christian doctrine or a dogmatic textbook which does not refer to it and even quote it; no account of pre-Nicene theology could possibly be complete without some extended treatment of it. And yet such constant use has somehow succeeded only in diverting from the work the undivided attention that it deserves in its own right. In the discussions of scholars CN has been relegated to an interesting but minor role — a luckily preserved fragment of a larger but now otherwise lost treatise from the earlier part of the Hippolytean corpus. Even recent and heated controversy about the extent of this corpus failed notably to make any new approach to CN. The view of CN accepted for the last two-and-a-half centuries has rarely been questioned: but now even the questioning seems to have stopped.

It is to the problem of CN as a text — to the exclusion, at least for the present, of other distracting issues — that the severely limited study which follows seeks to make a new approach. For this purpose many all-too-familiar landmarks in the discussion of CN will simply be missing. Thus, for instance, the problem of authorship will not be touched. It is presumed for the moment that there does not seem to be any clear reason why the accepted author, Hippolytus of Rome, could not have written CN: though it may be that the results of this study will make it harder to believe that he did. Again, the problem of the relationship between CN and the normally accepted Hippolytean corpus and other writings is carefully ignored. Again, neither all the theological problems in CN itself are brought to light, nor are those that are fully treated.

It is in the interest of a much-needed and new approach to CN that these problems have been passed by. Or rather, postponed. For this present study is based on the contention that unless and until certain basic questions concerning the character of CN as a text are properly approached and adequately solved, further discussion about the above-mentioned problems is bound to be fruitless. First, there is the question of *the text* of CN, preserved in a sole manuscript. What has to be asked and answered here is whether the ms-text is, as far as can be gauged, a sound one. For some three centuries or so no scholar seems to have consulted the ms; and of the two editions of the text published this century — where at least a photocopy of the ms was used — one is inaccessible and not entirely perfect (Schwartz) and the other is notoriously over-imaginative (Nautin). So in Chapter 2 of this study the text of CN, taken straight from the ms, is given. A glance at the *apparatus* will show that there is little reason to doubt its substantial integrity and reliability.

Once it is clear that the text of CN is fit for use, the second question to be asked is about *the structure* of CN. In Chapter 3 there are presented a set of new findings concerning the structuration of the work. Far from revealing no more than the two obvious halves of the whole, careful analysis shows that CN is constructed according to an impressively rigorous and elaborate plan. The body of the work is in two closely, indeed perfectly corresponding halves; and there is a dramatically told Introduction at the beginning, and a solemn Peroration at the end, corresponding exactly to one of the most important parts of the Introduction. The structure of CN is such as to preclude the possibility of its being a fragment of another work. CN stands plainly on its own feet. And it is this finding which is perhaps the most important result of this present study.

But not the only result. The solution of the question about the structure serves to bring up a further question about *the style* of CN. If CN is a work whose structure shows it to be a literary unity as it stands, what might be the literary genre of such a work? In Chapter 4 some hitherto unnoticed remarks of Norden on CN are for the first time fully developed to show, with the help of a brilliant style-analysis by Bultmann, that the style of CN, its modes of argument, and even, to some extent, its newly discovered structure, all point clearly to the influence of diatribe. Again the conclusion to be drawn is that CN is a popular discourse on a single theme, and not the end-fragment of a lost anti-heretical treatise.

It is the answering of such questions about CN that constitutes the new approach to CN which this study claims to be. A problem of very long standing is laid to rest. And to show how bogus and man-made a problem it was, Chapter 1 first traces its growth and progress at the hands of generations of scholars. The problem of CN, as normally conceived, has never really been that of the work itself, but always that of the supposed relationship of CN and its theology to other writings and their theology. But CN itself is too important a theological work to be treated thus peripherally. The need has been for attention to be refocussed on CN itself.

It remains only to thank my benign mentor, Fr Antonio Orbe, S.J., and Michael Walsh, whose editorial zeal has finally unearthed my findings.

Easter 1977, London   *Robert Butterworth*

ABBREVIATIONS

CSCO	*Corpus scriptorum christianorum orientalium,* ed. J.-B. Chabot *et al.,* Louvain − Rome − Paris, 1903−
CSHB	*Corpus scriptorum historiae byzantinae,* ed. B.G. Niebuhr, Bonn 1829−
GCS	*Die griechischen christlichen Schriftsteller der ersten drei Jahrhunderte,* Leipzig − Berlin, 1897−
JTS	*The Journal of Theological Studies,* London − Oxford, 1900−
MélSR	*Mélanges de science religieuse,* Lille, 1944−
NRT	*Nouvelle revue théologique,* (Louvain) Tournai − Paris, 1869−
PG	*Patrologia graeca,* ed. J.-P. Migne, Paris, 1857−66.
PL	*Patrologia latina,* ed. J.-P. Migne, Paris, 1844−64.
PO	*Patrologia orientalis,* ed. R. Graffin and F. Nau, Paris, 1907−
RAC	*Reallexikon für Antike und Christentum,* ed. T. Klauser, Stuttgart, 1950−
RechSR	*Recherches de science religieuse,* Paris, 1910−
RTAM	*Recherches de théologie ancienne et médiévale,* Louvain, 1929−
RBén	*Revue Bénédictine,* Maredsous, 1884−
RHE	*Revue d'histoire ecclésiastique,* Louvain, 1900−
RevSR	*Revue des sciences religieuses,* Strasbourg, 1921−
RSPT	*Revue des sciences philosophiques et théologiques,* Paris, 1907−
SC	*Sources chrétiennes,* ed. H. de Lubac and J. Daniélou, Paris, 1941−
TU	*Texte und Untersuchungen zur Geschichte der altchristlichen Literatur,* ed. O. von Gebhardt and A. von Harnack *et al.,* Leipzig, 1883−

1
THE GROWTH OF THE PROBLEM

Vaticanus graecus 1431 and CN

The problem of CN, as we shall come to see, is still very much alive. In a study of CN such as is undertaken here it will be necessary, before all else, to trace the growth of the problem as it exists today. For this purpose it is imperative to go back to the sole manuscript copy of CN, to describe its provenance and its setting in the florilegium where it is found, and then to show what generations of scholars have made of this important piece of theological writing.

CN is to be found, unconnected with any other work seemingly integral and under its own proper title, in a single ms, *Vaticanus graecus 1431*.[1] This superb parchment codex, whose purpose has been the subject of a number of studies,[2] appears to be in the main (f.22r2–360r1) a later copy of a dogmatic florilegium which Timothy Aelurus, the opponent of the Council of Chalcedon, composed

---

1 Two derived Vatican mss, *Ottobonianus gr. 384* and *Barberinianus gr. 497,* have not been used in the preparation of this study. See P. Nautin, *Hippolyte, Contre les Hérésies, Fragment,* Paris 1949, p. 77–8, for details. Some of the material reviewed in this present chapter has been helpfully collected by Nautin: but for a rather different purpose.

2 Notably: E. Schwartz, *Codex Vaticanus gr. 1431: eine antichalkedonische Sammlung aus der Zeit Kaiser Zenos,* in *Abhandlungen der Bayrischen Akademie der Wissenschaften,* Philosophisch-philologische und historische Klasse, XXXII, 6, Munich 1927; R. Draguet, *Le florilège antichalcédonien du Vatic. Graec. 1431,* in RHE 24 (1928) pp. 51–62; R. Devreesse, *Les premières années du monophysisme: une collection antichalcédonienne,* in RSPT 19 (1930) pp.251–265. The main issues debated in these historical studies are hardly relevant to the present one. Also of interest is: M. Richard, *Les florilèges diphysites du Ve et du VIe siècle,* in *Das Konzil von Chalkedon,* (ed. A. Grillmeier and H. Bacht) Würzburg 1951, I, pp.721–748.

during his exile in the Chersonese (A.D. 458–474).[3] According to Schwartz's analysis of the contents of the codex,[4] the florilegium is preceded (f.1r1–22r1) by an exchange of letters between Denis of Alexandria and Paul of Samosata, along with a letter of six bishops to the latter; and is followed (f.360r2–369v2) by two works, CN under the title ὁμιλία Ἱππολύτου ἀρχιεπισκόπου Ῥώμης καὶ μάρτυρος εἰς τὴν αἵρεσιν Νοητοῦ τινος (f.360r2–367r1), and the unascribed πρὸς Ἰουδαίους ἀποδεικτική (f.367r2–369v2). It is only with the former of these last two works that this present study is concerned.

It is difficult to offer a convincing reason for the sudden, unique appearance of CN in the codex. The early history of the codex itself does not help, since it can provide no more than the possible context in which the copy of an original collection of documents might have been made. The codex certainly came to the Vatican Library, though not directly, from the Greek Abbey at Rossano in Calabria.[5] The Abbey, soon to be called St Mary 'Hodigitria' or, more popularly, 'of the *Patir*', after its founding-father, Bartholomew of Simeri,[6] was chartered by Roger II of Calabria and Sicily in September 1103, and was exempted from the jurisdiction of the reluctant local Ordinary by a bull of Pascal II in August 1105.[7] The 'Life' of Bartholomew relates how, after his ordination and installation as first Abbot at Rossano, he left for Constantinople not only in order to collect religious objects for his first foundation, but also to gather manuscripts to help his monks in their zealous searchings of the Scriptures. Most probably he did not visit Mount Athos.[8] The manuscripts he brought back were shared out among several foundations. There is no evidence that he brought back from the East either Vat. gr. 1431 itself or any original of which Vat. gr. 1431 is a copy.

Perhaps a little more help concerning the appearance of CN in the collection can be derived from a consideration of the work of the two scribes who seem

---

3 This is the purpose as summarized in R. Devreesse, *Introduction à l'étude des manuscrits grecs,* Paris 1954, p.183. See his longer treatment in RSPT 19 (1930) pp.255–265, for the historical background.

4 Op.cit., pp.5–9; see also H. Lietzmann, *Apollinaris von Laodicea und seine Schule,* Tübingen 1904, I, pp.96–100.

5 P. Batiffol, *L'Abbaye de Rossano: Contribution à l'histoire de la Vaticane,* Paris 1891, Chapter I, pp.1–32, gives a reconstruction of the foundation and later decline of the Abbey. But see W. Holtzmann, *Die ältesten Urkunden des Klosters S. Maria del Patir,* in *Byzantinische Zeitschrift* 26 (1926) pp.328–351, as complementing Batiffol.

6 R. Devreesse, *Les manuscrits grecs de l'Italie méridionale,* Città del Vaticano 1955, p.14, n.2; and P. Batiffol, op. cit., p.7f.

7 R. Devreesse, op. cit., pp.13–14; P. Batiffol, op. cit., pp.2–6, gives a more circumstantial account of the foundation.

8 P. Batiffol, op. cit, p.6 with n.4.

to have a hand in the copying of the codex. The first scribe was responsible for the greater part of the codex. His work runs from f.1r1 to f.309v1; and then he takes up his work again at f.360r2, precisely with CN, and continues to the end of the codex, f.369v2. A second scribe appears to have been responsible for the intervening ff., 310r1 to 360r1.[9] There is general agreement that Lietzmann's date for the Greek script in the codex is too early;[10] but where Schwartz is sure that the codex was copied at the Rossano Abbey shortly after its foundation,[11] just as he is confident that the copy was made from an Alexandrian original,[12] Devreesse is much more cautious about both its provenance and date: 'no one up to now has succeeded in determing either its date or its country of origin; for the fact that it came to the Vatican from Rossano does not in the least imply that it had been copied in Southern Italy'.[13] This uninformative situation is further obscured by Devreesse's considered belief that the second scribe employed 'une écriture d'imitation'.[14] Even so there is a certain measure of agreement that the date of the ms could be placed either in the twelfth or thirteenth century;[15] and this itself may point to the codex's having been copied at Rossano. This in turn may be suggested by a further interesting fact. Batiffol had asked whether Bartholomew of Simeri himself might not have been an active copyist as well as a collector of mss;[16] and although Devreesse has criticised Batiffol's reconstruction of a Rossano school of copyists which imitated the style of Constantinople,[17] it is noteworthy that a scribe Pachomius appears to have copied a Rossano ms (now Vat. gr. 2000, dated to 1102) 'with the help of our Father Bartholomew'.[18] Of course

---

9 P. Nautin, op. cit., pp.73–74, gives a description of the codex and discusses the work of the two scribes. See also H. Lietzmann, op. cit., pp.96–97. P. Franchi de' Cavalieri et J. Lietzmann, *Specimina Codicum Graecorum Vaticanorum*², Berlin and Leipzig 1929, plate 33, clearly displays the two scripts of Vat. gr. 1431. Lietzmann's theory (*Apollinaris von Laodicea . . .*, p.99) that the codex is in fact two codices joined together, has not found acceptance: see E. Schwartz, op. cit., pp.4–5, for arguments against it.
10 E. Schwartz, op. cit., p.4; R. Devreesse, RSPT 19 (1930) p.251. Lietzmann wished to date the codex to the ninth or tenth century.
11 E. Schwartz, op. cit., p.3.
12 Idem, *Zwei Predigten Hippolyts,* in *Sitzungsberichte der Bayrischen Akademie der Wissenschaften,* Philosophisch-historische Abteilung, Munich 1936, 3, p.3.
13 *Introduction à l'étude . . .*, p.35. See Plate X for a reproduction of f.351v. P. Nautin, op. cit., p.75, reports that Cardinal G. Mercati was similarly hesitant about the provenance of the script.
14 Op. cit., p.35, n.3; see also P. Franchi de' Cavalieri et J. Lietzmann, op. cit., p.XV: 'formas saeculi IX/X imitatur'.
15 P. Franchi de' Cavalieri et J. Lietzmann, op. cit., note to plate 33 (twelfth century); R.·Devreesse, op. cit., note to plate X (thirteenth century).
16 P. Batiffol, op. cit., p.38.
17 R. Devreesse, *Les manuscrits grecs . . .*, pp.24–5.
18 Ibid., p.25; but especially p.39, n.2.

this fact could prove nothing about the identity of the copyists of Vat. gr. 1431; but it does show that copying work was shared at Rossano, as appears to have been the case with Vat. gr. 1431. The rough dates ascribed to the copying work fit in well enough with a conclusion, more tentative than that of Schwartz, that the codex might well have been copied in the Abbey at Rossano in the early years of that foundation. It becomes unlikely, in view of the supposition that the codex was merely copied and not compiled at Rossano, that CN would have been added to the collection there. CN would have belonged to the collection before it was copied. But of the presence of CN in the collection, as it stands a distinct entity unrelated to any other work and under its own title which, whatever its value, proclaims it to be an anti-heretical discourse in its own right, there emerges no satisfying explanation.

It may still be possible to suggest one. On the flyleaf of the codex Cardinal Angelo Mai (1782–1854), the Vatican Librarian, has written the following note: 'Auctor huius Collectionis haereticus monophysita est. Vide p.342.6. A. Maius.' The reference is to f.342v2 where, immediately after the 'Henotikon' of Zeno (f.341r1–342v2), and before the next rubric title, the second scribe has copied the following comment of the original compiler, also in rubric: ἀναγκαῖον δὲ ἡγησάμην καὶ ταῦτα προσθῆναι τῷ βιβλίῳ πρὸς εἴδησιν τῆς ἐν αὐτοῖς κακοπιστίας.[19] The καὶ ταῦτα would seem to refer to the five works which then follow and conclude the codex. Their rubric titles read as follows:

(1) ἐπιστολὴ λέοντος ἐπισκόπου ρώμης πρὸς φλαυϊνὸν ἐπισκόπου κωσταντινουπόλεως (f.342v2–350r1);

(2) ὅρος τῆς συνόδου τῆς ἐν χαλκήδονι with τὸ σύμβολον τῶν ρΗ (f.350r1–353r2);

(3) ἐπιστολὴ λέοντος ἐπισκόπου ρώμης πρὸς τὸν βασιλέα λέοντα (f.353r2–360r1); then with a reversal to the hand of the first scribe,

(4) CN and

(5) πρὸς Ἰουδαίους ἀποδεικτική.

These works, it is clear, were included because of what the heretical compiler considered to be their κακοπιστία, in fact for their orthodoxy. In the context of a short collection of such works it can be seen why CN was included. Not only does its title, even if somewhat exaggerated or wrong in its description of Hippolytus as 'Archbishop of Rome and Martyr', make it an obvious choice to be put alongside two letters of Leo, 'Bishop of Rome', but also its anti-

---

19 This has been noted both by P. Batiffol, op. cit., pp.64–5, and H. Lietzmann, op. cit., p.100. The comment is not a copyist's scholion in the margin, as Batiffol thinks; it is from the compiler of the original collection, as Mai implied.

monophysite content (in particular that of the Finale, 17.3–18.10 below*)
fits it to take its place alongside the Definition of the Council of Chalcedon.
CN had a place in the original collection because it was considered both Roman
and orthodox. It is difficult to understand why Schwartz should set apart the
last two works in the codex from the main 'Sammlung' as works 'die mit ihr
nichts zu tun haben'.[20] The change of scribes for CN at f.360r2 should not
have misled him into thinking this, since it marks no more than the return of
the first scribe who had copied most of the collection. But for the purpose of
the present study it is of importance to note that CN was included as an apparently independent literary and theological unit in a set of orthodox Roman
works.

First publication – in Latin

In the fourteenth and fifteenth centuries the Greek monasteries of southern
Italy and Sicily were in decline. By the sixteenth century the monks had sunk
to a scarcely believable state of ignorance and laxity.[21] The counter-reformation
Cardinal, Guglielmo Sirleto (1514–1585), himself a Calabrian, was charged
with the needed reform. He was pressed to come to grips with the Abbey at
Rossano: by the Vicar-General (1567), by the Town Council (1568 and 1572),
and by the Archbishop of Rossano himself (1574 and 1575). There were general
and local obstacles to the work of reform. But by 1579 it had been largely
effected: it was confirmed by Gregory XIII in 1580.[22]

The neglected library of the Abbey at Rossano had been of interest for some
time to the scholarly Sirleto, who was Vatican Librarian for the last thirteen
years of his life. A letter of the learned Spaniard, Francesco Torres (1509–
1584)[23] to Sirleto (17 October 1561) indicates that Sirleto, even at this date,
possessed a list of the mss of the Abbey.[24] It was from the Abbey that he

---

*   I use my new sectionalization of the traditional chapter-divisions in anticipation of my
    discussion of them.
20 *Codex Vaticanus gr. 1431 . . .*, p.5. No more satisfying on this count is Schwartz's
    later 'explanation' in *Zwei Predigten Hippolyts . . .*, p.3. R. Devreesse, RSPT 19
    (1930) p.252, n.4, leaves the last two works of the codex out of consideration.
21 See especially the letter (22 May 1581) of the Abbot of San Salvatore at Messina to
    Cardinal Sirleto, quoted by P. Batiffol, op. cit., pp.26–7.
22 P. Batiffol, op. cit., pp.27–30, for details.
23 For some details about the life and literary labours of Torres, who joined the Society
    of Jesus in 1566 and is, of course, better known as Franciscus Torrensis or Turrianus,
    see C. Sommervogel, *Bibliothèque de la Compagnie de Jésus,* Brussels–Paris 1898,
    Tome VIII, col. 113–126, s.v. *Torres.*
24 P. Batiffol, op. cit., pp.39–40.

eventually bought the later Vat. gr. 1431.[25] On 16 April 1582 Sirleto wrote a letter in which he reported that there had been found in the Abbey at Rossano the Liturgy of St Mark the Evangelist.[26] To this report Sirleto added that there had also been found there 'Dionysii Alex. adversus Noëtianos & Hippolyti Martyris adversus Noëti Haeresin, & contra Paulum Samosatenum opuscula, quae omnia curabimus accurate describenda, ut ad communem utilitatem conferantur'.[27] Batiffol has clearly shown that Sirleto has garbled this list of works. What the Cardinal meant to write was: 'Dionysii Alexandrini contra Paulum Samosatenum et Hippolyti Martyris adversus Noëtianos opuscula sunt inventa . . .'.[28] Sirleto is obviously referring to the later Vat. gr. 1431, which may already have been in his possession by this time. There is no need to follow the codex on its travels after the death of Sirleto through the libraries of Asconio Colonna and Giovanni Angelo Altemps, from whom Paul V finally purchased it along with about a hundred other Greek and Latin mss for the Vatican Library.[29] But it is worth noting that Sirleto seems never to have supposed that CN was anything but one of a number of 'opuscula'.

The first appearance of CN in print is in a Latin version, that made by Torres,[30] printed by G. Vossius in a miscellany of patristic writings which formed the second part of his Works of Gregory Thaumaturgus, published in Mainz in 1604.[31] The title prefixed to CN runs: *S. Hippolyti Martyris Homilia, De Deo*

---

25 R. Devreesse, *Les manuscrits grecs . . .*, p.18 with n.5.

26 The letter was to Johannes a S.Andrea, who later published the Liturgy in Paris in 1583. He had been in contact with Sirleto about the Liturgy almost six years earlier: P. Batiffol, op. cit., p.39 and n.2.

27 As quoted in J.A. Fabricius, *S.Hippolyti Episcopi et Martyris Operum Vol. II*, Hamburg 1718, *ad Lectorem*, p.1, n.*, from the preface to the 1583 edition of the Liturgy.

28 P. Batiffol, op. cit., *Excursus D: Le Codex Patirensis de saint Hippolyte et de saint Denys d'Alexandrie*, pp.75–77. E.Schwartz, *Codex Vaticanus gr. 1431 . . .*, p.4, concurs with Batiffol's explanation.

29 See E. Schwartz, op. cit., p.4 and n.1; P. Nautin, op. cit., p.75. Batiffol's view, that the codex passed to the Vatican Library on Sirleto's death, is incorrect.

30 Torres' version of CN is listed in C. Sommervogel, loc. cit., col.123, item 45.

31 *Sancti Gregorii Episcopi Neo-Caesariensis, cognomento Thaumaturgi, Opera Omnia, quotquot in insignioribus, praecipue Romanis bibliothecis reperiri potuerunt; una cum eiusdem Auctoris vita, graecè, & latinè. Interprete, et Scholiaste Reverendo D.Doct.* Gerardo Vossio *Borchlonio Germ. Praep. Tungrensi. Ediecta* [sic] *sunt Miscellanea Sanctorum aliquot Patrum Graecorum & Latinorum, omnia nunc primum in lucem edita, eodem D.Doct.* Gerardo Vossio *auctore et collectore.* The miscellany referred to is given its own title-page: *Miscellanea Sanctorum aliquot Patrum Graecorum et Latinorum ante hac non edita: quae hic S.Patris nostri Gregorii Thaumaturgi operibus adiicere visum fuit, ut ad iusti Voluminis magnitudinem Tomus excrescat. Auctore et Collectore Doct.* Gerardo Vossio, *praeposito Tungrensi.* Moguntiae, Apud Balthasarum Lippium, sumptibus Antonii Hierat. Anno M.DC.IV.

Trino, et Uno et de Mysterio Incarnationis, contra haeresim Noeti.[32] The work is printed without any chapter divisions, but there are numbered references to the fourteen short scholia, of a theological intent, which are appended.[33] At the end of the last Scholion Vossius writes: 'Ita eruditissimus R.P. Franciscus Torrensis, in praecedentem S. Hippolyti Homiliam elucubratus est, & commentatus'.[34] The version is adorned with Scripture references and some marginal notes. At one place an abbreviated Greek phrase from the original is given.[35] At another the type of argument employed is noted.[36] Only in two places is any indication given that the marginal notator was conscious that the work contained parts.[37] There is no indication that either Torres or Vossius thought that CN was anything but a 'Homilia' complete in itself. It was substantially as published by Vossius that CN became known in the seventeenth century.[38]

The beginning of the problem

But it was in the course of this century that the modern problem of CN began to take shape. It was noticed that Photius, in his *Bibliotheca*,[39] described a work by Hippolytus that closed with a treatment of the Noetian heresy. The full entry in Photius reads as follows:

> A Booklet (βιβλιδάριον) of Hippolytus against Heresies. There was read a booklet of Hippolytus – Hippolytus, a disciple of Irenaeus. It was the compendium (σύνταγμα) against 32 Heresies, starting with [the] Dositheans and dealing with each one up to Noetus and [the] Noetians. He says that these [heresies] were submitted in Irenaeus' discourses (ὁμιλοῦντος Εἰρηναίου) to refutations. By synopsizing these in turn (ὧν καὶ σύνοψιν. . . ποιούμενος), Hippolytus says that he has compiled this present book (βιβλίον). In what concerns expression he is clear and dignified and economical, although he does not pay much attention to the Attic style. He says a number of rather inaccurate things, including that the Letter to [the] Hebrews is not of the Apostle Paul. The story goes that this [Hippolytus] too discoursed (προσομιλεῖν) to the people in imitation of Origen, whose

---

32 CN is on pp.58–68 of the miscellany.
33 The Scholia are on pp.68–71.
34 P.71.
35 P.62 *marg.* δυνάμει καὶ διαθέσει ὁμοφρονίας.
36 P.66 *marg.* 'Si ratio generationis humanae non est enarrabilis, quanto minus erit generationis divinae.'
37 P.59 *marg.* 'Quandocumque confutatio falsae sententiae antecedit explicationem verae, ut hic: quandocumque explicatio verae confutationem falsam.' And p.63 *marg.* (at 8.4 below) has: 'Demonstratio, veritatis, de Deo trino, & uno.'
38 For instance, in the *Magna Bibliotheca Veterum Patrum et antiquorum scriptorum ecclesiasticorum . . .*, III, Cologne 1618, pp.19–22; and later in the *Maxima Bibliotheca Veterum Patrum . . .*, III, Lyons 1677, pp.261–264.
39 *Codex* 121. PG 103:401CD – 403B.

very close friend he became, and he was so fond of his speeches (λόγων) that he even exhorted him to write commentaries on Holy Scripture. He also placed secretaries at his disposal — seven shorthand-writers and the same number of fair-copyists; and he himself even bore the expense of these. And in doing him this service [it is said] that he made inexorable demands for work on him: hence he was also called a taskmaster in one of the letters from Origen. This [Hippolytus] is said to have written a great number of things too.

While allowance must be made for a number of erroneous or at least unverifiable details (λέγεται) in Photius' account of Hippolytus' *Syntagma against 32 Heresies,* there is no need to doubt that insofar as the account concerns the booklet itself and is taken from the booklet (φησὶ), it contains reliable information. Thus it is clear that the *Syntagma* was most probably a short work: not only because this is the obvious meaning of Photius' much-discussed description of it as a βιβλιδάριον, but also, and primarily, because the author says he merely compiled the little book (τὸ βιβλίον . . . συντεταχέναι) as a synopsis of refutations made by Irenaeus in his discourses. In other words the *Syntagma* of Hippolytus was most probably a short book because it was no more than a synoptical compilation of lecture-notes which refuted 32 heresies. There is no mention of a finale or peroration; nor of any introduction, save perhaps a note by Hippolytus giving the source of his material. In style the booklet is expressly stated to be clear and brief.

It was known from other sources that Hippolytus had, among his many works, written at least one anti-heretical work. Although there is no mention of the work in the list of writings on the right-hand back corner of the chair of the famous seated statue of Hippolytus,[40] Hippolytus himself appears to refer to some such earlier work in his *Elenchus*:[41] 'It is now a long time since we exposed the doctrine [of the heretics] in fair measure (μετρίως), not parading them in detail (οὐ κατὰ λεπτόν), but refuting them broadly (ἀδρομερῶς)'. Again, Eusebius attributed to Hippolytus a work entitled 'Against All the

---

40 An account of the finding and other details of the seated figure are given in G. Bovini, *Sant'Ippolito, Dottore e Martire del III secolo,* Rome 1943. See also J.-M. Hanssens, *La Liturgie d'Hippolyte.* (Orientalia Christiana Analecta 155), Rome 1959, pp.217–244: Chap. V, *La statue du Latran et ses inscriptions.* The statue has now been tastefully mounted in the entrance-hall of the Vatican Library, above the following judicious inscription: IOANNES XXIII PONT. MAX. STATUAM HIPPOLYTI ECCLESIASTICI VIRI DOCTISSIMI IN ADITU VATICANAE BIBLIOTHECAE COLLOCARI IUSSIT XVI KAL. AUGUSTI A.D. MCMLIX PONT. SUI ANNO I.

41 1, proem., 1 (GCS Hippolytus III, ed. Wendland, p.1,20–2,2).

Heresies',[42] and this attribution is taken up by Jerome,[43] Nicephorus Callistus,[44] and Georgius Syncellus.[45] If this 'Against All the Heresies' is not simply the *Elenchus* itself, then the title may refer to the same earlier work of Hippolytus as that indicated in his *Elenchus*. But although it must presumably be true that the earlier work was shorter than the *Elenchus*, as seems clear from Hippolytus' own memory of it, it would be foolhardy to identify it too readily with the *Syntagma* described by Photius. Most obviously, Photius does not say that the *Syntagma* in his library combatted all the heresies, but expressly 32 of them. But more importantly, in the *Elenchus* Hippolytus not only describes a work which must surely have been somewhat different from the Photian *Syntagma*, since it contained both exposition (ἐξεθέμεθα) and broad refutation (ἐλέγξαντες), apparently of his own devising; but also he makes no mention of any debt to Irenaeus, from whom the *Syntagma*, as Photius recounts, was closely derived. It is true that in the seventh-century *Chronicon Paschale* a passage of Hippolytus is said to be found ἐν τῷ πρὸς ἁπάσας τὰς αἱρέσεις συντάγματι;[46] but apart from the possible unreliability of the reference, σύνταγμα is a description applicable to any book generally, and so it could not be argued that the Photian *Syntagma* is meant, and that therefore the *Syntagma against 32 Heresies* and the 'Against All the Heresies' indicated possibly in the *Elenchus* and attributed in later tradition to Hippolytus, are one and the same work. Of course, they might be: but the identification is not certain and caution is advisable.

Again, it has been tempting to make a further dubious identification of certain fragments which are said to come from the Hippolytean corpus. Thus the extract in Theodoret[47] 'from the interpretation of Psalm 2', which appears in Latin in Gelasius[48] under the quaint title 'Hippolyti episcopi et martyris Arabum metropolis in memoria haeresium', has been identified as somehow derived from

---

42 Hist. Eccles. 6.22 (GCS Eusebius II,2, ed. Schwartz, p.568,20): πρὸς ἁπάσας τὰς αἱρέσεις.
43 De vir. inlustr. LXI (TU XIV,1, ed. Richardson, p.35, 26f.): Adversus omnes haereses.
44 Eccl. hist. 4.31 (PG 145:1052C): πρὸς πάσας τὰς αἱρέσεις.
45 *Chronographia* (CHSB I, ed. W. Dindorf, pp.674,21–675,1): πρὸς Μαρκίωνα καὶ τὰς λοιπὰς αἱρέσεις. See P. Nautin, op. cit., p.15 for a possible explanation of the change of title.
46.CHSB I, ed. L. Dindorf, pp.12,22–13,1.
47 *Eranistes II* (PG 83: 173C–176A).
48 *Tractatus III seu Gelasii episcopi Romani de duabus naturis in Christo adversus Eutychen et Nestorium,* in A. Thiel, *Epistolae Romanorum Pontificum Genuinae,* I, Braunsberg 1868, pp.545–6.

part of CN 18 (cf. 18.1–7 below).[49] This in turn has led to the overhasty
conclusion, based in particular on the phrase 'in memoria haeresium' of the
Gelasian lemma, that therefore CN itself must be the concluding fragment of
the 'Against All the Heresies' which Hippolytus is said to have written, and
which is often taken to be the *Syntagma* described by Photius.[50] Such reason-
ings simply will not do: especially in view of the fact that Hippolytus is
acknowledged to have been a repetitious writer who might easily have inserted
an adapted 'reprise' from some earlier work into a later one. Indeed Photius
himself almost says as much when he notices Hippolytus' commentary *In
Danielem* along with his earlier *De Christo et de Antichristo, ἐν ᾧ ἥ τε αὐτὴ
τῶν λόγων ἰδέα διαπρέπει, καὶ τὸ τῶν νοημάτων ἁπλούστερόν τε καὶ
ἀρχαιότροπον.*[51]

It is not the intention of the present study to discuss, still less to use, the above
literary distractions which have already trapped the imaginations of so many
earnest but incautious scholars. They are mentioned only to provide a background for the understanding of the shape that has been so unfortunately
imparted to the problem of CN.

'Hoc insigne ἀποσπασμάτιον'

Thus by the end of the seventeenth century Louis Sébastien Le Nain de
Tillemont (1637–1698) could propose that CN was no more than 'un fragment considérable . . . qui paroist estre la conclusion' of the 'Against All the
Heresies'. His arguments were two. First, Photius says that the last heresy
refuted in that work was the heresy of Noetus and the Noetians; and clearly
in CN this very heresy is dealt with immediately prior to what is obviously
the conclusion of the work. But secondly, the first words of CN, ἕτεροί τινες
ἑτέραν διδασκαλίαν παρεισάγουσιν, imply that it can only be 'une suite d'un
plus long discours' – the 'Against All the Heresies', for the reason given from

---

49 Thus L. Saltet, *Les Sources de l'Eranistes de Théodoret*, in RHE 6 (1905) pp.289–303;
513–536; 741–754; Saltet calls the extract in Theodoret 'an abbreviation' (p.517) of
the apparently relevant part of CN. A Thiel, op. cit., p.545, n.1, on the authority of
Döllinger, goes even further astray, saying simply: 'Est Hippolyti *contra haeres. Noëti*
locus'.

50 It is enough to instance P. Nautin, op. cit., pp.15–19, as an outstanding example of
the way in which 'les données' are managed. R. Puchulu, *Sur le Contre Noet
d'Hippolyte,* [Thèse de Doctorat], Lyons 1960, p.30, has given a convincing suggestion
which explains why Gelasius wrote 'in memoria haeresium': the first words of
Theodoret's commentary on Psalm 2 are: ἐν τῇ μνήμῃ τῶν ἀσεβῶν (PG 80:873B).

51 *Bibliotheca,* Codex 202 (PG 103:673C).

Photius.[52] By the time the Greek text of CN came to be first published, this view of the work had become accepted doctrine.

At the first attempt, Johannes Albertus Fabricius was unable to publish the Greek text in his Works of Hippolytus. In the *Ad Lectorem* of the first volume,[53] he explained that he was publishing CN, 'hanc egregiam lucubrationem', only in the Latin version of Torres, along with notes by Torres – the Scholia which had appeared in Vossius' edition – and by himself. He expressed the hope that 'beneficio viri doctrina & ingenio illustris' he would be able to give the Greek text, copied from the Vatican codex, in a subsequent volume of third-century patristic works. Fabricius' debt to Tillemont is clearly stated. In this *Ad Lectorem* Fabricius merely mentions the fact that 'Photius, Cod. CXXI, asserts that the last chapter of the Hippolytean work "Against the Heresies" had been aimed at Noetus', without developing this fact into an argument that therefore CN is a fragment of Hippolytus' work; and twice he refers to CN merely as a 'disputation against Noetus'. But it is in the long note on the title: 'CONTRA HAERESIN NOETI Francisco Turriano Interprete', under which he published Torres' version, that he argues that CN is a fragment. First there was an argument, taken from Tillemont, and based on Photius' description of the *Syntagma* and the abrupt opening words of CN:

> cum Photius testetur opus Hippolyti adversus haereses in oppugnatione Noëti desiisse, atque initium hujus scripti manifeste prodat alia processisse, in quibus de aliis dogmatibus, aliorum ut videtur haereticorum disseruit, eaque oppugnavit, habeo illud pro extrema parte libri Hippolytei adversus haereses, sive *memoria haeresium*, ut S. Gelasius appellat, quaedam ex hoc ἀποσπασμτίῳ referens ad verbum. . .

A second argument was evolved in answer to the obvious objection that the writer is addressing an audience and calls them ἀδελφοί, and that therefore CN is not likely to be part of an anti-heretical treatise: 'neque obstat quod fideles quandoque auctor alloquitur, ut in homiliis fieri solet, nam hoc etiam in scriptis facere veteres, & ad lectores respicere, tralatitium'.[54] The Latin text printed by Fabricius was divided into the eighteen chapters which are still in use today, and is accompanied by the notes of Torres and Fabricius himself.[55] But as a 'Homilia' CN was doomed. Fabricius' note to the title began with the fateful words: 'Hoc insigne ἀποσπασματίον . . .'

---

52 *Mémoires pour servir à l'histoire ecclésiastique des six premiers siècles justifiez par les citations des auteurs originaux,* par le sieur D.T., Tome III, Paris 1695, p.244.

53 *S. Hippolyti, Episcopi et Martyris Opera,* curante J. Alberto Fabricio, Hamburg 1716, *Ad Lectorem,* pp.VI–VII.

54 Op. cit., p.235, n.*

55 Op. cit., pp.235–244.

Two years later Fabricius published the promised volume.[56] In his *Ad Lectorem* he proudly presents both the *'Demonstratio adversus Judaeos'* and the *'praeclarus Adversus Noëtum commentarius'*. Both works, he says, are seeing the light of day for the first time: a copy had been taken from the Vatican codex, and had been sent to him from Paris by 'vir illustris eruditione & maximis in litteras meritis D. Bernardus à Montfaucon'[57] – the last great Maurist. Fabricius printed the newly-acquired Greek text and Torres' Latin version in parallel columns, along with his own and Torres' notes, and according to the chapter divisions of the 1716 edition.[58] In the note on the title, of which he still had no accurate copy, he repeated the arguments by which he supposed it proved that CN was a fragment.[59] But the possession of the Greek text inspired him to elaborate a third argument. This was based on a phrase which occurs later in the work, πᾶσαι τοσαῦται αἱρέσεις. . . (8.4 below), which Fabricius glossed: 'non Noëti tantum sed & aliae XXXI. quas hactenus Hippolytus oppugnaverat. Ex his verbis clarissime apparet clausulam hanc esse libri adversus haereses'.[60] All three arguments presented by Fabricius were to become the stock-in-trade of scholars who dealt with CN in the generations to come.

Fabricius' edition of CN was taken over by A. Gallandi (1709–1779) for his multi-volume Library of the Fathers, and was printed under the title given by Fabricius.[61] Gallandi makes his own the view that CN is the end-piece of the 'Against the Heresies', which 'prodire coepit imperante Alexandro sub anno CCXXX, ut proinde quod superest illius operis, pars ultima fuerit'.[62] Not that

---

56 *S. Hippolyti Episcopi et Martyris Operum Vol.II,* Hamburg 1718.

57 Op. cit., *Ad Lectorem,* p.1; also p.5, n.*. P. Nautin, op. cit., pp.78–9, gives an account of the Fabricius editions which, if read with Nautin's own correction of it in his later *Le Dossier d'Hippolyte et de Méliton dans les florilèges dogmatiques et chez les historiens modernes,* Paris 1953, p.130, shows that Fabricius had been hoping to see *Barberinianus gr. 497,* which contained (f.232r–238v) a copy of CN made from *Ottobonianus gr. 384* by Lukas Holste (Holstenius, 1596–1661), a convert Hamburgian who became in turn Secretary-Librarian of Cardinal Francesco Barberini and head of the Vatican Library. But Fabricius' patience in frustration was rewarded in time by a copy of CN made directly from Vat. gr. 1431.

58 Op. cit., pp.5–20.

59 Op. cit., p.5, n.*. The title in Fabricius' copy appears to have been: ὁμιλία Ἱππολύτου εἰς τὴν αἵρεσιν Νοητοῦ τινος. For his edition of the Greek text he invented, and misspelt, his own: ΙΠΠΟΛΥΤΟΥ ΑΡΧΙΕΠΙΣΚΟΠΟΥ ΚΑΙ ΜΑΡΤΥΡΟΣ ΕΙΣ ΤΗΝ ΑΙΡΕΣΙΝ ΝΟΕΤΟΥ [!] ΤΙΝΟΣ.

60 Op. cit., p.12, n.*.

61 *Bibliotheca Veterum Patrum antiquorumque scriptorum ecclesiasticorum,* cura & studio Andreae Gallandii Presbyteri Congregationis Oratorii, II, Venice, 1766, pp.454–465.

62 Op. cit., *Prolegomena,* cap. XVIII § VI, pp.XLVII–XLVIII.

his edition is slavish: although he repeats many of the Torres-Fabricius notes, he adds some of his own, and some selected from other theological writers. He can suggest textual improvement, and chooses at times to follow, in preference to Torres' version, one of the better translations which seem by then to have been available. His is a Catholic edition of CN; and at one point the Oratorian counteracts what he considered to be a sign of Fabricius' Protestantism.[63] Gallandi's edition was the one incorporated into J.-P. Migne's *Patrologia Graeca.*[64]

Martin Joseph Routh, the Oxford worthy, also used Fabricius' edition when he published CN in his collection of patristic opuscula.[65] Dr Routh repeats or refers to most of the Torres-Fabricius notes; occasionally he adds to them or substitutes others of his own, based on a study of the text of the LXX Old Testament, the New Testament and Epiphanius. But the most interesting part of his edition lies in the notes in which he most acutely compares Torres' Latin version and Fabricius' somewhat faulty Greek text, and thus argues to what must have been the original Greek in the Vatican codex. It is the measure of his enormous learning that he sometimes even turns out to be right. At other times his too simple trust in Torres' Latin leads him into making a number of ingenious but mistaken textual conjectures. He subscribes, however, to Fabricius' view of CN as the concluding fragment of the 'Against the Heresies' of Hippolytus. In fact, his Latin title runs: 'Hippolyti Episcopi contra haeresim Noeti cujusdam. Sive, extrema pars libri deperditi adversus omnes haereses'.[66] This title, along with much else from Dr Routh's edition, was later copied by P.A. de Lagarde in his collected Greek works of Hippolytus.[67]

By the mid-nineteenth century the Fabricius view had taken firm root. An eccentric like Freiherr von Bunsen might refuse to accept it. Bunsen claimed that CN's 'method and tone are those of a sermon, not of a historical work on doctrinal issues':[68] 'the book is a homily or a sermon, whether it was ever actually delivered or merely written in this form'.[69] But these arguments were

---

63 Op. cit., p.459, n.3. In a note (on 9.1 below) Fabricius (op. cit., p.12, n.+) had invoked a phrase of CN as 'insigne testimonium de S. Scripturae sufficientia'.
64 PG 10:803–830. This volume, published in Paris in 1857, is devoted mainly to the works of Hippolytus and Gregory Thaumaturgus.
65 *Scriptorum Ecclesiasticorum Opuscula Praecipua Quaedam,* Oxford 1832, I, pp.45–76. Torres' version is printed in double column at the foot of the Greek text. Dr Routh's annotations 'in S. Hippolyti contra Noëtum opus' are on pp.77–89.
66 Op. cit., p.49.
67 *Hippolyti Romani quae feruntur omnia graece,* a recognitione Pauli Antonii de Lagarde, Leipzig & London, 1858, pp.43–57.
68 C.C.J. Bunsen, *Hippolytus und seine Zeit,* I, Leipzig, 1852, p.88.
69 Ibid., p.182; cf. p.190.

perhaps too direct or too simple to be able to command a hearing. And so the problem of CN, as shaped by a century and a half of literary tradition, was ready to take on further elaborations. No longer was the discussion to concern itself with whether CN was a fragment: the question was, what was it a fragment of?

Discussion into the twentieth century

The discovery and partial publication of Hippolytus' *Elenchus* or *Philosophoumena* reawakened the interest of scholars in the study of early anti-heretical treatises.[70] Naturally enough, this interest brought with it the expression of views concerning the provenance and character of the fragment, CN. Sometimes, as in the case of Jacobi and Döllinger, the views expressed were not especially helpful. For Jacobi, CN was merely a fragment of a homily against the Patripassianists;[71] for Döllinger, the 'Schriftchen gegen Noetus', in order to explain how Gelasius could quote it as from Hippolytus' 'in memoria haeresium', was somehow related to the Photian *Syntagma*, 'welchem der Aufsatz gegen Noetus angehängt war, als ob er dazu gehöre'.[72] But Volkmar proposed a different solution, and one which was, at least for a time, to attract and convince Harnack. Volkmar claimed that the description of the *Syntagma* as a βιβλιδάριον precluded CN's belonging to it: the accumulated treatments of 32 heresies on the scale of the Noetians in CN would make up a volume which could not aptly be called a 'booklet'. But since CN was clearly the end-fragment of some anti-heretical work or other, and since it contained a mention of Theodotus (3.1 below), Volkmar proposed, in spite of the silence of the sources concerning any such work by Hippolytus, that CN must be the conclusion — in fact the second half — of a treatise against the Monarchians.[73]

Lipsius' attempts to discover the common anti-heretical 'Grundschrift' utilized by Ps.-Tertullian, Philastrius of Brescia and Epiphanius in their heresiological writings, led him to reassert the more traditional view that CN was the end of the *Syntagma* 'Against All the Heresies'. Briefly, Lipsius identified his 'Grundschrift' with the lost *Syntagma* of Hippolytus against 32 heresies, described,

---

70 The *Elenchus* was in fact first ascribed to Origen: *Origenis Philosophoumena sive Omnium Haeresium Refutatio e codice Parisino nunc primum edidit* Emmanuel Miller, Oxford 1851.
71 Cf. *Deutsche Zeitschrift für christl. Wissen und christl. Leben*, (1851) pp.217—220.
72 I. von Döllinger, *Hippolytus und Kallistus, oder Die römische Kirche in der ersten Hälfte des dritten Jahrhunderts*, Regensburg 1853, p.90.
73 G. Volkmar, *Die Quellen der Ketzergeschichte bis zum Nicänum*, I, *Hippolytus und die römischen Zeitgenossen*, Zurich 1855, p.93f.

as has been shown, by Photius. He further claimed that underlying both the *Syntagma* and the catalogue of heresies in Irenaeus, Adv. Haer. I, 23–27, he could discern an even older heresiological work, Justin's lost *Syntagma* against all the heresies.[74] It is not relevant to the present study to trace the course of Lipsius' investigations and the subsequent discussions of his findings. His views on CN are easily detachable, and his arguments not unfamiliar. He admits that the relationship of CN to the 'Against All the Heresies' of Hippolytus is controverted; but it is not a Homily, as the title would have it, but clearly, from its opening words, a fragment of a more comprehensive work which dealt with a number of other heresies besides the Noetian. Further, the mention of Theodotus (3.1), along with the πᾶσαι τοσαῦται αἱρέσεις phrase (8.4) and the τίς οὖν ἀποφαίνεται... passage (11.3), at once show that this is the case, and refute Volkmar's view.[75] The βιβλιδάριον objection, that the *Syntagma* could not be such an extensive work, did not convince Lipsius: in comparison with the *Elenchus*, the *Syntagma* would still rank as a βιβλιδάριον. Indeed, CN gives a wrong impression. Its second half (cc. 9–18) is, after all, the conclusion of the *whole* work, and a disproportionate amount of space and care has been given to the Noetian heresy, as being the chief heresy as far as Hippolytus was concerned. In fact the whole 'Against All the Heresies' need not have been larger than the tenth book of the *Elenchus*.[76]

Several years later Lipsius' views were attacked by Adolf von Harnack.[77] Harnack found the vulnerable part of Lipsius' arguments in his reply to the βιβλιδάριον objection. CN was simply too long to be the end-fragment of a 'booklet' dealing with 31 other heresies, and its final chapters (cc. 9–18) concern only the Noetian heresy. The πᾶσαι τοσαῦται αἱρέσεις phrase (8.4) could easily refer to the various types of Monarchianism: and so Harnack accepted Volkmar's view that CN was the second part of an unheard-of anti-Monarchian treatise by Hippolytus. Lipsius rose to defend himself.[78] He conceded that he had miscalculated the size of the lost *Syntagma*, which must have been at least twice as large as the tenth book of the *Elenchus*. Perhaps the βιβλιδάριον that Photius had read was in fact no more than a summary of the original *Syntagma*; and this might explain Photius' ὧν καὶ σύνοψιν ποιούμενος ...[79] But Lipsius could not agree with Harnack about the final

74 R.A. Lipsius, *Zur Quellenkritik des Epiphanios,* Vienna 1865.

75 Op. cit., pp.37–38 with p.37, n.2 and p.38, n.2.

76 Op. cit., pp.39–40.

77 In *Zeitschrift für die historische Theologie* 44 (1874) pp.141–226; esp. p.183ff.

78 R.A. Lipsius, *Die Quellen der Aeltesten Ketzergeschichte neu untersucht,* Leipzig 1875.

79 Op. cit., pp.124–5.

chapters of CN. Obviously there was a close link between these chapters and
the refutation of the Noetians: first, because they are contiguous sections,
and secondly because the Noetian heresy loomed largest in Hippolytus' mind.
But these final chapters do in fact envisage other heresies, which must therefore have been previously dealt with in the large, lost part of the *Syntagma*:
cc. 9–11 display anti-Gnostic traits; c.16 is anti-emanationist; cc.15–18 on
the reality of Christ's humanity are not anti-Monarchian. Nor had Harnack
convincingly disposed of the 'Hauptargument' drawn from CN 8.4, with its
telling phrases, καὶ ὁ Νοητός . . ., and πᾶσαι τοσαῦται αἱρέσεις . . .: to which
should be added the reference in 11.3 to the Gnostics etc. and πᾶσα ἐκείνων
φλυαρία.[80] So for Lipsius CN was to remain the end-fragment of Hippolytus'
Syntagma 'Against All the Heresies'. But he felt the need to add some explanation of the provenance of CN.[81] While it is true that the description in the
title, ὁμιλία, contradicts the data of 1.1, 8.4, etc., and the 'ganze Anlage' of
the work, it can be explained by the striking style of the final two chapters.
These chapters do manifest a quite distinct 'Predigtstil', and this is why CN
came to be separated from the *Syntagma*: the extracting of the final chapters
dragged the rest of CN along as well. Lipsius' views on the interpolations
detectable in CN will be related shortly.

In 1875 Caspari summarized the dispute between Lipsius and Harnack, while
inclining to the Volkmar-Harnack view of CN as the end of an anti-Monarchian
work. Caspari exposed the reasons for the traditional Fabricius-Lipsius view,
but the βιβλιδάριον objection and Harnack's submission that the final chapters
of CN (cc.9–18) concerned Christological heresies and did not envisage a
wider range of heresies won him to the camp of Volkmar and Harnack. As for
the πᾶσαι τοσαῦται αἱρέσεις phrase (8.4), he dismissed it as 'der subjektive
Ausdruck eines eifrigen Gegners, den man nicht pressen, und auf dem man
nicht zu viel bauen darf'.[82] Hilgenfeld, in 1884, saw in CN a fragment, but
not of the *Syntagma*, described by Photius as closing with the Noetian heresy:
rather 'es scheint eben zu den noch ὁμιλοῦντος Εἰρηναίου verfassten ἔλεγχος
des Hippolyts zu gehören'.This was a new view of CN, but it was not supported
by any arguments.[83] Lightfoot's reasons for supposing that CN 'is the peroration of [the Compendium against all the heresies], which is known to have

---

80 Op. cit., pp.129–131.
81 Op. cit., p.133: 'So gewiss es ursprünglich ein Bestandtheil eines grösseren Ganzes
   gebildet hat, so auffällig bleibt diese seine gesonderte Existenz'. See p.136f.
82 C.P. Caspari, *Ungedruckte, unbeachtete und wenig beachtete Quellen zur Geschichte
   des Taufsymbols und der Glaubensregel*, Christiania 1875, III, p.399, n.230.
83 Ad. Hilgenfeld, *Die Ketzergeschichte des Urchristentums, urkundlich dargestellt*,
   Leipzig 1884, p.615.

ended with the heresy of Noetus' will never be known. The relevant section of his work was never finished.[84] But in 1895 Rolffs drew from the treasure-house of his learning a view of CN that was both new and old. It was the end of a larger heresiological work which presented the Noetian heresy as the high-point of the heresies therein refuted. CN contains (9.3 below) phrases which have a clear reference to the Montanist type and method of inspiration. Further, research shows that both CN and the source-document of Epiphanius, *Panarion haer.* 48, belong to an anti-Montanist work against five heresies of this type; and CN is the end-fragment of this work. But the anti-Montanist work turns out to be none else than the concluding part of the *Syntagma* of Hippolytus described by Photius. The βιβλιδάριον objection should be discounted.[85] Two years later, Achelis was quite non-committal.[86]

With the turn of the century the closing phases of this period of the controversy concerning CN set in. An important article by J. Dräseke was to have great influence in rallying scholars to the traditional Fabricius-Lipsius view.[87] CN is a fragment, as 1.1, 3.1, 8.4, 11.3 show. The πᾶσαι τοσαῦται αἱρέσεις phrase is the convincing argument for CN's being a fragment of the *Syntagma*. In particular, πᾶσαι τοσαῦται, without the definite article, must be taken 'ganz allgemein in numerischer Bedeutung': the phrase refers to heresies which the writer has just refuted – 'sie hat der Verfasser im Vorhergehenden widerlegt, auf sie blickt er jetzt befriedigt zurück'.[88] Again, the close of the *Elenchus* shows that it is likely that Hippolytus concluded his earlier heresiological work in the same manner, as preserved in CN. Not all the heresies of the *Syntagma* will have been treated in the detail lavished on the Noetians. The βιβλιδάριον objection simply does not hold, especially in the light of the actual usage of the word.[89] The fatal flaw in the Volkmar-Harnack view is the complete absence of any mention in the sources of an anti-Monarchian work by Hippolytus. The description of CN as a Homily 'erklärt sich aus Ton und Haltung des Abschnitts Cap. 9–18'. The powerful impression made by these chapters, and above all by the last chapter (c.18), led to the ignoring of the data furnished in the previous chapters, which clearly point to the work's

---

84 J.B. Lightfoot, *The Apostolic Fathers, Part 1, S. Clement of Rome,* Vol. II, London 1890, pp.400; 413–418.

85 E. Rolffs, *Urkunden aus dem antimontanistischen Kampfe des Abendlandes,* TU XII, 4, Leipzig 1895, pp.126–9; 138–151.

86 H. Achelis, *Hippolytstudien,* TU N.F. I,4, Leipzig 1897, pp.21; 126, n.1; 173.

87 In *Zeitschrift für wissenschaftliche Theologie* 46 (1903) pp.58–80; 'Zum Syntagma des Hippolytos'.

88 Loc. cit., pp.60–64.

89 Loc. cit., pp.64f; 71–74.

being a fragment of a larger literary entity.[90] Although there was little new in Dräseke's article, it had the crucial effect of drawing Harnack from the Volkmar camp.[91] Two years later, d'Alès accepted the view of CN as the closing pages of the *Syntagma*, 'malgré son tour homilétique'.[92] Bardenhewer's singular view of CN as the closing fragment of yet another work, 'The Little Labyrinth', doubtfully ascribable to Hippolytus and contrasted with the *Elenchus*, which some may have known as 'The Labyrinth', was to find little support.[93] By the early years of the present century, then, the problem of the provenance of CN had been largely stilled, even if not entirely solved. The result of a long controversy which was most remarkable both for the originality of some of the guesses proposed and for the tedious repetition of the arguments in which the parties concerned saw their views supported, was that CN could be taken to be the final part of Hippolytus' *Syntagma* 'Against All the Heresies', largely lost but once described, perhaps misleadingly as a βιβλιδάριον, by Photius.

But if it had to a certain extent been agreed that as part of the *Syntagma* CN lacked literary integrity, other doubts concerning the textual integrity of the work had also arisen. Several participants in the discussion had noted that certain words and phrases – and even passages – in CN could be discounted as interpolations in an original text. These interpolated elements could be detected because they were either easily detachable from their immediate contexts, or in fact introduced overtones from what were obviously later heretical disputes. Bunsen had first remarked on the detachable references to the Holy Spirit in CN 14;[94] and Volkmar had suggested that certain words and phrases were suspect.[95] But it was Lipsius, in his second book, who pointed out a number of phrases and passages for exclusion: for instance, the references to the Holy Spirit in CN 14.2, 3, 5, 6, 8; the phrases λόγος ἔνσαρκος (12.5), ψυχὴ λογική (17.2), φῶς ἐκ φωτός (10.4 and 11.1); the whole passage, 12.3–5. On other elements he cast suspicion: αὐτὸς δὲ μόνος ὢν πολὺς ἦν (10.2), 15.7 as a whole, and even 16.3–7.[96] Dräseke approved of the view that many of the suggested elements were indeed interpolated;[97] while Harnack

90 Loc. cit., pp.62; 66–67.
91 A. Harnack, *Geschichte der altchristlichen Litteratur bis Eusebius*, 2/II, *Die Chronologie der Litteratur von Irenaeus bis Eusebius*, Leipzig 1904, pp.220–221, with p.221, n.2.
92 A. d'Alès, *La Théologie de Saint Hippolyte*, Paris 1906, pp.76–7, and p.76, n.1.
93 O. Bardenhewer, *Geschichte der altkirchlichen Literatur*[2], II, Freiburg im Breisgau 1914, pp.567–8.
94 C.C.J. Bunsen, op. cit., p.184ff.
95 G. Volkmar, op. cit., p.136, n.1.
96 R.A. Lipsius, op. cit., pp.134–137.
97 Loc. cit., pp.68–69.

could blandly declare that CN had been 'dogmatisch durchkorrigiert'.[98] Thus the question of interpolations in CN was to become another force in the shaping of the problem.

More recent discussion

In spite of all that had been written about CN and its literary and textual integrity since the days of its first publication in Torres' translation until well into the present century, none of the participants in the discussion had either given CN their undivided attention – all that had been written had been written in the course of conducting some other controversy – or had even consulted the original ms. All the more welcome, then, was the publication in 1936 of the text of CN along with a new study of it by E. Schwartz.[99] For the first time a reliable, but not wholly perfect, transcription of the text was available. But it is Schwartz's view of CN that is of interest at present. For Schwartz CN is an excerpt, and in fact the greater part, of a Homily by Hippolytus on Psalm 2.[100] That CN is a Homily is shown by the frequent use of $\dot{\alpha}\delta\epsilon\lambda\varphi\alpha\iota'$ – so conveniently explained away by so many scholars from Fabricius onwards – and by the lemmata of the Gelasius and Theodoret extracts.[101] That it is only part of an original whole is to be shown by the $\ddot{\epsilon}\tau\epsilon\rho\alpha\iota'\,\tau\iota\nu\epsilon\varsigma\,\dot{\epsilon}\tau\dot{\epsilon}\rho\alpha\nu$ phrase of 1.1, and by the $\kappa\alpha\iota'\,\dot{o}\,N o\eta\tau\dot{o}\varsigma$ of 8.4.[102] To Schwartz the $\beta\iota\beta\lambda\iota\delta\dot{\alpha}\rho\iota o\nu$ description of the *Syntagma* by Photius was key in showing that CN is not part of the *Syntagma*. A fragment of a short booklet could not contain the highly developed $\dot{\alpha}\nu\alpha\tau\rho o\pi\dot{\eta}$ and $\dot{\alpha}\pi\dot{o}\delta\epsilon\iota\xi\iota\varsigma$ which are to be found in CN. As for $\pi\hat{\alpha}\sigma\alpha\iota$ $\tau o\sigma\alpha\hat{\upsilon}\tau\alpha\iota\,\alpha\dot{\iota}\rho\dot{\epsilon}\sigma\epsilon\iota\varsigma$ (8.4), it implies nothing, since it is 'ohne Artikel, lediglich exclamativ'; and the list of heretics in 11.3 is an unchronological and purely rhetorical enumeration.[103] Only the beginning of the Homily is missing. Schwartz supposed that the lost beginning must have been short, and must have arrived quickly at the exposition of verse 7 of Psalm 2, where there arose an opportunity for Hippolytus to warn his hearers at some length against Christological heresy. Some treatment, but only short and without the detail given to Noetianism, of at least some other Christological heresy must have been present in the lost beginning.[104] The purpose of Hippolytus in the Homily

---

98 A. Harnack, op. cit., p.221, n.4.
99 E. Schwartz, *Zwei Predigten Hippolyts*, in *Sitzungsberichte der Bayrischen Akademie der Wissenschaften, Philosophisch-historische Abteilung*, Munich 1936, 3.
100 Op. cit., pp.23f; 26f; 32–35.
101 Op. cit., pp.23; 26.
102 Op. cit., pp.27; 34f.
103 Op. cit., pp.32–36.
104 Op. cit., pp.27; 34.

was not so much to deal with the Noetians as by defending his Logos-Christology to defend himself against Callistus and to attack the latter and his party. Noetus and the Noetians, in whom Hippolytus does not seem to be seriously interested, provided the cover for this purpose.[105] Schwartz's approach represented a refreshing re-appraisal of CN; but it was not without its difficulties. It is hard, for instance, to explain how the important beginning of the Homily came to be lost, why the Homily should not really be a Homily, and why there should be no reference or allusion to Psalm 2 in the substantial text that remains. Thus Schwartz won little support and soon came under attack.

In a careful article, Ch. Martin restated, against Schwartz, the claims of the traditional view of CN as the end of the *Syntagma*.[106] Martin began with a review of the external indications of what CN is: he sought to show that the description of CN as a ὁμιλία, along with other elements in the title, were not original. Just as 'Archbishop of Rome' and the curious Νοητοῦ τινος must be later elements, derived either from later unreliable tradition about Hippolytus, or, in the case of Νοητοῦ τινος, from the text of 1.1, so also with ὁμιλία: this too derives from the impression made on a later scribe by the recurring use of ἀδελφοί and ὁρᾶτε. The fact that Vat. gr. 1431, Theodoret and Gelasius have all preserved CN or part of it under three different titles should make for caution in accepting titles at their face-value. Gelasius' 'in memoria haeresium' should surely be especially significant in determining the source of the fragment CN; and Schwartz has not explained this convincingly in saying that it translates μνημονεύων τῶν αἱρεσέων – a phrase which was added to the original title preserved by Theodoret, 'From the interpretation of Psalm 2', in order to cover the ἀπόδειξις τῆς ἀληθείας – (cc. 9–18). In any case, if CN were part of a homily, it is difficult to see why Theodoret should say that an extract from it comes from a ἑρμήνεια. This latter implies not a short work, as Schwartz would have it, but, as πᾶσαι τοσαῦται αἱρέσεις also indicates, a long one. But the absence of any reference to Psalm 2 is very strange if CN is in fact the end-part of a commentary on that Psalm.[107]

In his consideration of the internal evidence provided by CN, Martin notes that the use of ἀδελφοί, while of interest, is not conclusive support for Schwartz's view of CN as a homily fragment. In Christian writing generally this mode of address is of special significance, and is by no means limited to homilies. Hippolytus commonly maintains close contact with his readers in his writings.[108]

---

105 Op. cit., pp.30–32.
106 In RHE 37 (1941) pp.5–23: *Le 'Contra Noetum' de Saint Hippolyte – fragment d'homélie ou finale du Syntagma?*
107 Loc. cit., pp.8–15.
108 Loc. cit., pp.15–18.

And so the way is still open for Martin to resume the consideration of the well-known evidence concerning the *Syntagma* as the source of the fragment CN. He tries to show once again how CN fits in with what can be learnt about the *Syntagma*, and sees in the parallelism between CN and the end of the *Elenchus* an indication that the former comes from a work of the same genre as the latter – the earlier *Syntagma*. Great weight is placed on Gelasius' 'in memoria haeresium'; the βιβλιδάριον objection is discounted, and the contents of cc. 9–18 are said to point to heresies other than simply Christological ones.[109] In the main Martin has little new to add to the traditional defence of the view of CN as the end of the *Syntagma*, even though he may have been successful in showing that all was not well with Schwartz's approach.

Perhaps the whole matter might have rested there had there not begun in France, not long after the end of the last war, a controversy among patristic scholars which was to last from 1947 to 1955, and which has still not been resolved. The controversy concerned the ascription of certain late works in the Hippolytean corpus, and particularly the ascription of the *Elenchus*, to Hippolytus of Rome. In the course of its eight years the controversy brought to light and to discussion almost every aspect of all the problems which surround the enigmatic figure of the first anti-Pope. Fortunately, for the purpose of the present study only one problem is strictly relevant: the place of CN in the corpus of Hippolytus' writings. This is a problem which few of the participants in the recent controversy, like their predecessors of the last century, deal with directly. It is rather a problem which once again emerges in the course of the controversy and makes it presence felt in occasional remarks and guarded footnotes and a few pages of summarily presented difficulties. A rapid sketch of the controversy will best show how the problem of CN was once again to emerge, and in what shape.[110]

P. Nautin opened the controversy in 1947 with two short notes which he contributed to *Recherches de Science Religieuse*.[111] In the first of them,[112] he established two points: first, that the *Spoudasma* against the heresy of Artemon cannot be ascribed to Hippolytus; and secondly, that the lemmata in the

---

109 Loc. cit., pp.19–23.

110 For an account of most of the controversy – up to 1952 – see G. Oggioni, *La questione di Ippolito,* in *La Scuola Cattolica* 78 (1950) pp.126–143; and also *Ancora sulla questione di Ippolito,* ibid., 80 (1952) pp.513–525. A fairly full bibliography is given by M. Richard in PO 27:271–272.

111 RechSR 34 (1947) pp.99–107 and pp.347–359: *Notes sur le catalogue des oeuvres d'Hippolyte.*

112 Now substantially reprinted in P. Nautin, *Le Dossier d'Hippolyte et de Méliton dans les florilèges dogmatiques et chez les historiens modernes,* Paris 1953, pp.115–120.

Eranistes of Theodoret are clearly unreliable. In the second note,[113] Nautin published a translation and a study of the πρὸς Ἰουδαίους ἀποδεικτική which is found along with CN in Vat. gr. 1431. On grounds of style, exegetical method, attitude to the Jews, and the anti-Arian theology which it contains, Nautin excluded this piece also from the corpus of Hippolytus' works. But these two notes, which in themselves contained no great surprises, were only signs of greater things to come. In the same year (1947) Nautin published the book which was to set the controversy alight.[114]

Briefly, the position which Nautin took up might be described as follows: the by now traditional ascription of the *Elenchus* to Hippolytus of Rome is not in fact on safe ground. This ascription was first arrived at, largely through the work of German scholars, by a process of elimination. Nautin claimed that the only safe ground on which to test the accepted ascription is the text of the *Elenchus* itself in comparison with other certain works of Hippolytus. Thus Nautin chose CN to be the basis of his comparative study. The obvious parallelism between the end of the *Elenchus* and CN makes the latter 'un terrain privilégié' for the work of comparison; and the Hippolytean authenticity of CN can be put beyond doubt.[115] Satisfied then with the authenticity of the text of CN as it has come down to the scholar of the present day, Nautin proceeded with his all-important comparison. From a consideration of four points – certain theological phenomena, heresiological method, mental-cultural formation and style – he arrived at the conclusion which was so to shock the world of patristic scholars: 'l'étude comparée de l'*Elenchus* et du fragment d'Hippolyte sur Noët montre ainsi nettement une différence d'auteur'.[116]

Not that Nautin was satisfied to stop there. He went on to show that CN does not precede the *Elenchus*, as the traditional view which saw in CN the end of the *Syntagma* would have it, but rather derives from the *Elenchus*. In fact CN is no more than a 'remaniement'[117] by Hippolytus of *Elenchus* material. Clearly Nautin could not stop at this point either. To the still unknown author of the *Elenchus* he ascribed both the *Synagoge* and the περὶ τῆς τοῦ παντὸς οὐσίας mentioned in the *Elenchus*. Since both of these two last-named works

---

113 See now P. Nautin, *Le Dossier d'Hippolyte . . .*, pp.109–114.

114 P. Nautin, *Hippolyte et Josipe, Contribution à l'histoire de la littérature chrétienne du troisième siècle*, Paris 1947.

115 *Hippolyte et Josipe*, p.35: The reasons given are that CN is quoted under the name of Hippolytus as early as the fifth century by Gelasius and Theodoret, and that it contains characteristic likenesses of idea and expression to *In Danielem* and *De Christo et de Antichristo*.

116 *Hippolyte et Josipe*, p.53.

117 Ibid., p.58.

have roughly equivalent titles inscribed on the famous statue, then this statue must represent not Hippolytus, as has been assumed since the statue was found in 1551, but the unknown author of this new corpus of works which has been detached from those usually ascribed to Hippolytus. From certain allusions in Photius' *Bibliotheca*, John Philoponus and the *Sacra Parallela*, Nautin discovered a name for his new author – Josipus. As for Hippolytus, he turns out to be a non-Roman, difficult to localize but probably from the eastern shores of the Mediterranean, who wrote in the middle of the third century. If Hippolytus' person and writings suffered in the course of this drastic treatment, scholars could console themselves with the acquisition of a new figure among writers of this patristic period. Nautin's thesis was not wholly novel. Some years previously G. da Bra had published a short book in which he too had challenged the ascription of the *Elenchus* to Hippolytus.[118] But it was Nautin's study which first roused patristic scholars.

The year 1948 brought the first reactions. G. Bardy opened the case for the defence of Hippolytus with a stout reassertion of the traditional position, with reference in particular to the priority of CN in relation to the *Elenchus*.[119] Bardy rehearsed the abundant evidence for the knowledge of Hippolytus' works, for his Roman attachments, for his date at the beginning of the third century, and for the identification of the seated figure of the statue with Hippolytus of Rome. While it may be true the Hippolytus is an enigmatic figure, Bardy saw no need to depart from the common view of his life and works through the postulating of a Josipus. In another article of the same year Bardy supported his views on the superfluity of Josipus by indicating the authority and popularity which Flavius Josephus enjoyed in Christian antiquity, thereby allowing for the possibility of the misattribution of works to him. Such misattributions might surprise a critical mind such as Photius,[120] but most Christians would look on the attribution of a work to Josephus as a case in which even an outsider to the faith was constrained by the evidence to testify to the Christian truth. Hence the traces of the name 'Josephus', which have wrongly made Nautin think of another Christian writer.[121]

As for CN, Bardy maintained, with Nautin, its authenticity; but, against Nautin, he held to the common view that its date must be early,[122] earlier certainly

---

118 G. da Bra, *I Filosofumeni sono di Ippolito?* Rome 1942. Da Bra followed this with another booklet, *Studio su S. Ippolito Dottore,* Rome 1944.

119 MélSR 5 (1948) pp.63–88: *L'énigme d'Hippolyte.*

120 Photius, *Bibliotheca,* Cod. 48, PG103:84C–85A.

121 RHE 43 (1948) pp.179–191: *Le souvenir de Josèphe chez les Pères.*

122 Bardy was especially struck by the resemblances between Tertullian's *Adversus Praxean* and CN. It was this resemblance which 'nous empêche à elle seule de fixer trop bas la rédaction de l'Antinoët', MélSR 5 (1948) p.83.

than the *Elenchus* by about fifteen or twenty years, and differing from the *Elenchus,* not for the reason of dual authorship proposed by Nautin, but for the very good reason that it is from a different sort of work with a different purpose, and from a different context. In a short review of Nautin's *Hippolyte et Josipe* Bardy even expressed certain vague reservations about CN: but this was a line of argument against Nautin which was to develop to more articulate proportions later in the controversy.[123]

Other reviews of Nautin's book were similarly negative. A critical notice by H. de Riedmatten went deep into the doubts which, for some at least, surround CN.[124] It was beginning to become clear that there were aspects of CN, especially with regard to the possible presence of doctrinal interpolations other than those on the subject of the Holy Spirit (which Nautin had dismissed[125]) that might make CN a much more unreliable touchstone of Hippolytean authenticity than Nautin had supposed. In a short notice of *Hippolyte et Josipe* J. Daniélou also refused allegiance to the new position of Nautin.[126] He stressed the clear resemblances between the *Elenchus* and CN, and the historical considerations which demand an earlier date for CN than for the *Elenchus.* M. Richard also reviewed *Hippolyte et Josipe*, along with other books on Hippolytus,[127] and while criticizing Bardy for misrepresenting Nautin's arguments, supported the traditional view on Hippolytus and his works. From Richard's review two main points became clear. First, that Richard had grave doubts about the value of CN in a discussion of the authenticity of works in the Hippolytean corpus: CN is simply not a sufficiently guaranteed witness of the thought of Hippolytus. The present text poses serious problems and these problems have not yet received satisfactory treatment. On the passages which mention the Holy Spirit he lays down two alternatives: either the text is authentic, or it has all been much more seriously altered than critics have been prepared to suppose. Richard himself was prepared to go so far as to admit that CN is no more than a late and inept compilation of Hippolytean material.[128] Second, that Richard's objections to Nautin's position were based on his disagreement with Nautin concerning chronographical details arising out of a

---

123 RHE 43 (1948) pp.197–200. See esp. p.198: '. . . ce fragment n'est peut-être pas, parmi les oeuvres attribuées à notre écrivain, celui dont l'authenticité est la mieux assurée. . .'
124 *Dominican Studies* 1 (1948) pp.168–173.
125 See *Hippolyte et Josipe,* Chap. II, pp.36–47.
126 RechSR 35 (1948) pp.596–598.
127 *Saint Hippolyte,* MélSR 5 (1948) pp.294–308.
128 '. . . ce que nous appelons le *Contre Noetum* pourrait bien n'être qu'une composition homilétique de l'époque byzantine, fabriquée assez maladroitement à partir d'extraits d'un ou plusieurs écrits d'Hippolyte.' Ibid., p.298.

comparison of the *Synagoge* with Hippolytus' commentary *In Danielem.*
Nautin's point was that certain discrepancies noted between the two works
could only be explained by postulating two authors, as with the *Elenchus* and
CN. Richard claimed that this explanation was not necessary. To a large extent
these two scholars fought in single combat on the battlefield of Hippolytean
questions for the next seven years. The details do not affect the present study,
but it is best to keep track of their contributions because CN was also mentioned in the course of what was to become, sadly, an acrimoniously personal
contest. Nautin first brought out the discrepancies which led him to hold to
different authors for the *Synagoge* (written by the author of the *Elenchus*)
and the commentary *In Danielem* in his *Hippolyte et Josipe,*[129] but he mentioned them for a second time in the course of a review of a new edition of
the *In Danielem;*[130] but it was two years later before Richard joined battle
with him.

Meanwhile Nautin's edition of CN appeared;[131] and he used the opportunity
to reply to the critics of *Hippolyte et Josipe.*[132] The reply was largely a restate-
ment of the thesis of *Hippolyte et Josipe* with special emphasis on the parts of
the thesis attacked by the critics. Already it was becoming apparent that the
result of the whole controversy would be the usual stalemate. Nautin stressed
four points against his critics: first, the author of the works *Elenchus-Synagoge-
περὶ τοῦ παντός* is certainly not Hippolytus, because of the complete divergence
which exists between the *Elenchus* and CN, and because of the chronographical
contradictions which exist between the *Synagoge* and the *In Danielem;* nor
can the divergence and the contradiction be explained by appealing to some
such theory as that which claims that Hippolytus' mind underwent certain
developments in the course of a long literary career, or by appealing to the fact
that Hippolytus was writing for different types of audience. Second, it is the
Elenchus which is used by the later fragment CN. Third, the name of the new
author is Josipus. Fourth, this Josipus is the person who is represented in the
statue. Nautin holds, of course, that CN is the finale of the *Syntagma:* both in
doctrine and in form it is clearly the authentic work of Hippolytus.[133]

---

129 pp.69–70.
130 See *Revue Biblique* 55 (1948) pp.315–317, where Nautin reviews Hippolyte,
    Commentaire sur Daniel. Introduction de Gustave Bardy; texte établi et traduit par
    Maurice Lefèvre. Paris 1947, *(Sources chrétiennes* 14).
131 *Hippolyte, Contre les Hérésies, Fragment. Etude et édition critique par Pierre Nautin.*
    Paris 1949, *(Etudes et textes pour l'histoire du dogme de la Trinité 2).*
132 See esp. *Contre les Hérésies,* Appendice II, *Retour sur Josipe,* pp.215–230.
133 Ibid., p.56.

It was in 1950 that B. Capelle made his contribution to the discussion, the most authoritative and eirenic in the whole course of the controversy.[134] He began by chasing Josipus from the scene, but then proposed to test, by a thorough reconsideration of the known facts, the hypothesis that the statue, the *Elenchus,* the *Synagoge* and the περὶ τοῦ παντός do not belong to Hippolytus. For Capelle, Nautin's concentration on CN as the best basis of comparison between the authentic works of Hippolytus and the *Elenchus* was especially unfortunate. Almost a quarter of a century before, Capelle had had occasion to express his doubts about certain parts of CN.[135] Now he pointed out that the text of CN seemed to him to have been re-worked, and its style was not in entire accord with the other works of Hippolytus.[136] Somewhat inconsistently perhaps, Capelle found Nautin's edition of CN fully satisfactory. In a footnote Capelle called Nautin's edition 'une critique magistrale du texte de l'Antinoët', but then went on to state that the transmission of the work is highly suspect and that he does not believe CN to be the work of Hippolytus pure and simple.[137] Later, too, Capelle launched into lavish praise of Nautin's edition while at the same time casting deep but unspecified suspicions on the reliability of the ms.[138] While this procedure was of admirable service to Capelle's undoubtedly eirenic intentions, it made it difficult to see exactly what he found wrong with the text of CN as it stands.

But Capelle proceeded with his re-evaluation of the known facts about Hippolytus. First, he established that the statue must be that of Hippolytus. Next, using the evidence available in Eusebius and Jerome, he concluded that the author of the *Elenchus,* the *Synagoge* and the περὶ τοῦ παντός must be Hippolytus. Then there follows the most original and valuable part of Capelle's article, in which he submitted certain aspects of Hippolytus' style to a close analysis. He separated Hippolytus' works into the two groups which led Nautin to suppose that they must have been written by different authors, and then, in impressive detail, he showed that both groups display such a common style, vocabulary and theology that they could only have been written by the same author, Hippolytus. But it is noteworthy that Capelle excluded CN from the main part of his analytical comparison, although he later admitted evidence from it,[139] to arrive at the traditional view of Hippolytus and his works, in opposition to Nautin. It is difficult to disagree with his general conclusion,

---

134 RTAM 17 (1950) pp.145–174: *Hippolyte de Rome.*
135 RBén 38 (1926) pp.321–330. For Capelle's restoration of CN 1, see p.325.
136 RTAM 17 (1950) p.148.
137 Ibid., n.10.
138 Ibid., p.170.
139 Ibid., pp.169–172.

which is that the texts of Hippolytus' works themselves, the literary evidence of antiquity, and the statue all point to the unity of one author, Hippolytus.[140]

In this same year (1950) and in the following one, Richard took up the question of the chronographical discrepancies in the commentary *In Danielem* and in the *Synagoge*.[141] In a long and careful treatment of the problems involved, Richard concluded against Nautin and showed that the *In Danielem*, the Paschal Table which is inscribed on the statue, and the *Synagoge* are closely linked with one another, and so must be attributed to the same author.[142] This was Richard's main conclusion; but he added for good measure yet another disturbing and unsupported remark on CN. Nautin, he said, was right in seeing CN as a *retractatio*. CN is a *retractatio*, but not of the end of Josipus' *Elenchus* by the later, non-Roman Hippolytus, but of the last chapter of Hippolytus' 'Against All the Heresies' 'par un inconnu d'âge à déterminer'.[143]

In 1951 B. Botte joined in the controversy, like the rest in opposition to Nautin, and proposed an interesting but little regarded solution to the problem of the differences between CN and the finale of the *Elenchus*.[144] Botte proposed that the finale of the *Elenchus* did not belong to the *Elenchus*. It is in fact, to judge from what can be gathered concerning the nature and contents of the *De Universo* (= περὶ τῆς τοῦ παντὸς οὐσίας [or αἰτίας] = περὶ τοῦ παντός on the statue) from the literary sources available, probably the finale of this latter work. But it has been incoherently tacked on to the *Elenchus* by Hippolytus. It belongs not to a work for Christians – which the *Elenchus* is – but to a work written for pagans, the περὶ τοῦ παντός. Hence the disharmony which Nautin has rightly diagnosed but wrongly cured, between the supposed finale of the *Elenchus* and CN. Further, Botte thought that there was no difficulty in explaining the ascription of the *De Universo* in antiquity to Flavius Josephus. It appears from the prologue and first chapter of the *Jewish Antiquities* of Josephus that he at least planned to write a philosophical exposé of the causes of the universe. A knowledgeable scribe, faced with an anonymous *De Universo,* might well have ascribed this work to Josephus. No need, then, to postulate a Josipus. Indeed it is even possible, according to Botte, that the confusion arose in an even more simple manner: an abbreviated form of the name Hippolytus in Greek capitals, alone or in combination with another word such as ΙΣΩΣ

---

140 'Funiculus triplex difficile rumpitur', ibid., p.174.
141 MélSR 7 (1950) pp.237–268, and 8 (1951) pp.19–50: *Comput et Chronographie chez Saint Hippolyte.*
142 MélSR 8 (1951) p.47.
143 Ibid., p.50.
144 RTAM 18 (1951) pp.5–18: *Note sur l'auteur du 'De Universo' attribué à Saint Hippolyte.*

or OMOIΩΣ, might easily lead to the construction of a name, IΩΣIIIΠ. . . . Botte's hypotheses are ingenious, and perhaps cast a certain light on possibilities which Nautin had not even considered, as well as giving a possible, if strictly unprovable, solution to the problem of the difference between the *Elenchus* and CN.

1952 was to be another busy year for the controversialists. More opposition to Nautin was expressed. Capelle insisted on his former proofs of the unity of author for Hippolytus' works,[145] and brought further evidence to bear on the early date of CN from R. Cadiou's *La Jeunesse d'Origène*. Cadiou points out the influence that Hippolytus had on Origen, in particular in the oldest part of the Commentary on the Psalms which Origen wrote prior to the year 222 A.D. And most interestingly, there appear to be even verbal likenesses between phrases in CN and in Origen's Commentary. This fact would help to date CN to before 222 A.D., which is decisively against the whole thesis of Nautin. But once again Capelle expressed his uncertainty of the text of CN.[146] A new figure now took his place among the anti-Nautin scholars. H. Elfers attacked not only *Hippolyte et Josipe* but also Nautin's edition of CN.[147] Elfers indicated some unacceptable textual emendations made by Nautin at the expense of the theology of CN, and claimed that CN was not so unspeculative as Nautin was inclined to suppose. Elfers had had a long acquaintance with CN, especially with regard to its links with the *Traditio Apostolica*.[148] On doctrinal questions arising from CN he showed himself hostile to Nautin, since he saw in CN a document which stands at a certain juncture in the history of the theology of the Trinity from which Nautin had unwittingly dislodged it.[149] But having raised a number of interesting questions and having propounded a number of theories, Elfers, as so many others before him, left the problem of CN to others.[150]

It was by now time again for Nautin to reply to some at least of his many adversaries.[151] Once again, the reply took the form of a reassertion of the position originally proposed in *Hippolyte et Josipe*. As far as CN is concerned, Nautin repeated, it follows the plan of the finale of the *Elenchus*, and it is from

---

145 RTAM 19 (1952) pp.193–202: *A propos d'Hippolyte de Rome*.
146 Ibid., p.202, n.31.
147 *Neue Untersuchungen über die Kirchenordnung Hippolyts von Rom*, in *Abhandlungen über Theologie und Kirche*, Festschrift für Karl Adam. In Verbindung mit H. Elfers und F. Hofman, herausgegeben von M. Reding. Düsseldorf 1952, pp.169–211.
148 *Die Kirchenordnung Hippolyts von Rom*, Paderborn 1938.
149 Ibid., p.187, on CN 14.
150 'Dieser ganze, für das Corpus Hippolyticum nicht unwichtige Fragenkomplex bedarf noch einer gründlichen Bearbeitung.' *Neue Untersuchungen . . .*, p.208.
151 RHE 47 (1952) pp.5–43: *La controverse sur l'auteur de l''Elenchos'*.

the point of view of this finale alone that CN can be adequately explained. CN, with all its additions, modifications and suppressions, becomes intelligible only when considered later than the *Elenchus* and as the work of a different author. Nautin claimed to have *proved* this; whereas no one has yet proved the opposite view, namely that CN is an earlier work of the author of the *Elenchus.* Then Nautin makes his reply to Richard concerning their chronographical dispute. At the end of this he took up the question of Richard's opinion of CN. Richard had supposed that CN was not the work of Hippolytus, whereas he held that the *Elenchus* was. To which Nautin replied that of the two works it should be CN which should be attributed to Hippolytus.[152] According to Nautin, Richard had seen the incompatibility that in fact exists between the two works; but had preferred to remove CN from the Hippolytean corpus to following Nautin himself in the postulating of another author for the *Elenchus.* The controversy waged between Nautin and Richard was to grow in bitterness in the next three years.

Next Nautin replied to Capelle. About the important analysis which Capelle made of the common elements, theological, stylistic and verbal, in the Hippolytean corpus, Nautin had little to say save that the expressions and phrases selected by Capelle were too general or stereotyped to prove much. What was required was an analysis and comparison of terms and doctrines which are characteristic; otherwise the concordance discovered did not arise above a merely material level. This was what was wrong, Nautin claimed, with the common traits between the *Elenchus* and CN which Capelle displays: they are either commonplaces or significant of no more than a material likeness. There is no proof of formal resemblance.[153] On Capelle's exclusion of CN from his main analysis Nautin was of the opinion that Capelle was taking something of an unfair advantage, since he would have discovered more contrasts than convergences had he included the fragment. Nautin found Capelle's reasons for excluding CN unsatisfactory: Capelle's doubts – and these have been already alluded to above – about the text of CN were unaccompanied by any supporting proofs. While it may be true that the text of CN contains defects, they are no more than such as would be expected in the ordinary transmission of a ms text. The text has not been reworked, and can easily be restored.[154] Neither in this article, nor in the appendix to it, in which he replied to Botte, did Nautin make the slightest concession to his adversaries. But he did call for a ten-year

---

152 [CN] 'qui offre une telle similitude d'esprit et d'expression avec toute l'oeuvre
    certaine d'Hippolyte et qui est du reste le seul des deux à porter son nom'. Ibid., p.27.
153 Ibid., p.35, n.1.
154 Ibid., p.36f.

respite, which, he hoped, would help to bring all scholars into agreement on essential points.[155]

Yet again, however, Richard came back to the attack.[156] On the chronographical issue between the two scholars there was still no progress. But on Richard's doubts and suspicions about CN there was much of interest, mostly in the second part of his long article. Richard pointed out that in the most authentic Hippolytean works there was a notable absence of Trinitarian formulae, and that in them, as in the *Elenchus*, Trinitarian doctrine has a ditheistic and subordinationist tendency. This fact, he claimed, makes the Trinitarianism of CN somewhat suspect, especially in the second part of the work: it could be much more seriously interpolated than had been supposed.[157] For Richard it is the text which Theodoret quotes as from a Commentary on Psalm 2 by Hippolytus which represents a fragment of what Hippolytus originally wrote. What we now have in CN, at least in the latter half, is an amplified and paraphrased version of a largely lost original. Coming down to particulars, Richard points to a single sentence,[158] which he asserted, contains three anachronisms: $\theta\epsilon\grave{o}\varsigma$ $\grave{\epsilon}\nu\sigma\acute{\omega}\mu\alpha\tau\sigma\varsigma$, which he said did not, for the second or third centuries, mean *incarnate* God, but material-corporeal God, and this sense was not, at the time of Hippolytus, in question; $\check{\alpha}\nu\theta\rho\omega\pi\sigma\varsigma$ $\tau\acute{\epsilon}\lambda\epsilon\iota\sigma\varsigma$, which supposes a problematic unknown in the third century, but fits well into the later Apollinarist crisis; and the phrase $\kappa\alpha\tau\grave{\alpha}$ $\varphi\alpha\nu\tau\alpha\sigma\acute{\iota}\alpha\nu$ $\mathring{\eta}$ $\tau\rho\sigma\pi\acute{\eta}\nu$, which, he said, did not appear as such before the sixth century. Richard said that he was dissatisfied with Nautin's explanation of these words and phrases. But it would have been better if Richard had been more thorough, and had made more clear what he thought was the full extent of the suspected amplification of the original text of CN.

Two more interventions of Nautin followed. The first[159] was a letter to the editor of *Mélanges de Science Religieuse* in which Nautin complained of Richard's personal attacks and accused him of having used a personal letter in the course of the published controversy. The second[160] was yet another chronographical battle with Richard; it is towards the end of this long article that Nautin replied to Richard's difficulties with the text of CN. This reply once again took the form of a straight reassertion of what Nautin had said before:

---

155 Ibid., p.38f.
156 MélSR 10 (1953) pp.13–52 and pp.145–180: *Encore le problème d'Hippolyte*.
157 Ibid., p.178. See n.4 for Richard's opinion that CN 1–7 is substantially Hippolytean.
158 CN 17.5 below.
159 MélSR 11 (1954) pp.215–218: *Encore le problème d'Hippolyte*.
160 RechSR 42 (1954) pp.226–257: *L'auteur du Comput pascal de 222 et de la Chronique anonyme de 235*.

ἐνσώματος is anti-docetic, and is 'paralleled' by σωματοποιεῖσθαι in *In Danielem* 3.14.6 (GCS Hippolytus I, ed. Bonwetsch, p. 150, 16); τέλειος is opposed to κατὰ φαντασίαν, and refers to Christ's authentic humanity; and τροπή means 'manner of speaking', or 'figure of speech', and is opposed to ἀληθῶς and again serves to bring out the reality of the manhood of Christ. For Nautin this reply constituted an effective rebuttal of Richard's doubts about CN. Nautin insists that it is a typical third-century text, well linked with Irenaeus, with Tertullian and so on. Once again the exchange of views between participants in the controversy about CN was to prove quite sterile.

Next year, 1955, was to bring the controversy to a long overdue conclusion. Richard made a final reply to Nautin on the chronographical problems which had exercised both of them for so long;[161] and he replied also to questions concerning CN, in particular concerning the anachronistic sentence mentioned above.[162] Ἐνσώματος, he said, came late into Christological terminology, whereas σωματοποιεῖσθαι was adopted in the second century. Τέλειος does not mean *real,* as Nautin would have it, but has to do with Hippolytus' doctrine whereby Christ in some way, after partial quasi-incarnation, finally becomes completely or pefectly incarnate as man only later.[163] Κατὰ τροπήν or τροπῇ is usually contrasted with ἀτρέπτως in later controversy.

Important recent work on CN, which has at least the merit of dealing with CN on its own terms and not in terms of alien issues – as has been the case for far too long – is contained in a doctoral thesis by R. Puchulu.[164] Puchulu examines the connection between the question about glorification in CN 1.6 and the important doxology of 18.10, in order to see if there is continuity of thought between these two *loci* and other mentions of glory/glorification and allied notions in CN. Interesting though such an investigation turns out to be, and stimulating though the arguments against Nautin and Richard are,[165] Puchulu's choice of theme is not a happy one. For while glory/glorification undoubtedly has its part to play in CN, it is hardly of primary importance; and Puchulu's treatment of it leaves untouched the more obviously fundamental aspects of CN both as a literary entity and a theological work.[166]

---

161 RechSR 43 (1955) pp.379–394: *Dernières remarques sur S. Hippolyte et le soi-disant Josipe.*

162 Op. cit., pp.393–394.

163 Op. cit., p.393.

164 R. Puchulu, *Sur le Contre Noet d'Hippolyte – Les attaches littéraires et doctrinales de la doxologie finale.* Thèse de Doctorat présentée à la Faculté de Théologie de Lyon par R.P. du Diocèse de Paris: Année académique 1959–1960.

165 Op. cit., pp.11–21 (against Nautin's view that the *Elenchus* should be ascribed to Josipus); pp.22–28 (against Richard's view on the 'interpolated' passages).

166 As Puchulu in fact admits: op. cit., p.148.

He holds, in the main, the Schwartz view of CN as substantially a homily, but one which, as its opening words seem to show, lacks perhaps one or two introductory phrases.[167] Unfortunately Puchulu's preoccupation with glory/glorification leads him to expend a disproportionate amount of ingenuity on puzzling out a solution for the 'lacuna' of CN 1.6,[168] – a problem which, as we shall see, can most probably be much more simply laid to rest.[169]

An abiding problem

Thus the way remains open for some more preliminary work on the fundamental problem of CN. Past controversy, to which even recent study clings too closely, has both produced and given abiding shape to a problem about CN which does not lie at the heart of the problem of CN itself. The growth of the problem as dictated by the interests of generations of scholars is largely an artificial growth, and it does not have its root in CN but in some other concern with other works in the Hippolytean corpus or with the sources of anti-heretical writings of the late second or early third century. CN has been regarded far too much *en passant.*

The growth of what has come to be accepted as the problem of CN has passed through a number of distinct phases. Firstly, there was a phase, lasting from the discovery of the work until it fell into the hands of the more critical, but not necessarily more wise, seventeenth-century scholars, during which CN was regarded as what it appeared to be from its sole ms, Vat. gr. 1431 – 'A Homily of Hippolytus . . . against the heresy of a certain Noetus'. Secondly, under the particularly strong influence of Fabricius' first edition of the Greek text, and lasting until the mid-nineteenth century, there was a phase when opinion changed and hardened, so that CN came to be considered as the end-fragment of the *Syntagma,* the name given by Photius to the 'Against All the Heresies' of Hippolytus. Thirdly, there followed a phase which lasted from the mid-nineteenth century until the beginning of the Second World War – a phase which was dominated by German patristic scholarship, and in which CN, while regarded as certainly the end-fragment of some work of Hippolytus, was

---

167 Op. cit., p.33. Well observed is what Puchulu says on CN as a literary unit (p.35f): 'on y trouve que la refutation des Noétiens et l'Exposé de la Verité sont placés par Hippolyte sur pied d'égalité et annoncés comme les deux parties de l'ouvrage [cf. CN 3.4–6]. Pareille division du discours ne semble guère indiquer que l'Apodeixis est la conclusion générale d'un recueil hérésiologique dont le Contre Noët ne serait qu'un fragment.' But Puchulu does not develop this remark. See Chapter 3 below.
168 Op. cit., pp.45–68.
169 See p. 37f. below.

ascribed by different scholars to different works. Although a number of works were considered as the possible whole to which the fragment CN was the conclusion – an otherwise unknown anti-Monarchian treatise and a Homily on Psalm 2 were the serious contenders – this phase, too, closed with the weight of opinion, probably much influenced by Harnack's conversion, on the side of CN's being the end-fragment of the *Syntagma*, in spite of the more or less extensive presence in it of certain interpolated elements. Fourthly, there is the latest phase, dominated by French scholars, in which CN has been both accepted without serious difficulty and subjected to vaguely aggressive suspicions and speculations from a number of different directions. Most of the participants in this phase of the controversy admitted that CN was indeed the end-fragment of the *Syntagma*; but disquiet about certain and possible interpolations grew as the phase proceeded, and even doubts about authorship were expressed by some.

And there the problem of CN stands, as it has been produced and shaped in the course of the four distinct phases of controversy. In general, it may be concluded that there is need of a fresh, if only preliminary, approach to CN which should involve single-minded enquiry and appraisal. No one, for instance, in spite of all the effort that has been expended on showing *that* it is a fragment, and *what* it is a fragment *of,* has ever managed to offer a convincing explanation of *why* it should be a fragment at all, or of *how* it ever came to be one. It has for far too long been the habit of scholars, in the heat of their personal controversies, to ignore the primary data of the sole ms authority, which claims, quite simply to present CN as a homily or discourse in its own right and complete in itself. It is the status of CN as a piece of writing that needs to be examined and clarified. The arguments for its being a fragment are old, thin and shaky. Will CN stand alone? What is its structure? its style? its literary character? Any further work on its provenance, for example, or on its theology will be possible only if there is a reliable textual basis.

2
THE TEXT OF CN

First, it is necessary to provide an acceptable text of CN taken directly from the sole ms. Along with this text there is provided a translation on the facing page. In anticipation of the results of Chapter 3, the translation (but not the text itself) has been divided, for the sake of later convenience, into the parts and sections which it has been discovered to contain. The translation itself is fairly free, and even at times rough: but then so is the original Greek. In view of what is discovered in the following chapters about the genre of which CN is seen to be an outstanding example, it would be a grave mistake — and one that has been made before — to try to smoothe out all the disharmonies and inconcinnities detectable in the Greek. If, for instance, Scripture quotations do not perfectly match one another in repetition, this is no reason for forcing them, in a procrustean way, to be identical. Again, if articles are omitted in the Greek, this is no reason for constantly supplying them, or for reading great significance into their omission. CN, as will be shown, is an excellent example of a popular and attractive kind of anti-heretical discourse. To make it conform to the standards of a scientific paper would be to do it the gravest injury.

The text

Textual criticism in any proper sense hardly comes into question where there is, as in the case of CN, only one independent ms-witness to the original text. The work involved in the presentation of a single ms-text can strictly go no further than *recensio*, the establishment, as P. Maas says in his wise pages, 'of what *must* or *may* be regarded as transmitted'. When the tradition of a text rests on a single witness, '*recensio* consists in describing and deciphering as accurately as possible the single witness'.[1] CN, it must be said, has suffered through the neglect of this principle.

Even so, precisely because there is no other witness available, the work of presentation must also aim at a tolerable and usable text. To quote Maas again:

If the tradition proves to be corrupt, we must attempt to remedy it by conjecture (*divinatio*). This attempt leads either to a self-evident emendation or to several more or less equally satisfying conjectures or to the recognition that a cure by conjecture has not been discovered – a crux. The typical conjecture consists in the removal of an anomaly. Now there are some anomalies which were admitted or intended by the author, while others are due to corruption. The assumption then in making a conjecture is that we recognize that an anomaly could not possibly have been admitted or intended by the author . . . As a rule, no writer will aspire to an anomaly for its own sake; an anomaly is the consequence of his desire to say something out of the ordinary for which the normal mode of expression was found to be inadequate. If we can show that he could, without any sacrifice, have expressed in a normal way what the tradition expresses anomalously, then the anomaly is probably based on a corruption . . . We must distinguish sharply between anomaly and *singularity*. What is unique is not for that reason alone to be regarded with suspicion.[2]

The stringent guide-lines laid down by Mass are those which have governed this present attempt to give a faithful yet tolerable and usable Greek text of CN. In fact, the sole ms seems to present a fairly good text of CN. The text has been copied with care and apparently with a certain amount of revision. It is easy to read, and, as will be seen from the *apparatus* devised below, needs only a few minor adjustments, most of which are generally accepted corrections of easily detectable misspellings.[3]

Corrections within the text

The number of insertions and corrections in the ms is indicative of the care with which the copy of CN was made and even, possibly, revised. Thus in 3.6 there is a marginal insertion of five words; in 10.3, of three words; in 5.1, of two words; and there are one-word marginal insertions in 10.3, 14.8 and 16.6.

---

1 P. Maas, *Textual Criticism,* Oxford 1958, p.1f.
2 Ibid., p.11f.
3 P. Nautin, *Hippolyte, Contre les Hérésies,* p.76, under-values the state of the text in the ms. His pessimistic assessment, along with other presuppositions, has encouraged him to make numerous alterations in the text of CN. This has seriously lessened the value of his edition. For the effects of his assessment etc. see ibid. Chap.V, pp.81–120, *L'Etat du Texte,* and his remarkable *'apparatus'* to the text, passim.

A dozen or more times a single letter seems to have been written in above the line; and twice, two letters. Once a single letter has been added in the margin. In 6.4 one word and a single letter have been written as a marginal insertion, even though they are in fact quite superfluous. Again, in 12.3 four words in the text have been cancelled; in 4.4, two words; and one word in 4.6, 6.4 and 6.6. A syllable has been cancelled in 6.4; and corrected in 8.3, 8.4, 18.7, 18.9: in 6.1 and 18.5, this has been done in the margin. In 8.3 a word has been corrected in the text. Twice an abbreviated καί has been erased. In spite of the unreliable accentuation, there is evidence that in about eight instances attempts have been made to correct accents. An odd feature is the random addition in rubric of odd letters of words in the text made in the margin on half-a-dozen occasions. Once, for instance, the second letter of ἐρωτήσατε has been decorated in the centre margin as an elaborate bird's-head. Thus by and large, there is reason to suppose that the sole ms of CN is a careful and even corrected copy of some lost ms.

Abbreviations

The copyist had at his disposal a regular system of abbreviations for some fourteen familiar words: and, God, Father, Son, Spirit, Jesus, Christ, Lord, Saviour, man, heaven, virgin, cross, said. He did not necessarily use the system consistently. At no point does any of these abbreviations cause difficulty. In the Greek text given here they have been written out in full. One single abbreviation has caused difficulty: παιον following πνεῦμα in 17.1. Ficker's completion of this as πα[νάγ]ιον is certainly the most convincing available, and it has been adopted in the text *ad loc.*[4] ν – mainly final – is written with a stroke some thirty-four times.

Punctuation etc.

The ms-text is not, of course, punctuated in any modern sense: rather it is broken up into short *cola* of an often haphazard kind. In the text given below a modern punctuation has been imposed, so as both to bring out what seems to be the obvious sense of the text, and to correspond to the style which, later in this study, is proposed as that of the whole work. Accents, breathings

---

4 G. Ficker, *Studien zur Hippolytfrage,* Leipzig 1893, pp.100–106 compares the ms-text of CN with Lagarde's text.

and subscript-iotas (of which there are none in the ms) have been given according to modern practice. There are a few misplaced Greek capital letters in the text: so capital letters have been introduced where sense required them.

Lacunae

There is a genuine lacuna detectable in the ms-text at 16.1. Probably it is no more than the omission of the verb. Such an omission is perhaps to be explained by the change of column which occurs at this point.

But in 1.6 there are in the ms clear signs of a lacuna in the text. f.360v1, line 17, consists only of the abbreviation X$\overline{\text{N}}$ followed by a stop and a blank to the end of the line. Towards the end of the blank line is written the abbreviation of ζήτει = *require*. These indications of a lacuna have attracted a number of scholars to attempt the restoration of what they suppose was the original text of CN. Thus, for instance, Capelle,[5] Nautin,[6] and Puchulu[7] have used considerable ingenuity in creating and proposing their various reconstructions. But in fact it seems unlikely that there is a true lacuna in the text at this point. The sense of Noetus' question is quite complete in itself, indeed cleverly naïve, if left as it stands. The reply of the presbyters is, dramatically, the reaction of orthodoxy expressed in well-known formulae. To reconcile the two sides textually with the dubious help of Epiphanius is to ruin the dramatic encounter between heresy and the Church. More will be said later about the dramatic structure of the two introductory chapters. In any case the blank line and ζήτει are, *prima facie*, merely signs of the lack of understanding on the part of the copyist. And it is possible to offer an explanation of this lack of understanding.[8] δοξάζεω – δοξάζεσθαι is of common enough occurrence in CN – seven times. But in the part of CN under discussion the copyist met δοξάζων for the first time. Now δοξάζεω has two clearly distinct senses. The more common sense of the word – especially perhaps for a Greek-speaking copyist – is 'to believe', 'to suppose', 'to be of the opinion that . . .' If the copyist took the word, on its first appearance, in this more common sense, it is easy to see how he was unable to make sense of Noetus' apparently unfinished question: 'What wrong am I in fact doing in supposing that Christ . . .?' Χριστόν became

5 RBén 38 (1926) pp.321–330: *Le cas du pape Zéphyrin.*
6 *Hippolyte, Contre les Hérésies,* p.235, 16–19: a drastic re-writing of the text. For Nautin's justification of the changes made, see op. cit., pp.85–87.
7 *Sur le Contre Noet d'Hippolyte,* pp.45–68.
8 This approach to the problem of the ms-lacuna has developed from private discussion with Fr E. Des Places S.J., Librarian and Professor of Greek Palaeography at the Pontifical Biblical Institute, Rome.

for the copyist the accusative in an expected accusative-with-infinitive construction: but no infinitive was forthcoming. Hence the blank and ζήτει. But if δοξάζων is taken in the less usual sense which it in fact has on all the occurrences of δοξάζειν — δοξάζεσθαι in CN (six other times), i.e. in the sense of 'to glorify', then Χριστόν becomes the object of δοξάζων and no further addition is needed to make good sense of Noetus' question: 'What wrong am I in fact doing in giving glory to Christ?' After all, Noetus was insisting that Christ was none other than the Father. Hence it may be concluded that this lacuna in the ms-text is a false lacuna, caused in the copyist's mind for the reasons given above, and to be ignored in the translation of CN. But its place in the Greek text has been clearly indicated.

The division of the text

A partly new system has been used in the division of the text, and has been introduced into both the Greek text and the English version. As CN stands in the ms, it contains no text-divisions. The chapter-divisions of CN which are given below are, with one minor adjustment at the beginning of chapter 13, those which were used by Fabricius, and which have remained in use ever since. They are still surprisingly serviceable. These eighteen traditional chapters have been newly subdivided into numbered parts, of an unequal but convenient length, in accordance with the sense they contain. For a full explanation and justification both of this sub-division of the chapters and of the additional new divisions which have been imported only into the English version, it will be necessary to consult Chapter 3 of the present study. In this study all references to the text of CN are given according to the traditional chapter and the new sub-division of the chapter. In the Greek text the traditional chapters are numbered in *Roman* numerals, while the new sub-divisions are numbered in *Arabic* numerals. This is simply to avoid confusion within the text. Elsewhere throughout the present study, both chapter and sub-division are given in Arabic numerals, since there is no possibility of confusion, and such numerals are simpler to read.

Special points

There are two places in the text as given below which deserve some short comment.

At 7.1 Nautin's addition of δύο has been adopted, with a corresponding change of the ms-reading ἐπει to ἐπί. It seems best to make this addition on grounds of haplography, much as in the case of 2.3.

The τριχής of 8.2 presents a more difficult problem. It remains possible that the word is in fact an adjective which is not normally found. Hence it has been left in the text on that supposition. The solutions of editors – except the unlikely one of Nautin – are noted in the *apparatus.* Certainly the most tempting change would be to τριχῆ, a common adverb. Cf., e.g., Irenaeus, Adv. Haer. 1.1.3 (Harvey I, 11), or Epiphanius, Panar. haer. 33.4.1 (GCS Epiphanius, ed. Holl, I, p.452, 13). It may be, however, that the adjective lies beneath 'tripartitum' in the following sentence from Irenaeus: 'Universorum quoque Pleroma, quid utique *tripartitum* est in octonationem, et decadem, et duodecadem: et non alterum quendam praeter hos numerum?' (Adv. Haer., 2.15.2, Harvey I, 303). At any rate, Reynders (*Lexique comparé* . . ., II, p.331) lists 'tripartitus' as an adjective.

Here a point about the translation may be added. CN has both παῖς and υἱός, as designations of the Word. The former has been translated as 'son', the latter as 'Son'. It is difficult to see that any important theological distinction is implied by the use of the two words.

The apparatus

The *apparatus* given at the foot of the Greek text is largely descriptive. For the most part it indicates the orthographical errors of the ms in those places where either the common correction of all the editors – which is enclosed in a square bracket,] – or the most convincing correction of some or one of them has been introduced into the Greek text. Sometimes other possible corrections are also given: but this has been done very selectively. Few conjectures for the betterment of the text of CN have ever been made on the basis of the sole ms. The copy of the ms from which Fabricius made his first edition of the Greek text contained errors which for two centuries – until Ficker's check on Lagarde's text – were simply repeated or allowed to engender further errors. There seems to be no point in displaying merely imaginative attempts at correction which simply will not square with the only ms available, or which in any case are unwarranted and unwanted. Scripture references have been inserted in the English version where they seem useful.

The following signs have been used in the text:

/	a new col. or fol.
⟨ ⟩	conjectural addition
. . . . . .	lacuna from ms.
⟦ ⟧	cancellation or erasure in ms.
⌐ ⌐	introduced into text from margin
[ ]	supplied where there is damage
⟨· · · ·⟩	conjectured lacuna

The following signs have been used in the *apparatus*:

V   = *Vaticanus graecus* 1431, ff. 360r2 – 367r1.

Vcorr   = a correction made by V.

f   = J.A. Fabricius, *S. Hippolyti Episcopi et Martyris Operum Volumen II*, Hamburg 1718, pp.5–20.

r   = M.J. Routh, *Scriptorum Ecclesiasticorum Opuscula praecipua quaedam*, Tom. I³, Oxford 1858, pp.49–80.

[r]   = a suggestion of Routh's, in square brackets in his text.

l   = P.A. de Lagarde, *Hippolyti Romani quae feruntur omnia graece*, Leipzig-London 1858, pp.43–57.

s   = E. Schwartz, *Zwei Predigten Hippolyts*, Munich 1936, pp.5–18.

n   = P. Nautin, *Hippolyte, Contre les Hérésies, Fragment*, Paris 1949, pp.235–265. But see also Nautin's retractations in his *Le Dossier d'Hippolyte* . . ., Paris 1953, p.130.

A DISCOURSE OF HIPPOLYTUS,
ARCHBISHOP OF ROME AND MARTYR,
AGAINST THE SECT OF A CERTAIN NOETUS

A Discourse of Hippolytus, Archbishop of Rome and Martyr, against the sect of a certain Noetus

1.1 – 2.8

Part 1

1.1 – 1.8

1.1

The disciples of Noetus

1.2

Noetus' vanity and his patripassianist heresy

1.3

The unclean and blasphemous spirit that inspired him explains the fact of his downfall

1.4

His trial for ambition and his lying denial

1.5

His deceitful formation of a sect of his own

1.6

His trial for heresy and condemnation: he openly defies authority

INTRODUCTION: THE PATRIPASSIANIST HERESY

Origins: The Doctrine, Decline and Fall of Noetus

Certain strangers are introducing a strange teaching, disciples as they are of a certain Noetus, who was a Smyrnaean by origin, and lived no great length of time ago.

The fellow put on airs and was led on into vanity. Carried away by an alien spirit's fancy, he said that Christ was the Father in person, and that the Father in person had been born and had suffered and died. You see the great vanity of heart and puffed-up pride of an alien spirit that found their way into him!

In fact the condemnation which the rest of his doings met with is enough to show that his pronouncements were coming from no pure spirit. For the fact is that he had been thrown out of holy office for blaspheming against the Holy Spirit *(cf. Lk 12, 10)*.

The fellow was saying that he himself was Moses and his brother Aaron. When the blessed elders heard all this, they called him in and questioned him closely in the name of the Church.* But he denied it and said that he was not aiming at the top ranks.

But afterwards he withdrew and hid behind a certain group of persons and gathered around himself wayward followers and subsequently he kept trying to establish his doctrine in its 'purity'.

Once again the blessed elders called him in

---

*or 'called him to face the Church and questioned him closely'.

Ὁμιλία Ἱ[π]πολύτου ἀρχ[ι]επισκόπου Ῥώμης καὶ   360r2

μάρτυρος εἰς τὴν αἵρεσιν Νοητοῦ τινος.

I. 1.   Ἕτεροί τινες ἑτέραν διδασκαλίαν παρεισάγ-

ουσιν γενόμενοί τινος Νοητοῦ μαθηταί · ὃς τὸ μὲν

5   γένος ἦν Σμυρναῖος, οὐ πολλοῦ χρόνου γενόμενος .

2. οὗτος φυσιωθεὶς εἰς ἔπαρμα ἀνήχθη. οἰήσει πνεύμ-

ατος ἀλλοτρίου ἐπαρθεὶς ἔφη τὸν Χριστὸν αὐτὸν εἶναι

τὸν Πατέρα, καὶ αὐτὸν τὸν Πατέρα γεγεννῆσθαι καὶ

πεπονθέναι καὶ ἀποτεθνηκέναι. ὁρᾶτε ὅσον ἔπαρμα

10   καρδίας καὶ φυσίωμα πνεύματος ἀλλοτρίου ὑπεισῆλθεν

εἰς αὐτόν. 3. ἤδη μὲν οὖν ἐκ τῶν ἑτέρων πράξεων

εἰς τοῦτο φέρεται ὁ ἔλεγχος αὐτῶν ὅτι μὴ καθαρῷ

πνεύματι ἐφθέγγετο. ὁ γὰρ εἰς πνεῦμα ἅγιον βλασ-

φημῶν ἔκβλητος γεγένηται κλήρου ἁγίου. 4. οὗτος

15   ἔλεγεν ἑαυτὸν εἶναι Μωυσῆν καὶ τὸν ἀδελφὸν αὐτοῦ

Ἀαρών. ταῦτα ἀκού/σαντες οἱ μακάριοι πρεσβύτεροι   360v1

προσκαλεσάμενοι ἐνώπιον τῆς ἐκκλησίας ἐξήταζον.

ὁ δὲ ἠρνεῖτο λέγων τὰς ἀρχὰς μὴ φρονεῖν. 5. ὕστ-

ερον δὲ ἐμφωλεύσας ἔν τισιν καὶ συσκευάσας ἑαυτῷ

20   συνπλανωμένους, καθαρῶς ὕστερον ἱστᾶν τὸ δόγμα

ἐβούλετο. 6. ὃν πάλιν προσκαλεσάμενοι οἱ μακάριοι

1   ὁμιλία]   ὁμειλία   V

10   ὑπεισῆλθεν]   ὑπησῆλθεν   V

18   ἠρνεῖτο]   ἠρνήτο   V

1.6 (continued)	and condemned him. But he stood up to them and said, 'What wrong am I in fact doing by giving glory to Christ?'
1.7 *The reaction of* *traditional orthodoxy*	The elders' reply to him runs: 'We too have knowledge of a single God — in the true way. We have knowledge of Christ. We know that the Son suffered as in fact he suffered, died as in fact he died; and rose up again on the third day and is at the right hand of the Father, and is coming to judge living and dead. And these things that we state are what we learnt.' Then they condemned the man and expelled him from the Church.
1.8 *Noetus' excommunication* *and final severance from* *the Church*	He reached such a pitch of bloated pride that he established a teaching centre.

Part 2

2.1 — 2.8 *(a) The Oneness of God:*	**Arguments** *a first pair of texts and an exposition*
2.1 *1st text: there is one* *God only*	It is these who are even trying to show how the doctrine is established by saying, 'He said in the Law: "I am the God of your fathers; you shall have no other gods besides me" *(Exod 3, 6; 20, 3).*
2.2 *2nd text: there is one* *God only*	And again elsewhere, "I am the first", he says, "and I am the last, and in addition to me there is no one" ' *(Isai 44, 6).*
2.3 *Patripassianist* *exposition*	This is the way they are claiming to establish a single God. They reply to queries by saying, 'Well, if I maintain that Christ is God, then he is the Father in person — if in fact he is God at all. But Christ, who is personally God, suffered. Then was it not the Father who suffered? After all, he was the Father in person.'

πρεσβύτεροι ἤλεγξαν. ὁ δὲ ἀνθίστατο λέγων, Τί οὖν

κακὸν ποιῶ δοξάζων τὸν Χριστόν ; .... 7. πρὸς

ὃν ἀνταποκρίνονται οἱ πρεσβύτεροι, Καὶ ἡμεῖς ἕνα

Θεὸν οἴδαμεν ἀληθῶς · οἴδαμεν Χριστόν · οἴδαμεν

5 τὸν Υἱὸν παθόντα καθὼς ἔπαθεν, ἀποθανόντα καθὼς

ἀπέθανεν, καὶ ἀναστάντα τῇ τρίτῃ ἡμέρᾳ καὶ ὄντα ἐν

δεξιᾷ τοῦ Πατρὸς καὶ ἐρχόμενον κρῖναι ζῶντας καὶ

νεκρούς. καὶ ταῦτα λέγομεν ἃ ἐμάθομεν. τότε

τοῦτον ἐλέγξαντες ἐξέωσαν / τῆς ἐκκλησίας. 8. ὃς 360v2

10 εἰς τοσοῦτο φυσίωμα ἠνέχθη ὡς διδασκαλεῖον συστῆσαι.

II. 1. οἳ καὶ δεῖξαι βούλονται σύστασιν τῷ δόγματι

λέγοντες, Εἶπεν ἐν νόμῳ, Ἐγὼ εἰμὶ ὁ Θεὸς τῶν πατέρων

ὑμῶν · οὐκ ἔσονται ὑμῖν θεοὶ ἕτεροι πλὴν ἐμοῦ. 2. καὶ

πάλιν ἐν ἑτέρῳ, Ἐγώ, φησίν, πρῶτος καὶ ἐγὼ ἔσχατος

15 καὶ μετ'ἐμὲ οὐκ ἐστιν οὐδείς. 3. οὕτω φάσκουσιν

συνιστᾶν ἕνα θεόν. οἳ ἀποκρίνονται λέγοντες, Εἰ

οὖν Χριστὸν ὁμολογῶ Θεόν, αὐτὸς ἄρα ἐστὶν ὁ Πατήρ,

εἰ γάρ ἐστιν ὁ Θεός. ἔπαθεν δὲ Χριστὸς αὐτὸς ὢν

Θεός. ἄρα οὖν ἔπαθεν Πατήρ ; < Πατὴρ > γὰρ αὐτὸς ἦν.

---

1 ἀνθίστατο lsn : ἀντίστατο V fr

2 lacunam (falsam!) fere unius lineae habet V, cum signo ⳨ᵀ

8 ἐμάθομεν frls : ἐμάθαμεν V n

10 διδασκαλεῖον] διδασκαλίον V

14 φησίν frln : φησι s, φᵛ V

18 εἰ γάρ V fr : εἴ γε [r]ls, εἷς γάρ Martin [RHE 37(1941)

19 sic n : alii aliter add.   p.6, n.1] n

<table>
<tr><td>

2.4

*Orthodox comment –
bad exegesis makes for
bad theology*

</td><td>

But this is not the case – because this is not the
way in which the Scriptures explain the matter.

</td></tr>
</table>

(b) The One God appeared on earth: a second pair of texts and an exposition plus an added testimony

<table>
<tr><td>

2.5

*1st text and
explanation*

</td><td>

But they go on to use other testimonies, too, and
say, 'Thus has it been written: "This is our God.
No other will be compared to him. He found out
the whole way of knowledge and gave it to Jacob
his son and to Israel who is his beloved. Afterwards
he was seen on earth and conversed with men"
(Bar 3,36–38). So you see', he says, ' that this is
the God who is one alone, and who subsequently
was seen and conversed with men.

</td></tr>
<tr><td>

2.6

*2nd text and
explanation*

</td><td>

And elsewhere', he says, 'he states: "Egypt laboured
and the markets of the Ethiopians and the giant
Sabaean men will come over to thee, and they will
be thy slaves, and they will walk behind thee with
their hands bound in chains, and thee they will
adore, because God is in thee; and to thee they
will make their prayers; and there is no God save
thee. For thou art God and we did not know, the
God of Israel, the Saviour" *(Isai 45, 14f)*. You see',
he says, 'how the Scriptures proclaim one God –
the one who is visibly revealed.

</td></tr>
<tr><td>

2.7

*Patripassianist
exposition*

</td><td>

On such testimonies as these, I am bound', says he,
'since the existence of a single one is maintained,
to submit this very one to suffering. For Christ was
God and suffered for us – he who was the Father
in person – so that he might be able also to save us.
And we cannot', he says, 'say anything else.

</td></tr>
<tr><td>

2.8

*The added testimony
of St Paul*

</td><td>

For, what is more, the Apostle maintains a single
God

</td></tr>
</table>

4. ἀλλ'οὐχ οὕτως ἔχει. οὐδὲ γὰρ οὕτως αἱ γραφαὶ
διηγοῦνται. 5. χρῶνται δὲ καὶ ἑτέραις μαρτυρίαις
λέγοντες, Οὕτω γέγραπται, Οὗτος ὁ θεὸς ἡμῶν · οὐ
λογισθήσεται ἕτερος πρὸς αὐτόν. ἐξηῦρεν πᾶσαν ὁδὸν
ἐπιστήμης καὶ ἔδωκεν / αὐτὴν 'Ιακὼβ τῷ παιδὶ αὐτοῦ 360^{bis}_{r1}
καὶ 'Ισραὴλ τῷ ἠγαπημένῳ ὑπ'αὐτοῦ. μετὰ ταῦτα ἐπὶ
γῆς ὤφθη καὶ τοῖς ἀνθρώποις συνανεστράφη. 'Ορᾷς οὖν,
φησίν, ὅτι οὗτός ἐστιν ὁ θεὸς ὁ μόνος ὢν καὶ ὕστερον
ὀφθεὶς καὶ τοῖς ἀνθρώποις συναναστραφείς. 6. <'Εν>
ἑτέρῳ δέ, φησίν, λέγει, 'Εκοπίασεν Αἴγυπτος καὶ
ἐμπόρια Αἰθιόπων καὶ οἱ Σαβαεὶμ ἄνδρες ὑψηλοὶ ἐπὶ σὲ
διαβήσονται καί σοι δοῦλοι ἔσονται καὶ πορεύσονται
ὀπίσω σου δεδεμένοι ἐν χειροπέδαις καὶ ἐν σοὶ προσ-
κυνήσουσιν, ὅτι ἐν σοὶ ὁ θεός ἐστιν, καὶ ἐν σοὶ προσεύξονται καὶ οὐκ ἔστιν θεὸς πλὴν σοῦ. σὺ γὰρ ἦς ὁ
θεὸς καὶ οὐκ ἤδειμεν, ὁ θεὸς τοῦ 'Ισραὴλ σωτήρ.
'Ορᾷς, φησίν, πῶς ἕνα θεὸν κηρύσσουσιν αἱ γραφαί,
τούτου ἐμφανοῦς δεικνυμένου. 7. Τούτων οὕτως μαρτυρ-
ουμένων ἀνάγκην, φησίν, ἔχω, ἑνὸς ὁμολογουμένου,
τοῦτον ὑπὸ πάθος φέρειν. / ⟦καὶ⟧ Χριστὸς γὰρ ἦν 360^{bis}_{r2}
θεὸς καὶ ἔπασχεν δι'ἡμᾶς, αὐτὸς ὢν Πατήρ, ἵνα καὶ
σῶσαι ἡμᾶς δυνηθῇ. ἄλλο δέ, φησίν, οὐ δυνάμεθα
λέγειν. 8. καὶ γὰρ ὁ ἀπόστολος ἕνα θεὸν ὁμολογεῖ

---

9 ὀφθείς 1sn: ὠφθείς V fr
συναναστραφείς] συναναστραφῆς V
<'Εν >] ? om. V
18 τούτων [r]1n : < ἐκ > τῶν s , των V fr

48

2.8 (continued)

when he says, "To them belong the fathers, and of their race, according to the flesh, is Christ, who is God over all, blessed for ever" ' *(Rom 9, 5)*.

3.1 – 3.6

SECTION A1 : PROGRAMMATIC NOTE
The use of Scripture and the programme to be followed

(a) On the use of Scripture

3.1

Heretics misuse Scripture and so do not attain the Truth

And this is the way they themselves, too, wish to explain these individual verses – using them in the way Theodotus spoke in his attempt to establish that [Christ] was a mere man. But neither they nor these latter have had a true thought, inasmuch as the Scriptures themselves, testifying as they do to the truth, prove their lack of learning.

3.2

E.g., the Patripassianists

You see, brethren, how rash and reckless a doctrine they introduced in saying quite shamelessly, 'The Father is himself Christ; he is himself the Son; he himself was born, he himself suffered, he himself raised himself up!'

3.3

Scripture is the norm of orthodoxy and truth

But this is not the case. It is the Scriptures that speak correctly, whatever other notions even Noetus might think up. And just because Noetus has no notion, this does not mean that it is the Scriptures that should be thrown out.

(b) On the programme to be followed

3.4

Of course, there is one God – plus the 'economy'

After all, would not everyone say that there is a single God? – but it is not everyone who would scrap the economy.

3.5

So Noetian exegesis must be refuted and a true exposition made

So really, in view of all this, the first of our two tasks must be to refute our opponents' understanding of the passages quoted, and to show what they mean in the light of the truth.

3.6

For a correct exposition of God's Fatherhood is all-important

This is because the primary aim really is to explain that there is 'one God, the Father, from whom is every family tie, through whom are all things, and from whom are all things; and we are in him' *(cf. 1 Cor 8, 6 with Eph 3, 15)*.

λέγων, ⸀Ων οἱ πατέρες, ἐξ ὧν ὁ Χριστὸς τὸ κατὰ σάρκα,
ὁ ὢν ἐπὶ πάντων Θεὸς εὐλογητὸς εἰς τοὺς αἰῶνας.

III. 1.   καὶ ταῦτα βούλονται οὕτω διηγεῖσθαι καὶ
αὐτοὶ μονόκωλα, χρώμενοι ὃν τρόπον εἶπεν Θεόδοτος
ἄνθρωπον συνιστᾶν ψιλὸν βουλόμενος.   ἀλλ'οὔτε ἐκεῖνοί
τι νενοήκασιν ἀληθὲς οὔθ'οὗτοι, καθὼς αὐταὶ αἱ γραφαὶ
ἐλέγχουσιν αὐτῶν τὴν ἀμαθίαν μαρτυροῦσαι τῇ ἀληθείᾳ.
2. ὁρᾶτε, ἀδελφοί, πῶς προαλὲς καὶ τολμηρὸν δόγμα
παρεισήνεγκαν ἀναισχύντως λέγοντες, Αὐτός ἐστι Χριστὸς ὁ Πατήρ, αὐτὸς Υἱός, αὐτὸς ἐγεννήθη, αὐτὸς ἔπαθεν,
αὐτὸς ἑαυτὸν ἤγειρεν.   3.   ἀλλ'οὐχ οὕτως ἔχει. αἱ
μὲν γραφαὶ ὀρθῶς λέγουσιν, ἄλλα ἂν καὶ Νοη/τὸς νοῇ. 360^bis_v1
οὐκ ἤδη δέ, εἰ Νοητὸς μὴ νοεῖ, παρὰ τοῦτο ἔκβλητοι
αἱ γραφαί.   4.   τίς γὰρ οὐκ ἐρεῖ ἕνα Θεὸν εἶναι ;
ἀλλ'οὐ τὴν οἰκονομίαν ἀναιρήσει.   5.   ὄντως μὲν οὖν
τὰ κεφάλαια διὰ ταῦτα πρότερον δεῖ ἀνατραπῆναι κατὰ
τὸν ἐκείνων νοῦν ˙ κατὰ δὲ τὴν ἀλήθειαν δειχθῆναι.
6. πρότερον γὰρ ὄντως ἐστὶν διηγήσασθαι ὅτι εἷς
Θεὸς ὁ Πατήρ, ἐξ οὗ πᾶσα πατριά, δι'οὗ τὰ πάντα ⌊καὶ
ἐξ οὗ τὰ πάντα⌋, καὶ ἡμεῖς ἐν αὐτῷ.

---

 9 ἀναισχύντως]   ἀναισχύντὄς V
12 νοῇ sn : νοή V ,   νοεῖ frl
13 νοεῖ frs : νοὴ V ,   νοῇ ln
17 τόν]   τῶν V

4.1 – 4.13

SECTION A2 : THE PRE–INCARNATE WORD
Isaiah 45 correctly interpreted

(a) Opening remarks: the importance of quoting passages in full

4.1

Our present refutation of Noetian exegesis will enable us to offer a true exegesis

As I was saying, let us see how he is refuted, then let us in this way come to explain the truth.

4.2

Noetus' use of Isaiah 45 illustrates their habit of mutilating the Scriptures

Now he says: 'Egypt laboured and the markets of the Ethiopians and the Sabaeans' *(Isai 45, 14)*, and the rest, so as to be able to say: 'For thou art the God of Israel, the Saviour' *(Isai 45, 15)* – having no thought for what has been said before this. In fact whenever they want to get up to their tricks, they hack the Scriptures to pieces.

4.3

The passage should be quoted in full

But let him quote passages in full, and he will discover the purpose behind what is being said. For the passage's beginning happens to be a little higher up, and it is from here that one must begin to show to whom and about whom he is speaking.

4.4

The passage quoted in full

Now starting from up above, the beginning of the passage goes like this:

> Question me about my sons and my daughters, and command me concerning the works of my hands? I made earth and man upon it. With my hand I made firm the heaven. I commanded all the stars. I raised him up, and all his ways are straight. This is he who will build my city and will reverse the captivity, not with ransoms and not with bribes, said the Lord Sabaoth. Thus spoke the Lord Sabaoth: 'Egypt laboured and the markets of the Ethiopians and the giant Sabaean men will come over to thee, and they will be thy slaves, and they will follow behind thee with their hands bound in chains. And thee they will adore, and to thee they will make their prayers, because God is in thee; and there is no God save thee. For thou art God and we did not know, the God of Israel, the Saviour'
> *(Isai 45, 11–15).*

IV. 1. ἴδωμεν, ὡς εἶπον, τὴν αὐτοῦ ἀνατροπήν, εἶθ'
οὕτως τὴν ἀλήθειαν διηγησώμεθα. 2. φησὶν γάρ, Ἐκοπ-
ίασεν Αἴγυπτος καὶ ἐμπόρια Αἰθιόπων καὶ οἱ Σαβαείμ καὶ
τὰ λοιπά, ἵνα εἴπῃ, Σὺ γὰρ ὁ θεὸς τοῦ Ἰσραὴλ σωτήρ,
οὐ νοῶν τὸ προειρημένον. ὁπόταν γὰρ θελήσωσιν πανουργ-
εύεσθαι, περικόπτουσι τὰς γραφάς. 3. ὁλοκλήρως δὲ
εἰπάτω καὶ εὑρήσει τὴν αἰτίαν πρὸς τίνα λέγεται.
ἀνωτέρω γὰρ / μικρὸν ἀρχὴ τοῦ κεφαλαίου τυγχάνει, 360bis v2
ὅθεν δεῖ ἀρξάμενον δεῖξαι πρὸς τίνα λέγει καὶ περὶ
τίνος. 4. ἄνωθεν γὰρ ἡ ἀρχὴ τοῦ κεφαλαίου τοῦτ'ἔχει,
Ἐρωτήσατέ με περὶ τῶν υἱῶν μου καὶ τῶν θυγατέρων μου
⟦ἐντελεῖσθαί μοι⟧ καὶ τῶν ἔργων τῶν χειρῶν μου ἐντείλασθέ
μοι. ἐγὼ ἐποίησα γῆν καὶ ἄνθρωπον ἐπ'αὐτῆς · ἐγὼ τῇ
χειρί μου ἐστερέωσα τὸν οὐρανόν · ἐγὼ πᾶσι τοῖς ἄστροις
ἐνετειλάμην. ἐγὼ ἤγειρα αὐτόν, καὶ πᾶσαι αἱ ὁδοὶ αὐτοῦ
εὐθεῖαι. οὗτος οἰκοδομήσει τὴν πόλιν μου καὶ τὴν
αἰχμαλωσίαν ἐπιστρέφει οὐ μετὰ λύτρων οὐδὲ μετὰ δώρων,
εἶπεν Κύριος Σαβαώθ. οὕτως εἶπεν Κύριος Σαβαώθ, Ἐκοπ-
ίασεν Αἴγυπτος καὶ ἐμπόρια Αἰθιόπων καὶ οἱ Σαβαείμ
ἄνδρες ὑψηλοὶ ἐπὶ σὲ διαβήσονται καί σοι ἔσονται δοῦλοι καὶ ὀπίσω σου ἀκολουθήσουσιν δεδεμένοι χειροπέδαις
καὶ ἐν σοὶ προσκυνη/σουσιν καὶ ἐν σοὶ προσεύξονται, ὅτι 361r1
ἐν σοὶ ὁ θεός ἐστιν καὶ οὐκ ἔστιν θεὸς πλὴν σοῦ. σὺ
γὰρ ἦς θεὸς καὶ οὐκ ἤδειμεν, ὁ θεὸς τοῦ Ἰσραὴλ σωτήρ.

---

1   ἴδωμεν] ἴδομεν V
9   δεῖ]   δὴ V
12 ἐντείλασθέ]   ἐντελεῖσθαί V
24 ἤδειμεν]   ἤδημεν V

(b) Correctly interpreted, the passage reveals the mystery of the economy, the existence of the Word

4.5

Certain phrases point to Christ, the Father's own Word

Now, 'In thee', he says, 'is God'. But in whom is God, except in Christ Jesus, the Father's own Word and the mystery of the economy?

4.6

and the Father's incarnate Son

Again, who is the revelation about when he points to the fact of his flesh: 'I raised him up with justice, and all his ways are straight'? Well? About whom is the Father testifying? It is about the Son that the Father says, 'I raised up with justice'. And that the Father raised up his Son in justice the Apostle Paul testifies when he says, 'But if the Spirit of him who raised Christ from the dead dwells in you, he who raised Jesus Christ from the dead will give life to your mortal bodies also, through his Spirit which dwells in you' *(Rom 8, 11)*. There you are! He has confirmed what had been said through the prophet:'I raised up with justice'.

4.7

In fact, to the Word who, as man, is Son

So the statement 'In thee is God' revealed the mystery of the economy — that once the Word had taken flesh and was among men, the Father was in the Son and the Son in the Father *(cf. Jn 14, 10)*, while the Son was living among men.

4.8

i.e., to the Word as mystery of the economy

So this, brethren, is what was being pointed out — that the mystery of the economy really was this very Word who fashioned from the Holy Spirit and the virgin an only Son for God.

(c) The pre-incarnate existence of the Word as Son of man

4.9

Christ himself says that he existed before the incarnation as Son of man in heaven

And this is not just my story, but he who came down from heaven is a witness to it himself. For he speaks as follows: 'No one has ascended into heaven but he who descended from heaven, the Son of man who is in heaven' *(Jn 3, 13)*.

4.10

The Word was not flesh before the incarnation: the flesh is the Word's self-offering as Son

So what is he after beyond what has been said? Surely he is not going to say that he was flesh while still in heaven? Now

5. Ἐν σοὶ οὖν, φησίν, ὁ Θεός ἐστιν. ἐν τίνι δὲ ὁ
Θεὸς ἀλλ'ἢ ἐν Χριστῷ Ἰησοῦ τῷ πατρῴῳ Λόγῳ καὶ τῷ
μυστηρίῳ τῆς οἰκονομίας ; 6. περὶ οὗ πάλιν δεικνύων
τὸ κατὰ σάρκα αὐτοῦ σημαίνει, Ἐγὼ ἤγειρα αὐτὸν μετὰ
δικαιοσύνης, καὶ πᾶσαι αἱ ὁδοὶ αὐτοῦ εὐθεῖαι. τί οὖν ;
περὶ τίνος μαρτυρεῖ Πατήρ ; περὶ τοῦ Υἱοῦ ⟦αὐτοῦ⟧
Πατὴρ λέγει, Ἐγὼ ἤγειρα μετὰ δικαιοσύνης. ὅτι δὲ
Πατὴρ ἤγειρεν αὐτοῦ τὸν Υἱὸν ἐν δικαιοσύνῃ μαρτυρεῖ
ὁ ἀπόστολος Παῦλος λέγων, Εἰ δὲ τὸ πνεῦμα τοῦ ἐγείραντος
Χριστὸν ἐκ νεκρῶν οἰκεῖ ἐν ὑμῖν, ὁ ἐγείρας ἐκ νεκρῶν
Χριστὸν Ἰησοῦν ζωοποιήσει καὶ τὰ θνητὰ σώματα ὑμῶν
διὰ τοῦ ἐνοικοῦντος αὐτοῦ πνεύματος ἐν ὑμῖν. ἰδοὺ
συνέστηκεν τὸ διὰ τοῦ προφήτου / εἰρημένον, Ἐγὼ ἤγειρα 361r2
μετὰ δικαιοσύνης. 7. τὸ δὲ εἰπεῖν, Ὅτι ἐν σοὶ ὁ
Θεός ἐστιν, ἐδείκνυεν μυστήριον οἰκονομίας · ὅτι
σεσαρκωμένου τοῦ Λόγου καὶ ἐνανθρωπήσαντος ὁ Πατὴρ ἦν
ἐν τῷ Υἱῷ καὶ ὁ Υἱὸς ἐν τῷ Πατρί, ἐνπολιτευομένου τοῦ
Υἱοῦ ἐν ἀνθρώποις. 8. τοῦτο οὖν ἐσημαίνετο, ἀδελφοί,
ὅτι ὄντως μυστήριον οἰκονομίας ἐκ πνεύματος ἁγίου ἦν
οὗτος ὁ Λόγος καὶ παρθένου ἕνα Υἱὸν Θεῷ ἀπεργασάμενος.
9. τοῦτο δὲ οὐκ ἐγὼ λέγω, ἀλλ'αὐτὸς μαρτυρεῖ ὁ καταβὰς
ἐκ τοῦ οὐρανοῦ. οὕτως γὰρ λέγει, Οὐδεὶς ἀναβέβηκεν εἰς
τὸν οὐρανὸν εἰ μὴ ὁ ἐκ τοῦ οὐρανοῦ καταβάς, ὁ υἱὸς τοῦ
ἀνθρώπου ὁ ὢν ἐν τῷ οὐρανῷ. 10. τί οὖν ζητεῖ παρὰ τὸ
εἰρημένον ; μήτι ἐρεῖ ὅτι ἐν οὐρανῷ σὰρξ ἦν ; ἔστιν μὲν

---

18   ἐσημαίνετο] ἐσημένετο V

4.10 (continued)

flesh is what was offered up by the Father's own Word as a gift — flesh which had been shown forth as God's perfect Son from the Spirit and the virgin. So it was plain to see that he himself was offering himself up to the Father.

4.11

In heaven the Word was without flesh

But there was no flesh previous to this in heaven. Who, then, was he in heaven but the fleshless Word — he who was sent for the purpose of showing that he who is on earth is in heaven too? For he was Word, he was Spirit, he was Power *(cf. Lk 1, 35).*

4.12

In becoming man he became what he had been called from the beginning — the Son of man

He was taking to himself the name which is common among men and understood by them; and this — 'the Son of man' — he was called from the beginning with a view to the future, even though he was not yet a man.

4.13

This is confirmed by Daniel 7

Just as Daniel attests when he says: 'I looked, and behold! on the clouds of heaven there was one coming like a Son of man' *(Dan 7, 13).* So he said quite justifiably that the Word of God, who has this name from the beginning, is in heaven, and is called it from the beginning.

5.1 – 5.5

SECTION A3 : THE INCARNATE WORD
Baruch 3 correctly interpreted — The incarnate Word is the visible expression of the Father's will

5.1

The text points to another besides the Father

'But what', he says, 'does he mean in the other text: "This is God; no other will be compared to him" *(Bar 3, 36)*?' It is well said. After all, who is there to be compared to the Father? In what he says — 'This is our God; no other will be compared to him. He has found out the whole way of knowledge, and has given it to Jacob his son, and to Israel who is his beloved' *(Bar 3, 36f)* — he puts it well.

5.2

The beloved Son of the Gospels

For who is Jacob his son, Israel who is his beloved

οὖν σάρξ ἡ ὑπὸ τοῦ Λόγου τοῦ πατρῴου προσενεχθεῖσα
δῶρον, ἡ ἐκ πνεύματος καὶ παρθένου τέλειος Υἱὸς Θεοῦ
ἀποδεδειγμένος. πρό/δηλον οὖν ὅτι αὐτὸς ἑαυτὸν προσ- 361v1
έφερεν τῷ Πατρί. 11. πρὸ δὲ τούτου ἐν οὐρανῷ σάρξ
οὐκ ἦν. τίς οὖν ἦν ἐν οὐρανῷ ἀλλ'ἢ Λόγος ἄσαρκος,
ὁ ἀποσταλεὶς ἵνα δείξῃ αὐτὸν ἐπὶ γῆς ὄντα εἶναι καὶ
ἐν οὐρανῷ ; Λόγος γὰρ ἦν, πνεῦμα ἦν, δύναμις ἦν.
12. ὃς τὸ κοινὸν ὄνομα καὶ παρὰ ανθρώποις χωρητὸν
ἀνελάμβανεν εἰς ἑαυτόν, τοῦτο καλούμενος ἀπ'ἀρχῆς,
υἱὸς ἀνθρώπου, διὰ τὸ μέλλον, καίτοι μήπω ὢν ἄνθρωπος.
13. καθὼς ὁ Δανιὴλ μαρτυρεῖ λέγων, Εἶδον καὶ ἰδοὺ
ἐπὶ τῶν νεφελῶν τοῦ οὐρανοῦ ἐρχόμενον ὡς υἱὸν ἀνθρώπου.
δικαίως οὖν ἐν τῷ οὐρανῷ ὄντα ἔλεγεν τὸν τῷ ὀνόματι
τούτῳ ἀπ'ἀρχῆς ὄντα καλεῖσθαι ἀπ'ἀρχῆς, Λόγον Θεοῦ.

V. 1. ἀλλὰ τί μοι, φησίν, λέγει ἐν ἑτέρῳ, Οὗτος ὁ
θεός · οὐ λογισθήσεται ἕτερος πρὸς αὐτόν ; καλῶς
εἶπεν. πρὸς γὰρ τὸν Πατέρα τίς λογισθήσεται ; ὁ
δὲ λέγει, Οὗτος ὁ Θεὸς / ἡμῶν · οὐ λογισθήσεται 361v2
ἕτερος πρὸς αὐτόν · ἐξηῦρεν πᾶσαν ὁδὸν ἐπιστήμης
καὶ ἔδωκεν αὐτὴν 'Ιακὼβ τῷ παιδὶ αὐτοῦ καὶ 'Ισραὴλ
τῷ ἠγαπημένῳ ὑπ'αὐτοῦ, ⌊καλῶς λέγει⌋. 2. τίς γάρ
ἐστιν 'Ιακὼβ ὁ παῖς αὐτοῦ, 'Ισραὴλ ὁ ἠγαπημένος ὑπ'

---

1   τοῦ πατρῴου frls : τοῦ πατρὅου V   τῷ πατρί n
8   ὅς[r]lsn : εἰς   Vfr
11   εἶδον]   ἴδον V
19   ἐξηῦρεν rn :   εξεῦρεν Vfls

5.2 (continued)

but the very one about whom he cries out with the words, 'This is my beloved Son with whom I am well pleased: him you must hear' *(Mt 17, 5)*?

5.3

The perfect Israel, the true Jacob, who received all knowledge from the Father and came on earth as man

So the perfect Israel, the true Jacob, received the whole of knowledge from the Father, and 'afterwards he appeared on earth and lived among men' *(Bar 3, 38)*.

5.4

This man-who-sees-God has alone revealed the Father's will

And who is Israel but 'man-seeing-God'? But there is no one who sees God save only the son and perfect man, and he who alone made known the mind of the Father.

5.5

This is confirmed by John 1 and 3

After all, John too says: 'No one has even seen God; the only-begotten Son who is in the bosom of the Father has himself made him known' *(Jn 1, 18)*. And again: 'He who has come down from heaven bears witness to what he has seen and heard' *(Jn 3, 13.32)*. So this is he to whom the Father gave all knowledge. He it is who 'appeared on earth and lived among men'.

6.1 – 7.7

SECTION A4 : THE UNITY AND DISTINCTION OF GOD
Romans 9 correctly interpreted

(a) Christ and the Father are one God

6.1

The text shows that Christ is God, and Christ himself said as much

And what the Apostle says – 'To them belong the fathers, and of their race, according to the flesh, is Christ, who is God over all, blessed for ever' *(Rom 9, 5)* – gives a good and clear exposition of the mystery of the truth. He is, since he is over all, God. After all, he speaks quite openly as follows: 'All things have been delivered to me by the Father' *(Mt 11, 27)*. He who is blessed God over all has been born, and, having become man, is God

αὐτοῦ, ἀλλ'ἦ οὗτος περὶ οὗ βοᾷ λέγων, Οὗτός ἐστιν
ὁ Υἱός μου ὁ ἀγαπητός, εἰς ὃν ηὐδόκησα · τούτου
ἀκούετε ; 3. πᾶσαν οὖν τὴν ἐπιστήμην παρὰ τοῦ Πατρὸς
λαβὼν ὁ τέλειος 'Ισραήλ, ὁ ἀληθινὸς 'Ιακώβ, μετὰ
ταῦτα ἐπὶ τῆς γῆς ὤφθη καὶ τοῖς ἀνθρώποις συνανεστράφη.
4. 'Ισραὴλ δὲ τίς ἐστιν ἀλλ'ἦ ἄνθρωπος ὁρῶν τὸν Θεόν ;
ὁρῶν δὲ τὸν Θεὸν οὐδεὶς εἰ μὴ μόνος ὁ παῖς καὶ τέλειος
ἄνθρωπος καὶ μόνος διηγησάμενος τὴν βουλὴν τοῦ Πατρός.
5. λέγει γὰρ καὶ 'Ιωάννης, Θεὸν οὐδεὶς ἑώρακεν πώ-
ποτε · μονογενὴς Υἱὸς ὁ ὢν εἰς τὸν κόλπον τοῦ Πατρὸς
αὐτὸς διηγήσατο. καὶ πά/λιν, Ὁ ἐκ τοῦ οὐρανοῦ κατα-   362r1
βὰς ὃ ἤκουσεν καὶ ἑώρακεν μαρτυρεῖ. οὗτος οὖν ἐστιν
ᾧ πᾶσαν ἐπιστήμην Πατὴρ ἔδωκεν · ὃς ἐπὶ γῆς ὤφθη καὶ
τοῖς ἀνθρώποις συνανεστράφη.

VI. 1. ὃ δὲ λέγει ὁ ἀπόστολος, Ὧν οἱ πατέρες, ἐξ
ὧν ὁ Χριστὸς τὸ κατὰ σάρκα, ὁ ὢν ἐπὶ πάντων Θεὸς
εὐλογητὸς εἰς τοὺς αἰῶνας, καλῶς διηγεῖται καὶ λαμπρὸν
τὸ τῆς ἀληθείας μυστήριον. οὗτος ὢν ἐπὶ πάντων, θεός
ἐστιν. λέγει γὰρ οὕτω μετὰ παρρησίας, Πάντα μοι
παραδέδοται ὑπὸ τοῦ Πατρός. ὁ ὢν ἐπὶ πάντων θεὸς
εὐλογητὸς γεγέννηται, καὶ ἄνθρωπος γενόμενος θεός

---

5   τοῖς]   τῆς V
12 ἑώρακεν] ἑόρακεν V
13 πᾶσαν] πᾶσα V
17 διηγεῖται V corr : διηγῆται V
20 παραδέδοται]   παραδέδωται V

58

6.1 (continued)

for ever.

6.2

This is confirmed by John, who calls Christ 'Almighty', using Christ's own testimony

For John too spoke as follows: 'He who is and who was and who is to come, God the Almighty' *(Apoc 1, 8)*. He was quite right to say that Christ is Almighty, because he has said exactly what Christ will testify to him too. For Christ testified to this when he said, 'All things have been delivered to me by the Father' *(Mt 11, 27)*. And he does exercise his might over all. Christ was established as Almighty by the Father.

6.3

And Paul had already said the same in 1 Corinthians 15

And Paul too had already spoken thus, when he revealed that all things had been delivered to him:

Christ is the first-fruits, then at his coming those who belong to Christ. Then comes the end, when he delivers the kingdom to God the Father after destroying every rule and every authority and power. For he must reign until he has put all his enemies under his feet. The last enemy to be destroyed is death . . . But when it says, 'all things are put in subjection under him', it is plain that he is excepted who put all things under him. Then he himself will also be subjected to him who put all things under him, so that God may be all in all *(1 Cor 15, 23–28)*.

6.4

although, of course, Christ is ultimately subject to the Father

If therefore all things have been put in subjection under him except him who subjected them, he exercises his might over all; but the Father over him, so that in all things a single God may be revealed, to whom all things are subjected along with Christ, to whom the Father subjected all things apart from himself.

6.5

and Christ himself, in John 20, calls the Father his God

For this is what Christ said when in the Gospel he acknowledged him who is both his own Father and his God. For his words run

ἐστιν εἰς τοὺς αἰῶνας. 2. οὕτως γὰρ καὶ 'Ιωάννης
εἶπεν, 'Ο ὢν καὶ ὁ ἦν καὶ ὁ ἐρχόμενος, ὁ Θεὸς ὁ παντοκράτωρ. καλῶς εἶπεν παντοκράτορα Χριστόν. τοῦτο
γὰρ εἶπεν ὅπερ καὶ αὐτῷ μαρτυρήσει ὁ Χριστός. μαρτυρῶν γὰρ Χριστὸς ἔφη, Πάντα μοι πα/ραδέδοται παρὰ   362r2
τοῦ Πατρός. καὶ πάντων κρατεῖ · παντοκράτωρ παρὰ
Πατρὸς κατεστάθη Χριστός. 3. ἤδη δὲ καὶ Παῦλος,
δεικνὺς ὅτι πάντα αὐτῷ παραδέδοται, οὕτως ἔφη, 'Απ-
αρχὴ Χριστός, ἔπειτα οἱ τοῦ Χριστοῦ ἐν τῇ παρουσίᾳ
αὐτοῦ, εἶτα τὸ τέλος, ὅταν παραδιδῷ τὴν βασιλείαν
τῷ θεῷ καὶ Πατρί, ὅταν καταργήσῃ πᾶσαν ἀρχὴν καὶ
πᾶσαν ἐξουσίαν καὶ δύναμιν. δεῖ γὰρ αὐτὸν βασιλεύειν
ἄχρι οὗ θῇ πάντας τοὺς ἐχθροὺς ὑπὸ τοὺς πόδας αὐτοῦ.
ἔσχατος ἐχθρὸς καταργεῖται ὁ θάνατος. ὅταν δὲ εἴπῃ,
πάντα ὑποτέτακται αὐτῷ, δῆλον ὅτι ἐκτὸς τοῦ ὑποτάξαντος αὐτῷ τὰ πάντα. τότε καὶ αὐτὸς ὑποταγήσεται
τῷ ὑποτάξαντι αὐτῷ τὰ πάντα, ἵνα ᾖ ὁ θεὸς πάντα ἐν
πᾶσιν. 4. εἰ οὖν τὰ πάντα ὑποτέτακται αὐτῷ ἐκτὸς
τοῦ ὑποτάξαντος, ⟦καὶ⟧ πάντων κρατεῖ · αὐτοῦ / δὲ   362v1
ὁ Πατήρ, ἵνα ἐν πᾶσιν εἷς θεὸς φανῇ, ᾧ τὰ πάντα ὑπο-
τάσσεται ἅμα Χριστῷ, ᾧ τὰ πάντα Πατὴρ ὑπέταξε παρὲξ
ἑαυτοῦ. 5. τοῦτο γὰρ Χριστὸς ἔφη, ὡς ἐν τῷ εὐαγγελίῳ καὶ Πατέρα ἴδιον καὶ Θεὸν ὡμολόγησεν. λέγει γὰρ

8	παραδέδοται]	παραδέδωται	V
11	καταργήσῃ]	καταργήσει	V
14	καταργεῖται]	καταργῆται	V
15	τοῦ]	τῷ	V
18	post **οὖν** inser. V marg. **πάντα** ū : sed superflue.		
20	**ὑποτάσσεται** V corr: **ὑποτά⟦υπ⟧σσεται** V		

6.5 (continued)

as follows: 'I am going to my Father and your Father, my God and your God' *(Jn 20, 17)*.

6.6

What objection could Noetus have to this, which is so clear in Scripture?

Now if Noetus has the effrontery to say that he [Christ] is the Father in person, to what Father will he say Christ is going, according to the Gospel quotation? And if he imagines that we are to abandon the Gospel and believe in his nonsense, he is wasting his time — for we 'must obey God rather than man' *(Acts 5, 29)*.

(b) Yet, as Son, Christ is distinct from the Father

7.1

John 10 reveals distinct persons, but a single Power

And if he were to say, 'He himself said: "I and the Father are one" ' *(Jn 10, 30)*, let him apply his mind to the matter and learn that he did not say, 'I and the Father *am* one', but '*are* one'. 'We are' is not said with reference to one, but with reference to two. He revealed two persons, but a single Power.

7.2

This is confirmed by John 17

And Christ himself resolved the problem when he spoke about the disciples to his Father: 'The glory thou gavest me, I gave to them, that they may be one even as we are one, so that the world may know that thou hast sent me' *(Jn 17, 22—23)*.

7.3

The Son is the single Mind of the Father

What have the Noetians got to say to this? Surely not that all of us 'is' actually one body in terms of substance! Rather we become one virtually, by our disposition towards singlemindedness. Well, in the same way the son, sent and not recognized by those who are in the world *(cf. Jn 1, 10)*, maintained that he is in the Father — virtually, as a disposition. For the son is the Father's 'single Mind'. Those of us

οὕτως, Ὑπάγω πρὸς τὸν Πατέρα μου καὶ Πατέρα ὑμῶν,
καὶ Θεόν μου καὶ Θεὸν ὑμῶν.   6. εἰ οὖν Νοητὸς τολμᾷ
λέγειν αὐτὸν εἶναι τὸν Πατέρα, ⟦καὶ⟧ πρὸς ποῖον Πατέρα
ἐρεῖ πορεύεσθαι Χριστὸν κατὰ τὴν εὐαγγελικὴν φωνήν ;
εἰ δὲ ἀξιοῖ καταλείψαντας ἡμᾶς τὸ εὐαγγέλιον τῇ αὐτοῦ
ἀφροσύνῃ πιστεύειν, μάτην κάμνει. Πειθαρχεῖν γὰρ δεῖ
θεῷ μᾶλλον ἢ ἀνθρώποις.   VII. 1.   ἐὰν δὲ λέγῃ, Αὐτὸς
εἶπεν, Ἐγὼ καὶ ὁ Πατὴρ ἓν ἐσμέν, ἐπιστανέτω τὸν νοῦν
καὶ μανθανέτω ὅτι οὐκ εἶπεν ὅτι ἐγὼ καὶ ὁ Πατὴρ ἓν εἰμί,
ἀλλ' ἓν ἐσμέν.   τὸ γὰρ ἐσμὲν οὐκ ἐφ'ἑνὸς λέγεται, ἀλλ'
ἐπὶ δύο · ⟨δύο⟩πρόσωπα ἔδειξεν, δύναμιν δὲ μίαν.
2. αὐτὸς δὲ αὐτὸ / ἀπέλυσεν εἰπὼν περὶ μαθητῶν πρὸς 362v2
τὸν Πατέρα, Τὴν δόξαν ἣν ἔδωκάς μοι, ἔδωκα αὐτοῖς,
ἵνα ὦσιν ἓν καθὼς ἡμεῖς ἕν, ἐγὼ ἐν αὐτοῖς καὶ σὺ
ἐν ἐμοί, ἵνα ὦσιν τετελειωμένοι εἰς ἕν, ἵνα γινώσκῃ
ὁ κόσμος ὅτι σύ με ἀπέστειλας.   3.   τί πρὸς ταῦτα
ἔχουσιν λέγειν Νοητιανοί ;   μὴ πάντες ἓν σῶμά ἐστιν
κατὰ τὴν οὐσίαν ; ἢ τῇ δυνάμει καὶ τῇ διαθέσει τῆς
ὁμοφρονίας ἓν γινόμεθα.   τὸν αὐτὸν δὴ τρόπον ὁ παῖς
ὁ πεμφθεὶς καὶ ὑπ'αὐτῶν μὴ γινωσκόμενος ὄντων ἐν
κόσμῳ ὡμολόγησεν εἶναι ἓν τῷ Πατρὶ δυνάμει, διαθέσει.
εἷς γὰρ νοῦς Πατρὸς ὁ παῖς · οἱ

---

7   λέγῃ lsn :   λέγει   Vfr
11 ἐπὶ frn: ἔπει V, ἐπεὶ [r]ls, ἐκεῖ Giet [RevSR 24 (1950)
                                              p.317]
    ⟨δύο⟩ sic add. n.
15 γινώσκῃ]   γινώσκει   V
19 δὴ]   δει   V

7.3 (continued)

who have the Father's Mind are thereby believers. But those who are not so 'minded' have denied the Son *(cf. 1 Jn 5, 12).*

(c) An objection answered: Philip's question about the Father

7.4

Pace the Noetians, Christ's answer to Philip in John 14 brings out the same distinction

But supposing they were to try also to quote the fact that Philip asked about the Father: 'Show us the Father and we shall be satisfied' *(Jn 14, 8);* and the Lord answered him with the words: 'Have I been with you so long, Philip, and yet you do not know me? He who has seen me has seen the Father. Do you not believe that I am in the Father and the Father is in me?' *(Jn 14, 9–10)* – and they want to say that thereby their doctrine prevails, since [Christ] maintains that he himself is the Father. They should realize that they are putting an enormous obstacle in their own path, and stand condemned by the quotation itself.

7.5

Christ in fact showed himself to be Son – and Philip did not see it

For although Christ declared and revealed himself to be the Son in everything, they attained no knowledge of him, and could not grasp or see the force [of his words]. And Philip did not take in the very thing that was there to see, and was expecting to look at the Father. The Lord said to him, 'Philip, have I been with you so long, and yet you do not know me? He who has seen me has seen the Father. How is it that you are saying, "Show us the Father"?' *(Jn 14, 9).*

7.6

And therefore also Image of the Father, through whom the Father can be known

In other words, 'If you have seen me, through me you can know the Father. For through the image which has real likeness, the Father becomes easy to know. But if you do not recognize the image – which

δὲ νοῦν Πατρὸς ἔχοντες οὕτω πιστεύομεν. οἱ δὲ τὸν

νοῦν μὴ ἔχοντες τὸν Υἱὸν ἤρνηνται. 4. εἰ δὲ καὶ

Φίλιππον ἐπερωτᾶν περὶ Πατρὸς βούλοιντο λέγειν –

Δεῖξον ἡμῖν τὸν Πατέρα καὶ ἀρκεῖ ἡμῖν · πρὸς ὃν

ἀπε/κρίθη ὁ Κύριος λέγων, Τοσοῦτον χρόνον μεθ'ὑμῶν   363r1

εἰμι, Φίλιππε, καὶ οὐκ ἔγνωκάς με ; ὁ ἑωρακὼς ἐμὲ

ἑώρακε τὸν Πατέρα · οὐ πιστεύεις ὅτι ἐγὼ ἐν τῷ Πατρὶ

καὶ ὁ Πατὴρ ἐν ἐμοί ἐστιν ; – καὶ θέλουσιν λέγειν

διὰ τούτου κρατύνεσθαι τὸ δόγμα αὐτῶν, ὁμολογοῦντος

αὐτοῦ ἑαυτὸν Πατέρα, γνώτωσαν ὅτι μέγιστον ἑαυτοῖς

ἐναντίωμα ἐπιφέρουσιν, ὑπ'αὐτοῦ τοῦ ῥητοῦ ἐλεγχόμενοι.

5. τοῦ γὰρ Χριστοῦ ἑαυτὸν ἐν πᾶσιν Υἱὸν εἰπόντος καὶ

δείξαντος οὐκ ἐπέγνωσαν · οὐδὲ καταλάβεσθαι ἢ ἀτεν-

ίσαι τὴν δύναμιν ἐδυνήθησαν. καὶ τοῦτο μὴ χωρήσας

Φίλιππος καθ'ὃ ἦν ἰδεῖν τὸν Πατέρα ἠξίου βλέπειν.

πρὸς ὃν ὁ Κύριος ἔφη, Φίλιππε, τοσοῦτον χρόνον μεθ'

ὑμῶν εἰμι καὶ οὐκ ἔγνωκάς με ; ὁ ἑωρακὼς ἐμὲ ἑώρακε

τὸν Πατέρα. πῶς σὺ λέγεις, Δεῖξον ἡμῖν τὸν Πατέρα ;

6. τοῦτ'ἔστιν, εἰ ἐμὲ ἑώρακας, δι'ἐμοῦ τὸν Πατέρα

γνῶναι δύνῃ. / διὰ γὰρ τῆς εἰκόνος ὁμοίας τυγχανούσης   363r2

εὔγνωστος ὁ Πατὴρ γίνεται. εἰ δὲ τὴν εἰκόνα, ἥτις

---

3   ἐπερωτᾶν]   ἐπερωτᾶ V

9   ὁμολογοῦντος]   ὡμολογοῦντος V

17   εἰμι]   ἡμὶ V

19   ἑώρακας]   ἑώρακες V

20   ὁμοίας]   ὁμοίως V

7.6 (continued)

is the Son — how is it that you want to see the Father?'

7.7

Other statements confirm this distinction between the Son and the Father

Statements prior and subsequent to the passage quoted clearly show that this is the case, pointing as they do to the Son who has been put forth *(cf. Rom 3, 25)*, sent out from the Father *(cf.Jn 5, 36)*, and returning to the Father *(cf. Jn 14, 12)*.

8.1 – 8.3

SECTION A5 :
CONCLUSION OF SECTION A (2 – 4)

8.1

In fact the whole of Scripture forcefully testifies to the truth of the threefold distinction of the Godhead

And there are many other passages too — in fact it would be truer to say that all of them testify to the truth. So even an unwilling person is obliged to confess the Father as God Almighty, and Christ Jesus, the Son of God, as the God who became man — him to whom the Father subjected all things except himself *(cf. 1 Cor 15, 27)* — and the Holy Spirit; and that these really are three.

8.2

There is a single divine Power, revealed triply, as we shall show

But if he wants to learn how God is shown to be one, he must know that this [God] has a single Power; and that as far as the Power is concerned, God is one: but in terms of the economy the display [of it] is triple — as will be shown later when we give our account about the truth.

8.3

For there is a single, sovereign God – Noetus can say nothing against our view

Well then, brethren, what we have said is shown to be consistently said: and the reason is that there is one God, in whom we must believe; but he does not become, cannot suffer, cannot die: and he makes all things as he wills, in the way he wills, when he wills *(cf. Ps 134, 6 LXX)*. What, then, will Noetus, who has no notion of the truth, dare to say to this?

ἐστὶν ὁ Υἱός, οὐκ ἔγνως, πῶς ἰδεῖν θέλεις τὸν Πατέρα ;

7. ὅτι ταῦθ' οὕτως ἔχει, τὰ ἐπικείμενα τῷ κεφαλαίῳ καὶ ὑποκείμενα ἀπολύει, τὸν προκείμενον Υἱὸν ἀπεσταλμένον παρὰ Πατρὸς καὶ πρὸς Πατέρα πορευόμενο⟨ν⟩ σημαίνοντα.

VIII. 1.　　　πολλὰ δὲ καὶ ἕτερα, μᾶλλον δὲ πάντα ἐστὶ μαρτυροῦντα τῇ ἀληθείᾳ. ἀνάγκην οὖν ἔχει καὶ μὴ θέλων ὁμολογεῖν Πατέρα θεὸν παντοκράτορα καὶ Χριστὸν Ἰησοῦν Υἱὸν θεοῦ θεὸν ἄνθρωπον γενόμενον · ᾧ πάντα Πατὴρ ὑπέταξε παρεκτὸς ἑαυτοῦ καὶ πνεύματος ἁγίου · καὶ ταῦτ' εἶναι ὄντως τρία. 2. εἰ δὲ βούλεται μαθεῖν πῶς εἷς θεὸς ἀποδείκνυται, γιγνωσκέτω ὅτι μία δύναμις τούτου · καὶ ὅσον μὲν κατὰ τὴν δύναμιν εἷς ἐστιν θεός, ὅσον δὲ κατὰ τὴν οἰκονομίαν τριχῆς ἡ ἐπίδειξις, ὡς ὕστερον ἀποδειχθήσεται ἀποδιδόντων / ἡμῶν περὶ ἀληθ- 363v1 είας λόγον. 3. ταῦτα μὲν οὖν, ἀδελφοί, δείκνυται ἡμῖν συμφώνως εἰρημένα · εἷς γὰρ θεός ἐστιν, ᾧ δεῖ πιστεύειν, ἀλλ' ἀγένητος ἀπαθὴς ἀθάνατος, πάντα ποιῶν ὡς θέλει, καθὼς θέλει, ὅτε θέλει. τί οὖν πρὸς ταῦτα τολμήσει Νοητὸς μὴ νοῶν τὴν ἀλήθειαν ;

11　　ταῦτ' sn : τούτους frl, ταύτης V
14　　τριχῆς Vfrl: τριχῶς [r], τριχῇ s
16　　ταῦτα Vcorr : ταῦ V
17　　συμφώνως] συμφώνος
18　　ἀπαθής Vcorr: ἀπαθείς V

8.4 – 9.3

SECTION B1 : PROGRAMMATIC NOTE
The use of Scripture and the programme to be followed

(a) On the use of Scripture

8.4

Let us proceed to the Demonstration of the Truth which conquers all heresies

Seeing, then, that even Noetus now stands refuted, let us move on to the demonstration of the truth, with a view to establishing the truth against which none of the great sects has even been able to say a single word.

9.1

Scripture is the sole source of our knowledge of the one true God and the true religion

There is one God, and we acquire knowledge of him from no other source, brethren, than the Holy Scriptures. For just as in the case of a person who might wish to practise the wisdom of this age *(cf. 1 Cor 2, 6)*, he will not be able to get at it otherwise than by meeting it in the philosophers' teachings, in exactly the same way those of us who want to practise true piety will not learn how to practise it from any other source than from the utterances of God *(cf. Rom 3, 2)*.

(b) On the programme to be followed

9.2

Following Scripture, let us make our religion fully trinitarian in the way the Father has willed that it should be

Well, let us look at what the Sacred Scriptures proclaim, and let us acquire knowledge of what they teach. And let us in future believe in the way the Father wills to be believed, and let us glorify [the Son] in the way he wills the Son to be glorified, and let us receive [the Holy Spirit] in the way he wills the Holy Spirit to be imparted.

9.3

It is not by following private preference that we shall learn how God has willed to reveal himself to us

Not in accordance with private choice, nor private interpretation, nor by doing violence to the things that God has given — but rather let us look at things in the way God himself resolved to reveal them through the Holy Scriptures.

VIII. 4. ἐπειδὴ οὖν ἤδη καὶ ὁ Νοητὸς ἀνατέτραπται,
ἔλθωμεν ἐπὶ τὴν τῆς ἀληθείας ἀπόδειξιν, ἵνα συστήσ-
ωμεν τὴν ἀλήθειαν καθ'ἧς πᾶσαι τοσαῦται αἱρέσεις γεγένηνται μηδὲν δυνάμεναι εἰπεῖν. IX. 1. εἷς θεός, ὃν
οὐκ ἄλλοθεν ἐπιγινώσκομεν, ἀδελφοί, ἢ τῶν ἁγίων γραφῶν.
ὃν γὰρ τρόπον ἐάν τις βουληθῇ τὴν σοφίαν τοῦ αἰῶνος
τούτου ἀσκεῖν, οὐκ ἄλλως δυνήσεται τούτου τυχεῖν, ἐὰν
μὴ δόγμασιν φιλοσόφων ἐντύχῃ, τὸν αὐτὸν δὴ τρόπον καὶ
ὅσοι θεοσέβειαν ἀσκεῖν βουλόμεθα, οὐκ ἄλλοθεν ἀσκήσομεν / ἢ ἐκ τῶν λογίων τοῦ θεοῦ. 2. ὅσα τοίνυν 363v2
κηρύσσουσιν αἱ θεῖαι γραφαὶ ἴδωμεν, καὶ ὅσα διδάσκουσιν
ἐπιγνῶμεν. καὶ ὡς θέλει Πατὴρ πιστεύεσθαι πιστεύσωμεν,
καὶ ὡς θέλει Υἱὸν δοξάζεσθαι δοξάσωμεν, καὶ ὡς θέλει
πνεῦμα ἅγιον δωρεῖσθαι λάβωμεν. 3. μὴ κατ'ἰδίαν
προαίρεσιν μηδὲ κατ'ἴδιον νοῦν μηδὲ βιαζόμενοι τὰ
ὑπὸ τοῦ θεοῦ δεδομένα, ἀλλ'ἢ ὃν τρόπο<ν> αὐτὸς ἐβουλήθη διὰ τῶν ἁγίων γραφῶν δεῖξαι, οὕτως ἴδωμεν.

---

2   ἔλθωμεν   V corr: ἔλθομεν V
14   δωρεῖσθαι]   δωριεῖσθαι V

10.1 – 12.4

SECTION B2 : THE PRE-INCARNATE WORD –
expressive of the Father's will in Creation and
the Prophets

(a) The pre-incarnate Word and Creation

10.1

Creation depends on the will of the sole Creator God

While God was existing alone, and had nothing contemporaneous with himself, he resolved to create the world. What comes into being is at once there before him, as he willed it – what he performed, just as he willed it. So for us it is enough simply to know that there was nothing contemporaneous with God except himself.

10.2

who is eternally and internally complex

But alone though he was, he was manifold. For he was not Word-less nor Wisdom-less nor Power-less nor Mind-less. But everything was in him, and he was himself the All.

10.3

The process of willing creation required the Word

When he willed, in the way he willed, at times he had fixed, he showed forth his Word, through whom he made all things. Just as when he wills, he makes, so when he puts his mind to it, his work is done; and when he gives utterance, he shows forth, and when he forms [things] he displays his Wisdom. For everything that has come into being he contrives through Word and Wisdom – creating by Word and setting in due order by Wisdom. So it is that he made [things] in accordance with his will. After all, he was God.

10.4

and revealed the Word in the world

But as Leader *(cf. Acts 3, 15)* and Counsellor *(cf. Isai 40, 13)* and Craftsman *(cf. Prov 8, 22 LXX)* for what was coming into being, he brought forth the Word. This Word which he has in himself and is invisible to the world that is being created, he makes visible. In uttering what was formerly a sound, and in bringing forth light out of light, he sent forth in the creation, as its Lord, his own Mind, which previously was visible to himself alone. And him who was invisible to the world that is coming into being, he makes visible, so that through his appearance the world might be able to see and be saved.

11.1

as other, but not different from God – the one Power of the Father

And so it is that another took his stand beside him. Now when I say 'other', I am not saying there are two gods.

Χ. 1.   θεὸς μόνος ὑπάρχων καὶ μηδὲν ἔχων ἑαυτῷ σύνχρονον, ἐβουλήθη κόσμον κτίσαι. ὃν κόσμον ἐννοηθεὶς
θελήσας τε καὶ φθεγξάμενος ἐποίησεν · ᾧ παραυτίκα
πάρεστι τὸ γινόμενον ὡς ἠθέλησεν, ὃ ἐτέλεσεν καθὼς
ἠθέλησεν. αὔταρκες οὖν ἡμῖν ἐστιν μόνον εἰδέναι ὅτι
σύνχρονον θεοῦ οὐδὲν πλὴν αὐτὸς ἦν. 2. αὐτὸς δὲ
μόνος ὢν πολὺς ἦν. οὔτε γὰρ ἄλογος οὔτε ἄσοφος /
οὔτε ἀδύνατος οὔτε ἀβούλευτος ἦν. πάντα δὲ ἦν ἐν   364r1
αὐτῷ, αὐτὸς δὲ ἦν τὸ πᾶν. 3. ὅτε ἠθέλησεν, καθὼς
ἠθέλησεν, ἔδειξεν τὸν Λόγον αὐτοῦ καιροῖς ὡρισμένοις
παρ'αὐτῷ · δι'οὗ τὰ πάντα ἐποίησεν. ὅτε μὲν θέλει,
ποιεῖ · ὅτε δὲ ἐνθυμεῖται, τελεῖ · ὅτε δὲ φθέγγεται,
δεικνύει · ὅτε πλάσσει, σοφίζεται. πάντα γὰρ τὰ
γενόμενα διὰ Λόγου καὶ σοφίας τεχνάζεται, ⌊Λόγῳ μὲν
κτίζων⌋, σοφίᾳ δὲ κοσμῶν. ἐποίησεν ⌊οὖν⌋ ὡς ἠθέλησεν ·
θεὸς γὰρ ἦν. 4. τῶν δὲ γινομένων ἀρχηγὸν καὶ σύμ-
βουλον καὶ ἐργάτην ἐγέννα Λόγον. ὃν Λόγον ἔχων ἐν
ἑαυτῷ ἀόρατόν τε ὄντα τῷ κτιζομένῳ κόσμῳ ὁρατὸν ποιεῖ.
προτέραν φωνὴν φθεγγόμενος καὶ φῶς ἐκ φωτὸς γεννῶν,
προῆκεν τῇ κτίσει κύριον τὸν ἴδιον νοῦν αὐτῷ μόνῳ
πρότερον ὁρατὸν ὑπάρχοντα · τῷ δὲ γινομένῳ κόσμῳ
ἀόρατον ὄντα ὁρατὸν ποιεῖ, ὅπως διὰ τοῦ φανῆναι ἰδὼν
ὁ / κόσμος σωθῆναι δυνηθῇ. ΧΙ. 1.   καὶ οὕτως αὐτῷ   364r2
παρίστατο ἕτερος. ἕτερον δὲ λέγων οὐ δύο θεοὺς λέγω,

2	δν ?Vn	:	δ [κόσμον] s,	ὁ κόσμον frl
4	πάρεστι s :	πάρεστη V ,	παρέστη frln
10	ὡρισμένοις]	ὁρισμένοις	V
12	ἐνθυμεῖται]	ἐνθυμεῖτε	V
24	**ἕτερος**]	ἑτέρως	V

11.1 (continued)

But it is like light out of light, or like water out of a spring, or like a sunbeam out of the sun. For there is a single Power that comes out of the All. But the All is the Father, and the Power that comes out of him is the Word.

11.2

and the Mind of God, alone directly from the Father; his Son

And this is the Mind which went forth in the world and was revealed as son of God. Now everything is through him *(cf. Jn 1,3)*, but he himself alone is out of the Father.

11.3

even certain Gnostic heretics agree in fact that ultimately there is one God who willed to create all things

So who is proposing a whole crowd of gods being emitted, one after another, at different times? In fact everybody was bound to agree, unwilling though they might be, that the All is ultimately reducible to a single One. Now if all things are ultimately reducible to a single One — even according to Valentinus, and according to Marcion and Cerinthus and all their rubbish — and unwilling though they are, they have fallen in with the view which would agree that the One is the cause of all things, then even those who have no desire to do so in fact concur with the truth which says that one God made [things] as he willed.

(b) The pre-incarnate Word and the prophets

11.4

The inspired prophets proclaimed the Father's design and will

Now this is he who gave the Law and the Prophets; and in giving them, he forced the latter through the Holy Spirit to give utterance, so that they caught a breath of the Father's own Power and announced the resolve and the will of the Father.

12.1

In them, in fact, the Word, unrecognized, was heralding his own coming

Now while he found his home in these [prophets], the Word was giving utterance about himself. For he himself was already acting as his own herald in revealing that the Word was going to appear among men. That is the reason he cried out with the words: 'I was being made manifest to those who did not seek me; I was found by those who did not ask for me' *(Isai 65, 1)*.

12.2

In sending his Word, the Father was revealing his own authority

And who is he who was made manifest but the Word of the Father? And in sending him the Father was showing men the Power which was from himself. Thus, then, the Word was becoming manifest, just as

ἀλλ'ὡς φῶς ἐκ φωτὸς ἢ ὡς ὕδωρ ἐκ πηγῆς ἢ ὡς ἀκτῖνα
ἀπὸ ἡλίου. δύναμις γὰρ μία ἡ ἐκ τοῦ παντός · τὸ δὲ
πᾶν Πατήρ, ἐξ οὗ δύναμις Λόγος. 2. οὗτος δὲ νοῦς,
ὃς προβὰς ἐν κόσμῳ ἐδείκνυτο παῖς θεοῦ. πάντα τοίνυν
δι' αὐτοῦ · αὐτὸς δὲ μόνος ἐκ Πατρός. 3. τίς τοίνυν
ἀποφαίνεται πληθὺν θεῶν παραβαλλομένην κατὰ καιρούς ;
καὶ γὰρ πάντες ἀπεκλείσθησαν εἰς τοῦτο ἄκοντες εἰπεῖν
ὅτι τὸ πᾶν εἰς ἕνα ἀνατρέχει. εἰ οὖν τὰ πάντα εἰς
ἕνα ἀνατρέχει - καὶ κατὰ Οὐαλεντῖνον καὶ κατὰ Μαρκίωνα
Κήρινθόν τε καὶ πᾶσαν τὴν ἐκείνων φλυαρίαν - καὶ
ἄκοντες εἰς τοῦτο περιέπεσαν ἵνα τὸν ἕνα ὁμολογήσωσιν
αἴτιον τῶν πάντων, ἆρα συντρέχουσιν καὶ αὐτοὶ μὴ
θέλοντες τῇ ἀληθείᾳ ἕνα θεὸν λέγειν ποιήσαν/τα ὡς 364v1
ἠθέλησεν. 4. οὗτος δὲ ἔδωκεν νόμον καὶ προφήτας ·
καὶ δοὺς διὰ πνεύματος ἁγίου ἠνάγκασεν τούτους φθέγξ-
ασθαι, ὅπως τῆς πατρῴας δυνάμεως ἀπόπνοιαν λαβόντες
τὴν βουλὴν καὶ τὸ θέλημα τοῦ Πατρὸς καταγγείλωσιν.

XII. 1. ἐν τούτοις τοίνυν πολιτευόμενος ὁ Λόγος
ἐφθέγγετο περὶ ἑαυτοῦ. ἤδη γὰρ αὐτὸς **ἑαυτοῦ** κῆρυξ
ἐγίνετο δεικνύων μέλλοντα Λόγον φαίνεσθαι ἐν ἀνθρώποις.
δι'ἣν αἰτίαν οὕτως ἐβόα, Ἐμφανὴς ἐγενόμην τοῖς ἐμὲ
μὴ ζητοῦσιν · εὑρέθην τοῖς ἐμὲ μὴ ἐπερωτῶσιν. 2. τίς
δέ ἐστιν ὁ ἐμφανὴς γενόμενος ἀλλ'ἢ ὁ Λόγος τοῦ Πατρός,
ὃν ἀποστέλλων Πατὴρ ἐδείκνυεν ἀνθρώποις τὴν παρ'ἑαυτοῦ
ἐξουσίαν ; οὕτως οὖν ἐμφανὴς ἐγένετο ὁ Λόγος καθὼς

---

6 ἀποφαίνεται]   ἀποφένεται V
10 **Κήρινθον**]   κίρινθον V
11 ὁμολογήσωσιν] ὁμολογίσωσιν V
16 πατρῴας]   πατρόᾱς V

12.2 (continued)   he says.

(c) One and the same Word is operative in Creation and the Prophets and is revealed in them.

12.3

Passages in John 1 sum up the Word's function in creation and the prophets

For the blessed John sums up what has been said through the prophets in showing that this was the Word through whom all things came into being. For he speaks as follows: 'In the beginning was the Word, and the Word was with God, and the Word was God. All things were made through him, and without him was made nothing' *(Jn 1, 1.3)*. And further on he said: 'the world came into being through him, and the world knew him not. He came to his own, and his own people received him not' *(Jn 1, 10–11)*.

12.4

The Word of creation and in the prophets is visibly revealed

Well, if he said, 'the world has come into being through him', just as the prophet says, 'By the word of the Lord were the heavens made strong' *(Ps 32, 6)*, then this Word is the one who is also shown forth as manifest.

12.5— 13.4

SECTION B3 : THE INCARNATE WORD –
sent as the visible will of the Father

12.5

It is the incarnate Word on whom our religion is based, as God willed it

Then surely it is the Word incarnate that we behold. It is through him that we get the idea of the Father, but it is in the Son that we believe, and by the Holy Spirit that we adore *(cf. Jn 4, 23)*.

13.1

Jeremiah called God's Word 'visible'

So let us look at what has been written. That it was the Word who was going to be manifest who was being proclaimed, Jeremiah says, too: 'Who has stood in the presence of the Lord and has seen his Word?' *(Jer 23, 18)*.

13.2

It is this visible Word who was sent

Now only God's Word is visible – that of man is audible. Where he talks of seeing the Word, I can only believe that it is this visible Word that has been sent. But he who has been sent is none other than the Word.

13.3

As we know from Acts 10 – 'through the preaching of Jesus Christ'

And that he was sent, Peter declares to the centurion Cornelius when he says: 'God sent out

λέγει. 3. ἀνακεφαλαιοῦται γὰρ ὁ μακάριος 'Ιωάννης
τὰ διὰ τῶν προφητῶν εἰρημένα δεικνὺς τοῦτον εἶναι
τὸν Λόγον δι'οὗ τὰ πάντα / ἐγένετο. φησὶν γὰρ οὕτως, 364v2
'Εν ἀρχῇ ἦν ὁ Λόγος καὶ ὁ Λόγος ἦν πρὸς τὸν θεὸν καὶ
θεὸς ἦν ὁ Λόγος [[ἦν πρὸς τὸν Θεόν]] . πάντα δι'αὐτοῦ
ἐγένετο καὶ χωρὶς αὐτοῦ ἐγένετο οὐδὲ ἕν. ὑποβὰς δὲ
ἔφη, 'Ο κόσμος δι'αὐτοῦ ἐγένετο καὶ ὁ κόσμος αὐτὸν
οὐκ ἔγνω · εἰς τὰ ἴδια ἦλθεν καὶ οἱ ἴδιοι αὐτὸν οὐ
παρέλαβον. 4. εἰ οὖν ἔφη, 'Ο κόσμος δι'αὐτοῦ γεγένηται, καθὼς λέγει ὁ προφήτης, Τῷ Λόγῳ Κυρίου οἱ οὐρ-
ανοὶ ἐστερεώθησαν, ἆρα οὗτός ἐστιν ὁ Λόγος ὁ καὶ
ἐμφανὴς δεικνύμενος.

XII. 5. οὐκοῦν ἔνσαρκον Λόγον θεωροῦμεν; Πατέρα
δι'αὐτοῦ νοοῦμεν, Υἱῷ δὲ πιστεύομεν, πνεύματι ἁγίῳ
προσκυνοῦμεν. XIII. 1.   ἴδωμεν οὖν τὰ γεγραμμένα.
ὅτι μὲν ἐμφανὴς ὁ Λόγος ἐσόμενος ἐκηρύσσετο, καὶ
'Ιερεμίας λέγει, Τίς ἔστη ἐν ὑποστήματι Κυρίου καὶ
εἶδεν τὸν Λόγον αὐτοῦ ; 2. Λόγος δὲ Θεοῦ μόνος
ὁρατός, ἀνθρώπου δὲ ἀκουστός. ὅπου ὁρᾶν τὸν Λόγον
λέγει, ἀνάγκην ἔχω πιστεύειν τὸν ὁρατὸν τοῦτον 365r1
ἀπεσταλμένον. ὁ δὲ ἀπεσταλμένος οὐκ ἄλλος ἦν ἀλλ'
ἢ ὁ Λόγος. 3. ὅτι δὲ ἀπεστάλθη, μαρτυρεῖ Πέτρος
πρὸς τὸν ἑκατόνταρχον Κορνήλιον λέγων, 'Εξαπέστειλεν

---

2 τῶν]   τὸν V
9 παρέλαβον] παρέλαβων V
12 ἐμφανής]   ἐμφανεὶς V
18 εἶδεν rlsn: ἴδεν   V f

13.3 (continued)

his Word to the sons of Israel, through the preaching of Jesus Christ. He it is who is God, the Lord of all' *(Acts 10, 36)*.

13.4

So this means that Jesus Christ is the Father's will

But then if it is the Word who is sent out through Jesus Christ, the will of the Father is Jesus Christ.

14.1 – 16.7

SECTION B4 : THE UNITY AND DISTINCTION OF GOD

(a) The three Persons of the Trinity are One God

14.1

What the Scriptures say of the economy appears in John 1

Well then, brethren, all this is what the Scriptures point out to us. This economy the blessed John, too, passes on to us through the witness of his Gospel, and he maintains that this Word is God, with the words: 'In the beginning was the Word, and the Word was with God, and the Word was God' *(Jn 1,1)*.

14.2

John's words do not imply two Gods, but one God – two persons, not forgetting a third economy of the Holy Spirit

But then if the Word, who is God, is with God, someone might well say: 'What about this statement that there are two gods?' While I will not say that there are two gods – but rather one – I will say there are two persons; and that a third economy is the grace of the Holy Spirit.

14.3

i.e., one Father, two persons, plus the Holy Spirit

For though the Father is one, there are two persons – because there is the Son as well: and the third, too, – the Holy Spirit.

14.4

The relative functions of Father and Son

The Father gives orders, the Word performs the work, and is revealed as Son, through whom belief is accorded to the Father. By a harmonious economy the result is a single God.

14.5

The relative functions of Father, Son and Holy Spirit

This is because there is one God. For the one who commands is the Father, the one who obeys is the Son, and the one who promotes mutual understandings is the Holy Spirit. He who is Father is over all things, and the Son is through all things, and the Holy Spirit is in all things *(cf. Eph 4,6)*.

14.6

Only fully trinitarian faith leads to a true notion of God

We can get no idea of the one God other than by really believing in Father and

ὁ Θεὸς τὸν Λόγον αὐτοῦ τοῖς υἱοῖς Ἰσραὴλ διὰ κηρύγ-
ματος Ἰησοῦ Χριστοῦ · οὗτός ἐστιν ὁ Θεὸς ὁ πάντων
Κύριος. 4. εἰ δὲ οὖν Λόγος ἀποστέλλεται διὰ Ἰησοῦ
Χριστοῦ, τὸ θέλημα τοῦ Πατρός ἐστιν Ἰησοῦς Χριστός.

XIV. 1. ταῦτα μὲν οὖν, ἀδελφοί, σημαίνουσιν ἡμῖν
αἱ γραφαί. ταύτην τὴν οἰκονομίαν παραδίδωσιν ἡμῖν
καὶ ὁ μακάριος Ἰωάννης ἐν εὐαγγελίῳ μαρτυρῶν, καὶ
τοῦτον τὸν Λόγον Θεὸν ὁμολογεῖ οὕτως λέγων, Ἐν ἀρχῇ
ἦν ὁ Λόγος καὶ ὁ Λόγος ἦν πρὸς τὸν Θεὸν καὶ Θεὸς ἦν
ὁ Λόγος. 2. εἰ δὲ οὖν ὁ Λόγος πρὸς τὸν Θεὸν Θεὸς
ὤν, τί οὖν, φήσειεν ἄν τις, δύο λέγειν θεούς ; δύο
μὲν οὐκ ἐρῶ θεούς, ἀλλ' ἢ ἕνα · πρόσωπα δὲ δύο, /
οἰκονομίαν τε τρίτην τὴν χάριν τοῦ ἁγίου πνεύματος. 365r2
3. Πατὴρ μὲν γὰρ εἷς, πρόσωπα δὲ δύο, ὅτι καὶ ὁ
Υἱός · τὸ δὲ τρίτον καὶ ἅγιον πνεῦμα. 4. Πατὴρ
ἐντέλλεται, Λόγος ἀποτελεῖ, Υἱος δὲ δείκνυται δι'
οὗ Πατὴρ πιστεύεται. οἰκονομία συμφωνίας συνάγεται
εἰς ἕνα Θεόν. 5. εἷς γάρ ἐστιν ὁ Θεός. ὁ γὰρ
κελεύων Πατήρ, ὁ δὲ ὑπακούων Υἱός, τὸ δὲ συνετίζον
ἅγιον πνεῦμα. ὁ ὢν Πατὴρ ἐπὶ πάντων, ὁ δὲ Υἱὸς διὰ
πάντων, τὸ δὲ ἅγιον πνεῦμα ἐν πᾶσιν. 6. ἄλλως τε
ἕνα Θεὸν νοῆσαι οὐ δυνάμεθα, ἐὰν μὴ ὄντως Πατρὶ καὶ

---

6   παραδίδωσιν]   παραδήδωσιν   V
19   συνετίζον]   συνετίζων   V
22   ὄντως]   ὄντὸς   V

14.6 (continued)

Son and Holy Spirit. Of course the Jews glorified the Father, but they offered no thanksgiving *(cf. Rom 1, 21)*, since they had no knowledge of the Son. The disciples did have knowledge of the Son, but not in the Holy Spirit, so they even denied [him].

14.7

The Father's own Word, in accordance with the Father's will, passed on a fully trinitarian faith whereby God is perfectly glorified

Now the Father's own Word was aware of the economy and the will of the Father — that the Father is determined to be glorified in no other way than this. So after his resurrection he passed this on to his disciples with the words: 'Go and make disciples of all nations, baptizing them in the name of the Father and of the Son and of the Holy Spirit' *(Mt 28, 19)* — showing that all those who miss out any one of these did not glorify God perfectly.

14.8

The whole of Scripture testifies to this trinitarian faith

For it is by means of this Triad that the Father is glorified. For the Father willed, the Son brought it about, the Spirit made it clear. Now the whole of the Scriptures are a proclamation about this.

(b) Yet it was the Word, distinct from the Father, who became man and suffered as Son

15.1

It is said that you cannot take John literally

But someone will say to me: 'It sounds strange to me when you call the Son "Word". Of course John says "Word", but he is speaking merely figuratively'.

15.2

You can — cf. further, Apocalypse 19

He is not speaking merely figuratively. For this is how he shows that the Word of God existed as such from the beginning and has now been sent, when someway down in the Apocalypse he said: 'And I saw heaven opened, and behold! a white horse. And he who sits upon it is faithful and true, and in righteousness he judges and makes war. His eyes

Υἱῷ καὶ ἁγίῳ πνεύματι πιστεύσωμεν. Ἰουδαῖοι μὲν
γὰρ ἐδόξασαν Πατέρα, ἀλλ'οὐκ ηὐχαρίστησαν · Υἱὸν
γὰρ οὐκ ἐπέγνωσαν. μαθηταὶ ἐπέγνωσαν Υἱόν, ἀλλ'οὐκ
ἐν πνεύματι ἁγίῳ · διὸ καὶ ἠρνήσαντο. 7. γινώσκων

5   τοίνυν ὁ πατρῷος Λόγος τὴν οἰκονομίαν καὶ τὸ θέλημα
τοῦ Πατρὸς ὅτι οὐκ ἄλλως βούλεται δοξάζεσθαι ὁ Πατὴρ
ἢ οὕτως, ἀ/ναστὰς παρέδωκεν τοῖς μαθηταῖς λέγων, 365v1
Πορευθέντες μαθητεύσατε πάντα τὰ ἔθνη βαπτίζοντες
αὐτοὺς εἰς τὸ ὄνομα τοῦ Πατρὸς καὶ τοῦ Υἱοῦ καὶ τοῦ

10 ἁγίου πνεύματος, δεικνύων ὅτι πᾶς ὃς ἂν ἕν τι τούτων
ἐλλίπῃ, τελείως Θεὸν οὐκ ἐδόξασεν. 8. διὰ γὰρ τῆς
τριάδος ταύτης Πατὴρ δοξάζεται. Πατὴρ γὰρ ἠθέλησεν,
Υἱὸς ἐποίησεν, πνεῦμα ἐφανέρωσεν. πᾶσαι τοίνυν αἱ
γραφαὶ περὶ τούτου κηρύσσουσιν.

15 XV. 1. ἀλλ'ἐρεῖ μοί τις, Ξένον μοι φέρεις Λόγον
λέγων Υἱόν. Ἰωάννης μὲν γὰρ λέγει Λόγον, ἀλλ'
ἄλλως ἀλληγορεῖ. 2. οὐκ ἄλλως ἀλληγορεῖ. οὕτως
γὰρ δεικνύων τὸν Λόγον τοῦ Θεοῦ τοῦτον ὄντα ἀπ'
ἀρχῆς καὶ νῦν ἀπεσταλμένον, ὑποβὰς ἐν τῇ Ἀποκαλύψει

20 ἔφη, Καὶ εἶδον τὸν οὐρανὸν ἠνεῳγμένον καὶ ἰδοὺ ἵππος
λευκὸς καὶ ὁ καθήμενος ἐπ'αὐτοῦ πιστὸς καὶ ἀληθινὸς
καὶ ἐν δικαιο/σύνῃ κρίνει καὶ πολεμεῖ · οἱ δ'ὀφθαλμοὶ 365v2

---

6   ἄλλως] ἄλλος
11 ἐλλίπῃ = ἐνλίπῃ V : ἐκλίπῃ frln,   ἐγλίπῃ s
15 ἀλλ'] ἀλ V
20 εἶδον ln: ἴδον Vfr,   εἶδεν s

78

15.2 (continued)

are a flame of fire; there are many diadems on his head. And he has a name inscribed which no one knows but himself; and he is clad in a robe sprinkled with blood, and the name he has been called is The Word of God' *(Apoc 19, 11–13)*.

15.3

This passage indicates symbolically that it was the Word who suffered in the flesh

So you see, brethren, how the robe sprinkled with blood symbolically expressed the flesh through which even the impassible Word of God underwent suffering, just as I find the prophets attesting.

15.4

And Micah 2 confirms this

For the blessed Micah speaks as follows: 'The house of Jacob provoked the Spirit of the Lord to anger. These are their doings. Are not his words good for them? and do they not walk uprightly? And they rose up in enmity; from the face of his peace they have stripped off his glory' *(Mic 2, 7–8)*. This refers to his suffering in the flesh.

15.5

So does Paul in Romans 8, speaking of God's own Son in the flesh

In just the same way the blessed Paul, too, says: 'For God [has done] what the Law, weakened as it was, could not do: sending his own Son in the likeness of sinful flesh, he condemned sin in the flesh, in order that the just requirement of the Law might be fulfilled in us, who walk not according to the flesh but according to the Spirit' *(Rom 8, 3–4)*.

15.6

This Son in the flesh must be the Word — to call him Son expresses God's love for man

Now what Son of his own has God sent down through the flesh if not the Word, whom he addressed as Son in view of the fact that he was going to become such in future? And in being called Son, he assumes the common name for loving affection between one man and another.

αὐτοῦ φλὸξ πυρός, διαδήματα πολλὰ ἐπὶ τὴν κεφαλὴν
αὐτοῦ, ἔχων ὄνομα γεγραμμένον δ οὐδεὶς οἶδεν εἰ μὴ
αὐτός, καὶ περιβεβλημένος ἱμάτιον ῥεραντισμένον αἵματι,
καὶ κέκληται τὸ ὄνομα αὐτοῦ ὁ Λόγος τοῦ Θεοῦ. 3. ὁρᾶτε,
οὖν, ἀδελφοί, πῶς ἐν συμβόλῳ τὸ ἱμάτιον τὸ ῥεραντισμένον αἵματι τὴν σάρκα διηγήσατο, δι'ἧς καὶ ὑπὸ
πάθος ἦλθεν ὁ ἀπαθὴς τοῦ Θεοῦ Λόγος, καθὼς μαρτυροῦσί
μοι οἱ προφῆται. 4. λέγει γὰρ οὕτως ὁ μακάριος
Μιχαίας, Οἶκος 'Ιακὼβ παρώργισε πνεῦμα Κυρίου ·
ταῦτα τὰ ἐπιτηδεύματα αὐτοῖς ἐστιν · οὐχ οἱ λόγοι
αὐτοῦ καλοὶ μετ'αὐτῶν καὶ ὀρθοὶ πορεύονται, καὶ αὐτοὶ
ἀνέστησαν εἰς ἔχθραν, κατὰ πρόσωπον τῆς εἰρήνης αὐτοῦ
τὴν δόξαν ἐξέδειραν αὐτοῦ. τοῦτ'ἐστὶν τὸ σαρκὶ πα/θεῖν   366r1
αὐτόν. 5. ὡσαύτως καὶ ὁ μακάριος Παῦλος λέγει, Τὸ
γὰρ ἀδύνατον τοῦ νόμου, ἐν ᾧ ἠσθένει, ὁ θεὸς τὸν
ἑαυτοῦ Υἱὸν πέμψας ἐν ὁμοιώματι σαρκὸς ἁμαρτίας,
κατέκρινεν τὴν ἁμαρτίαν ἐν τῇ σαρκί, ἵνα τὸ δικαίωμα
τοῦ νόμου φανερωθῇ ἐν ἡμῖν τοῖς μὴ κατὰ σάρκα περι-
πατοῦσι, ἀλλὰ κατὰ πνεῦμα. 6. ποῖον οὖν Υἱὸν ἑαυτοῦ
ὁ Θεὸς διὰ τῆς σαρκὸς κατέπεμψεν ἀλλ'ἢ τὸν Λόγον, ὃν
Υἱὸν προσηγόρευε διὰ τὸ μέλλειν αὐτὸν γενέσθαι ;
καὶ τὸ κοινὸν ὄνομα τῆς εἰς ἀνθρώπους φιλοστοργίας

---

6 διηγήσατο]   διηγίσατο   V
9 Μιχαίας]   μιιχαίας   V
   παρώργισε]   παρώργεισαι V
14 ὡσαύτως]   ὁσαύτος   V

15.7

In fact, without flesh the Word is not perfect Son: the flesh belongs to the Word and reveals that the Word is the one perfect Son of God

For the Word was not a perfect Son when he was fleshless and on his own, although because he was Word, he was perfect Only-begotten. Nor could the flesh exist on its own apart from the Word, because it has its subsistence in the Word. So in this way a single perfect Son of God was made manifest.

16.1

This shows that it was the Word and not the Father who became man

While these are the testimonies about the incarnation of the Word [that we have seen], there are, of course, a great number of others as well. But let us keep our eyes on the subject in hand: that it really was the Father's own Power, brethren, — which is the Word — that came down from heaven, and not the Father in person.

16.2

cf. John 16 – The Word came out of the Father

This is what he says: 'I came out from the Father, and have come' *(Jn 16, 27f)*. What is the subject of 'I came out from the Father' if not the Word? What is it that has been born from him if not Spirit — that is, the Word?

(c) An objection answered: we cannot hope to understand how the distinction between Father and Son arose

16.3

The problem remains – how was the Son born? Even in the case of a man we do not know

But you will say to me: 'How was he born?' Now in your own case you could not provide the explanation of how you came to be born, even though every day you see what causes a human being, and you cannot give an accurate account of the 'economy' at work behind this.

16.4

We do not know how God produces a man, let alone his Word

After all, it is not for you to know the skilled and inexplicable technique of the Creator.

ἀναλαμβάνει Υἱὸς καλούμενος. 7. οὔτε γὰρ ἄσαρκος
καὶ καθ᾽ἑαυτὸν ὁ Λόγος τέλειος ἦν Υἱός, καίτοι
τέλειος, Λόγος ὤν, μονογενής · οὔθ᾽ἡ σὰρξ καθ᾽
ἑαυτὴν δίχα τοῦ Λόγου ὑποστῆναι ἠδύνατο διὰ τὸ ἐν
Λόγῳ τὴν σύστασιν ἔχειν. οὕτως οὖν εἷς Υἱὸς τέλειος
Θεοῦ ἐφανερώθη. XVI. 1. καὶ ταύτας μὲν περὶ
σαρκώσεως τοῦ Λό/γου μαρτυρίας ⟨........⟩· ἔστιν δὲ   366r2
καὶ ἕτερα πλεῖστα. ἴδωμεν δὲ καὶ τὸ προκείμενον, ὅτι
ὄντως, ἀδελφοί, ἡ δύναμις ἡ πατρῴα, ὅ ἐστιν Λόγος,
ἀπ᾽οὐρανοῦ κατῆλθεν καὶ οὐκ αὐτὸς ὁ Πατήρ. 2. λέγει
γὰρ οὕτως, Ἐγὼ ἐκ τοῦ Πατρὸς ἐξῆλθον καὶ ἥκω. τί
δέ ἐστιν τὸ Ἐξῆλθον ἐκ τοῦ Πατρός, ἀλλ᾽ἢ Λόγος ;
τί δὲ τὸ ἐξ αὐτοῦ γεννηθὲν ἀλλ᾽ἢ πνεῦμα, τοῦτ᾽ἐστὶν
ὁ Λόγος ; 3. ἀλλ᾽ἐρεῖς μοι, Πῶς γεγέννηται ;
τὴν μὲν κατὰ σὲ διήγησιν, ὡς γεγέννησαι, οὐ δύνῃ
ἐξειπεῖν, καίτοι ἑκάστης ἡμέρας ὁρῶν τὴν κατὰ ἄνθρωπον
αἰτίαν, καὶ τὴν περὶ τοῦτον οἰκονομίαν ἀκριβῶς ἐξειπεῖν οὐ δύνασαι. 4. οὐ γὰρ πάρεστίν σοι γιγνώσκειν
τὴν τοῦ δημιουργήσαντος ἔμπειρον καὶ ἀνεκδιήγητον

---

4 ὑποστῆναι rl : ὑποστάναι V, ὑποστᾶναι fn, ὑφεστάναι s
7 deesse videtur verbum: fortasse addend.   εἴδομεν vel simile.
9 ὄντως] ὄντος V
10 οὐκ αὐτός frln: οὐχ αὐτός V, οὐχ αὐτός s
15 γεγέννησαι rlsn: ἐγέννησε V, ἐγέννησαι f
   δύνῃ] δύνει V
18 δύνασαι] δύνασε V

16.4 (continued)

All you can do, when you see it, is to realize and believe that man is a work of God. Yet you are enquiring after the origin of the Word — he whom the Father brought forth as he willed, according to his decision!

16.5

Just as it must suffice to know **that** *God created the world, not to mention* **whence**

Is it not enough for you to be told that God created the world? Do you also make so bold as to try to discover what he made it out of as well?

16.6

So it must suffice to know **that** *the Son of God was revealed to save us, never mind* **how**

Are you not satisfied to be told that the Son of God was made manifest for your salvation, if you would have but faith? But in your meddling curiosity do you look for how he was born according to the Spirit? Not more than two people have been entrusted with the explanation of his birth even according to the flesh — yet you dare to try and find out the explanation according to the Spirit! — an explanation which the Father keeps to himself, and which he will reveal later to those who are saints and worthy to look upon his face.

16.7

Let Christ's word suffice, John 3 — it is a matter of the Spirit and thus mysterious: cf. Psalm 109

Let what has been said by Christ be enough for you: that 'that which is born of Spirit is Spirit' *(Jn 3, 6)*. While God indicates through the prophet the fact that the Word has been born, he reserves the explanation of the fact for a later time which he has fixed for the future revelation of it. And he speaks as follows: 'From the womb before the day-star, I gave thee birth' *(Ps 109, 3)*.

τέχνην, ἀλλ'ἢ μόνον ὁρῶντα νοεῖν καὶ πιστεύειν ὅτι
ἔργον θεοῦ ἄνθρωπος · περὶ δὲ Λόγου γένεσιν ζητεῖς,
ὅνπερ βουληθεὶς ὁ θεὸς Πατὴρ ἐγέννησεν ὡς ἠθέλησεν. /
5. οὐ γὰρ αὔταρκές σοί ἐστιν μαθεῖν ὅτι κόσμον ὁ   366v1
θεὸς ἐποίησεν ; ἀλλὰ καὶ πόθεν ἐποίησεν τολμᾷς ἐπιζητεῖν ; 6. ἢ οὐκ αὔταρκές σοί ἐστιν μαθεῖν ὅτι
Υἱὸς Θεοῦ σοι ἐφανερώθη εἰς σωτηρίαν, ἐὰν πιστεύσῃς ;
ἀλλὰ καὶ πῶς ἐγεννήθη κατὰ πνεῦμα πολυπραγμονεῖς ;
καὶ τὴν μὲν κατὰ σάρκα γέννησιν αὐτοῦ οὐ πλείονες
ἐπιστεύθησαν διηγήσασθαι πλὴν δύο, καὶ σὺ τολμᾷς
ἐπιζητεῖν τὴν κατὰ πνεῦμα διήγησιν, ἣν παρ'ἑαυτῷ
φυλάττει Πατὴρ ἀποκαλύπτειν μέλλων τότε ⌊τοῖς⌋ ἁγίοις
καὶ ἀξίοις ἰδεῖν τὸ πρόσωπον αὐτοῦ. 7. αὔταρκές
σοι ἤτω τὸ εἰρημένον ὑπὸ τοῦ Χριστοῦ ὅτι τὸ γεγενν-
ημένον ἐκ τοῦ πνεύματος πνεῦμά ἐστιν. καθὼς διὰ τοῦ
προφήτου τὴν τοῦ Λόγου γέννησιν σημαίνων ὅτι γεγέννηται, τὸ δὲ πῶς φυλάσσει καιρῷ ὡρισμένῳ παρ'αὐτῷ
μέλλων ἀποκαλύπτειν · λέγει δὲ οὕτως, Ἐκ γαστρὸς
πρὸ ἑωσφόρου ἐξεγέννησά σε. /

---

2 ζητεῖς] ζητεῖν V
7 πιστεύσῃς] πιστεύσις V
8 πολυπραγμονεῖς] πολυπραγμονής V
12 φυλάττει] φυλάτγει V
13 ἰδεῖν] εἰδεῖν V
16 σημαίνων] σημαίνον V
19 ἑωσφόρου] ἐοσφόρου V

17.1 – 17.2

SECTION B5 :
CONCLUSION OF SECTION B (2–4)

17.1

For us, the true faithful,
these testimonies suffice –
the faithless will not
believe anyway

These testimonies satisfy the faithful who are living
the truth. But the faithless believe in nothing.
Indeed, the all-holy Spirit, in the person of the
Apostles, declared this in saying: 'Lord, who
believed what he heard from us?' *(Isai 53, 1)*.
So let us not become faithless, lest the saying
should ever be fulfilled in us.

17.2

So let us believe what
tradition tells us about
the saving incarnation of
the Word

So let us in future believe, blessed brethren, in
accordance with the tradition of the Apostles,
that God the Word came down from the heavens
into the holy virgin Mary, so that once he had
taken flesh out of her, and taken a soul of the
human kind – a rational one, I mean – and had
become everything that a man is, sin excepted
(cf. Heb 4, 15) he might save fallen Adam and
procure incorruption for such as believe in his
name.

17.3 – 18.10

THE PERORATION – a Meditation on 1.7 in
the Introduction

(a) 'We too have knowledge of a single God – in the true way'

17.3

Our work of Demonstration
is ended concerning the
one Father and his Word
sent to save

Thus, then, from every point of view, we have
demonstrated our account of the truth: that there
is a single Father and his Word, through whom he
made all things, is at his side. He it was whom the
Father at subsequent times, as we have stated
further back, sent for the salvation of men.

(b) 'We have knowledge of Christ'

17.4

This Word was foretold
by the prophets, born of
the virgin and the Spirit,
a new man

This was he who was proclaimed through the Law
and Prophets

XVII. 1. αὐτάρκεις αὗται αἱ μαρτυρίαι πιστοῖς ἀλήθειαν 366v2
ἀσκοῦσιν · οἱ δὲ ἄπιστοι οὐδενὶ πιστεύουσιν. καὶ γὰρ
τὸ πνεῦμα πανάγιον ἐκ προσώπου τῶν ἀποστόλων διεμαρτ-
ύρατο λέγον, Κύριε, τίς ἐπίστευσεν τῇ ἀκοῇ ἡμῶν ; ὥστε
μὴ γενώμεθα ἄπιστοι, μήποτε ἐφ' ἡμῖν τελεσθῇ τὸ εἰρημένον. 2. πιστεύσωμεν οὖν, μακάριοι ἀδελφοί, κατὰ
τὴν παράδοσιν τῶν ἀποστόλων ὅτι θεὸς Λόγος ἀπ'οὐρανῶν
κατῆλθεν εἰς τὴν ἁγίαν παρθένον Μαρίαν, ἵνα σαρκωθεὶς
ἐξ αὐτῆς, λαβὼν δὲ καὶ ψυχὴν τὴν ἀνθρωπείαν, λογικὴν
δὲ λέγω, γεγονὼς πάντα ὅσα ἐστὶν ἄνθρωπος ἐκτὸς ἁμαρτίας,
σώσῃ τὸν πεπτωκότα 'Αδὰμ καὶ ἀφθαρσίαν ἀνθρώποις
παράσχῃ τοῖς πιστεύουσιν εἰς τὸ ὄνομα αὐτοῦ.

XVII. 3. ἐν πᾶσιν οὖν ἀποδέδεικται ἡμῖν τῆς ἀληθείας
λόγος, ὅτι εἷς ἐστιν ὁ Πατήρ, οὗ πάρεστι Λόγος, δι'οὗ
τὰ πάντα ἐποί/ησεν · ὃν ὑστέροις καιροῖς, καθὼς 366bisr1
εἴπαμεν ἀνωτέρω, ἀπέστειλεν ὁ Πατὴρ πρὸς σωτηρίαν
ἀνθρώπων. 4. οὗτος διὰ νόμου καὶ προφητῶν ἐκηρύχθη

---

1 αὐτάρκεις] αὐτάρκις V
3 πανάγιον Ficker [Studien z. Hippolyt.104] = παίον V,
τὸ ἅγιον frln, πνέον s
4 λέγον lsn : λέγων Vfr
5 γενώμεθα] γενόμεθα V
9 ἀνθρωπείαν sn: ἀνθρωπίαν V , ἀνθρωπίνην frl
10 γεγονώς] γεγονὸς V
12 παράσχῃ] παράχη V
13 ἀποδέδεικται] ἀποδέδικται V
15 ὑστέροις] οἰστέροις V

17.4 (continued)

as destined to come into the world. So in the very same way in which he was proclaimed, he became present as well, and manifested himself by becoming a new man from the virgin and the Holy Spirit. While, as Word, he has the heavenly element that he gets from his Father, he has the earthly element he gets by taking flesh from the old Adam through the virgin.

17.5

He was God embodied, revealed as true man

This is he who went forth into the world and was manifested as God embodied, going forth as perfect man — for he truly became man, and not just in appearance or figuratively speaking.

(c) 'We know that the Son suffered as in fact he suffered'

18.1

He lived a human life

Thus although he was God clearly revealed, he did not disown what was human about himself as well — when he is hungry and exhausted and weary and thirsty, and takes fright and flees, and is troubled when he prays, and sleeps on a pillow — he who as God has a nature which knows no sleeping.

18.2

and suffered in a human way

And he asks to be excused the suffering of the chalice — he who was present for this very reason in the world. And in his agony he sweats, and is strengthened by an angel — he who strengthens those who believe in him, and has taught them by his example to treat death with contempt.

18.3

at the hands of human beings

And he is betrayed by Judas — he who knows what Judas is; and he is dishonourably treated by Caiaphas — he who, God as he was, was earlier declared priest by him; and he is scorned by Herod — he who is the future judge of all the earth; and he is flogged by Pilate — he who took upon himself our infirmities; and

παρεσόμενος εἰς τὸν κόσμον. καθ'ὅν οὖν τρόπο‹ν›
ἐκηρύχθη κατὰ τοῦτον καὶ παρών, ἐφανέρωσεν ἑαυτὸν
ἐκ παρθένου καὶ ἁγίου πνεύματος, καινὸς ἄνθρωπος
γενόμενος · τὸ μὲν οὐράνιον ἔχων τὸ πατρῷον ὡς Λόγος,
τὸ δὲ ἐπίγειον ὡς ἐκ παλαιοῦ 'Αδὰμ διὰ παρθένου
σαρκούμενος. 5. οὗτος προελθὼν εἰς κόσμον θεὸς
ἐνσώματος ἐφανερώθη, ἄνθρωπος τέλειος προελθών ·
οὐ γὰρ κατὰ φαντασίαν ἢ τροπήν, ἀλλὰ ἀληθῶς γενόμενος
ἄνθρωπος. XVIII. 1. οὕτως οὖν καὶ τὰ ἀνθρώπινα
ἑαυτοῦ οὐκ ἀπαναίνεται ἐνδεικνύμενος θεὸς ὤν, ὅτε
πεινᾷ καὶ κοπιᾷ καὶ κάμνων διψᾷ καὶ δειλιῶν φεύγει
καὶ προσευχόμενος λυπεῖται καὶ ἐπὶ προσκεφάλαιον
καθεύδει, ὁ ἄυπνον ἔχων τὴν φύσιν ὡς / θεός. 2. καὶ 366bis r2
ποτηρίου πάθος παραιτεῖται, ὁ διὰ τοῦτο παραγεγονὼς
ἐν κόσμῳ, καὶ ἀγωνιῶν ἱδροῖ καὶ ὑπὸ ἀγγέλου ἐνδυναμ-
οῦται, ὁ ἐνδυναμῶν τοὺς εἰς αὐτὸν πιστεύοντας καὶ
θανάτου καταφρονεῖν ἔργῳ διδάξας. 3. καὶ ὑπὸ
'Ιούδα παραδίδοται, ὁ γινώσκων τὸν 'Ιούδαν τίς ἐστιν,
καὶ ἀτιμάζεται ὑπὸ Καιάφα, ὁ πρώην ὑπ'αὐτοῦ ἱερατ-
ευόμενος ὡς θεός, καὶ ὑπὸ 'Ηρώδου ἐξουθενεῖται, ὁ
μέλλων κρῖναι πᾶσαν τὴν γῆν, καὶ μαστίζεται ὑπὸ
Πιλάτου, ὁ τὰς ἀσθενείας ἡμῶν ἀναδεξάμενος, καὶ ὑπὸ

---

2 παρών] παρὸν V
4 γενόμενος] γενώμενος V
10 ἀπαναίνεται] ἀπανένεται V
18 παραδίδοται] παραδίδωται V

| 18.3 (continued) | he is made the sport of soldiers — he at whose side stand a thousand thousands and ten thousand times ten thousand angels and archangels; and by the Jews he is fixed to the wood — he who fixed the heaven like a vault. |

(d) 'who died as in fact he died'

| 18.4 *He died a human death* | And with a cry he delivers up the Spirit to the Father — he who is inseparable from the Father; and bowing down his head he breathes his last — he who said: 'I have power to lay down my life, and I have power to take it up again' *(Jn 10, 18)*. But [to show] that, as Life, he was not being mastered by death, he said, 'I lay it down of my own accord' *(ibid.)*. And he is struck in the side by a lance — he who grants to all the favour of life. |

(e) 'who rose again on the third day'

| 18.5 *He was buried to rise again — all for us* | And he is wrapped in a shroud and placed in a tomb — he who raises the dead; and he is raised again after three days by the Father — he who is himself the Resurrection and the Life. And he has successfully accomplished all these things for us — he who became one of us on our account. For he took upon himself our infirmities and bore our sicknesses and underwent suffering on our account, just as the prophet Isaiah said *(cf. Isai 53, 4)*. |

(f) 'and is at the right hand of the Father and is coming to judge living and dead'

| 18.6 *His hidden life showed him to be God* | This is he who is carolled by angels and gazed on by shepherds, and is long expected by Simeon and witnessed to by Anna. He is sought out by the Magi, and is signalled by a star, and he finds himself at home in his Father's house, too, and is pointed out by John. He received the witness of the Father from above: |

στρατιωτῶν παίζεται, ᾧ παραστήκουσιν χίλιαι χιλιάδες
καὶ μύριαι μυριάδες ἀγγέλων καὶ ἀρχαγγέλων, καὶ ὑπὸ
'Ιουδαίων ξύλῳ προσπήγνυται, ὁ πήξας ὡς καμάραν τὸν
οὐρανόν. 4. καὶ πρὸς Πατέρα βοῶν παρατίθεται τὸ
πνεῦμα, ὁ ἀχώριστος τοῦ Πατρός, καὶ κλίνων κεφαλὴν
ἐκπνεῖ, ὁ εἴπας, 'Εξουσίαν / ἔχω θεῖναι τὴν ψυχήν 366bis v1
μου καὶ ἐξουσίαν ἔχω πάλιν λαβεῖν αὐτήν · ὅτι δὲ
οὐκ ἐκυριεύετο ὑπὸ τοῦ θανάτου ὡς ζωή, εἶπεν, 'Εγὼ
ἀπ'ἐμαυτοῦ τίθημι αὐτήν. καὶ πλευρὰν λόγχῃ νύσσεται,
ὁ τὴν ζωὴν πᾶσιν χαριζόμενος. 5. καὶ σινδόνι ἐλ-
ισσόμενος ἐν μνημείῳ τίθεται, ὁ τοὺς νεκροὺς ἐγείρ-
ων, καὶ τριήμερος ὑπὸ Πατρὸς ἀνίσταται, αὐτὸς ὢν
ἡ ἀνάστασις καὶ ἡ ζωή. ταῦτα γὰρ πάντα ἡμῖν κατώρθωσεν ὁ δι'ἡμᾶς γεγονὼς καθ'ἡμᾶς · αὐτὸς γὰρ τὰς
ἀσθενείας ἡμῶν ἀνεδέξατο καὶ τὰς νόσους ἐβάστασεν
καὶ περὶ ἡμῶν ὠδυνᾶτο, καθὼς εἶπεν 'Ησαίας ὁ προφήτης. 6. ὁ ὑπὸ ἀγγέλων ὑμνούμενος καὶ ὑπὸ ποι-
μένων θεωρούμενος καὶ ὑπὸ Συμεῶνος προσδοκώμενος
καὶ ὑπὸ "Αννας μαρτυρούμενος, οὗτος ἦν · ὁ ζητούμενος
ὑπὸ μάγων καὶ σημαινό/μενος ὑπὸ ἀστέρος, ὁ καὶ ἐν 366bis v2
οἴκῳ Πατρὸς πολιτευόμενος καὶ ὑπὸ 'Ιωάννου δακτυλοδεικτούμενος, ὁ ὑπὸ Πατρὸς ἄνωθεν μαρτυρούμενος,

---

5   κλίνων] κλίνον   V
9   πλευράν] πλευρᾶ   V
12 αὐτός Vcorr: αυτῶς   V
13 κατώρθωσεν] κατόρθωσεν   V
21 δακτυλοδεικτούμενος]   δακτυλοδικτούμενος   V

18.6 (continued)

'This is my beloved Son; hear ye him' *(Mt 3, 17)*.

18.7

and so did his public ministry and death

This is he who is crowned in victory against the devil; this is Jesus the Nazarene, who was invited to the wedding in Cana, and changed the water into wine; and reproves the sea which is tossed by the force of the winds. And he walks on the sea as on dry land, and makes a man born blind see, and makes Lazarus, a four-day-dead corpse, rise again, and performs all sorts of acts of power, and forgives sins and gives authority to his disciples. And struck by a spear, he released blood and water from his holy side.

18.8

at his death natural phenomena confirmed this

For his sake the sun is darkened, the day has no light, the rocks are rent, the veil is torn apart, the foundations of the earth are shaken, tombs are opened, and the dead are raised up, and the chief powers are deeply shamed. For on the Cross they beheld him who sets the universe in order, and his eyes are closed; and when creation saw that he had given up the Spirit, it was deep disturbed, and in its inability to take in his superabounding glory, it grew dark.

18.9

as did his post-resurrection appearances and ascension

He it is who by breathing on them gives the Spirit to the disciples, and enters through closed doors. And in full sight of his disciples he is taken up by a cloud into the heavens, and sits at the right hand of the Father, and of the living and the dead

Οὗτός ἐστιν ὁ Υἱός μου ὁ ἀγαπητός, ἀκούετε αὐτοῦ. 7.
οὗτος στεφανοῦται κατὰ διαβόλου, οὗτός ἐστιν 'Ιησ-
οῦς ὁ Ναζωραῖος, ὁ ἐν Κανὰ ἐν γάμοις κληθεὶς καὶ τὸ
ὕδωρ εἰς οἶνον μεταβαλών, καὶ θαλάσσῃ ὑπὸ βίας ἀνέμων
κινουμένῃ ἐπιτιμῶν, καὶ ἐπὶ θαλάσσης περιπατῶν ὡς
ἐπὶ ξηρᾶς γῆς, καὶ τυφλὸν ἐκ γενετῆς ὁρᾶν ποιῶν, καὶ
νεκρὸν Λάζαρον τετραήμερον ἀνιστῶν, καὶ ποικίλας
δυνάμεις ἀποτελῶν, καὶ ἁμαρτίας ἀφίων, καὶ ἐξουσίαν
διδῶν μαθηταῖς, καὶ αἷμα καὶ ὕδωρ ἐξ ἁγίας πλευρᾶς
ῥεύσας λόγχῃ νυγείς. 8. τούτου χάριν ἥλιος σκοτ-
ίζεται, ἡμέρα οὐ φωτίζεται, ῥήγνυνται πέτραι, σχίζεται καταπέτασμα, / τὰ θεμέλια τῆς γῆς σείεται, 367r1
ἀνοίγονται τάφοι καὶ ἐγείρονται νεκροὶ καὶ ἄρχοντες
καταισχύνονται. τὸν γὰρ κοσμήτορα τοῦ παντὸς ἐπὶ
σταυροῦ βλέποντες καμμύσαντα τὸν ὀφθαλμὸν καὶ παρα-
δώσαντα τὸ πνεῦμα ἰδοῦσα ἡ κτίσις ἐταράσσετο, καὶ
τὴν αὐτοῦ ὑπερβάλλουσαν δόξαν χωρῆσαι μὴ δυναμένη
ἐσκοτίζετο. 9. οὗτος ἐμφυσῶν δίδωσι πνεῦμα μαθηταῖς καὶ θυρῶν κεκλεισμένων εἰσέρχεται, καὶ βλεπ-
όντων μαθητῶν ὑπὸ νεφέλης ἀναλαμβάνεται εἰς οὐρανούς,
καὶ ἐκ δεξιῶν Πατρὸς καθέζεται καὶ ζώντων καὶ νεκρῶν

---

1 ἀκούετε] ακούεται V
8 ἀφίων sn: ἀφείων V, ἀφείς frl
10 νυγείς Vcorr frl: νυγίς V , νυγείσης sn
11 σχίζεται] σχήζεται V
19 κεκλεισμένων Vcorr : κεκλισμένων V

92

18.9 (continued)   he is there as judge.

(g) The Doxology

18.10

He is God made man for us — to him be glory and power ... Amen

This is God who became man on our behalf — he to whom the Father subjected all things. To him be glory and power as well as to the Father and the Holy Spirit in the Holy Church, both now and always and from age to age. Amen.

παραγίνεται κριτής.   10.   οὗτος ὁ Θεὸς ὁ ἄνθρωπος
δι' ἡμᾶς γεγονώς, ᾧ πάντα ὑπέταξεν Πατήρ.

αὐτῷ ἡ δόξα καὶ τὸ κράτος ἅμα Πατρὶ καὶ
ἁγίῳ πνεύματι ἐν τῇ ἁγίᾳ ἐκκλησίᾳ καὶ
νῦν καὶ ἀεὶ καὶ εἰς τοὺς αἰῶνας τῶν αἰώνων.

ἀμήν.

3
THE STRUCTURE OF CN

To speak of the structure of CN is not to break entirely new ground. As has been shown in Chapter 1, at CN's first appearance in the Latin version of Torres, it was noted in the margin, at two places, that the work possessed two parts, different but somehow complementary in purpose.[1] These two main parts, labelled rather obviously 'The Noetians' (cc.1–8) and 'Demonstration of the Truth' (cc.9–18), appear in Nautin's edition of CN, suitably sub-divided in accordance with a superficial appreciation of their contents. But closer study of the text of CN shows that there is need of a deeper and more detailed description of the elaborate structure which is to be found in the work.

Several factors prompt a completely new approach to the structure of CN as a whole. In the first place, the original description of CN in the sole ms as a ὁμιλία apparently complete in itself, together with the fact that the view of CN as a fragment of some larger anti-heretical work, probably the *Syntagma* of Hippolytus, is of a later origin, invites an examination of the structure of CN which treats CN as an integral literary entity. Certainly the fluctuations which the view of CN as a fragment has undergone do not inspire confidence in that view; and in any case it would be wrong to exclude *a priori* the possibility that the primitive description of CN is right. In the second place, the chapter-divisions which are used in Fabricius' edition, first of the Latin version of CN and then in the *editio princeps* of the Greek text, and which were thenceforth to become the traditional divisions of the text, are not at all haphazard. More often than not they correspond closely to definite sections in the text and coincide with easily observable transitions from one topic to another. In fact they provide a sort of evidence for some kind of inner structure in CN. In the

---

1 See n.37 to Chapter 1.

third place, there occurs in the first part of CN a slight, little noticed displacement which requires some explanation. In 2.5–8, a sub-section where the second of two pairs of Scripture texts and an exposition of their meaning are given as a sample of patripassianist argument, along with an added testimony to the same effect from St Paul, the order in which the texts are quoted is as follows: (1) Baruch 3, 36–38, (2) Isaiah 45, 14f, (3) Romans 9, 5. But in the subsequent refutation of the patripassianist exegesis of these texts – which in fact makes up the main body of the first part of CN – the order in which the texts are treated is changed: (1) Isaiah 45, (2) Baruch 3, (3) Romans 9. It would be wrong to treat the reversal in order of Isaiah 45 and Baruch 3 as insignificant. Considerable space and care is devoted to developing the exegesis of these two passages, and it must be supposed that there is some underlying reason for dealing with them in this new order. In other words, it looks as though within the first part of CN, after the preliminary introduction of the texts to be discussed, the writer has fitted them into a certain structure which for one reason or another he had in mind. In the fourth place, even a cursory reading of CN reveals the presence of two short, roughly equal passages which stand at the beginning of the two main parts of the work, and which deal, in slightly different ways, with a common theme and refer to what is to follow them. Thus 3.1–3.6 presents a note on the use of Scripture and an indication of the programme which is to be followed in subsequent sections. Thus also 8.4–9.3, while marking the transition from the first part of CN to the second, comments on the value and use of Scripture and indicates the programme which it is hoped to fulfil in subsequent sections.

All these four factors, but especially the third and fourth, seem to show that it would be worthwhile examining CN, not as a fragment of a larger work, but as a work complete in itself, yet possessing a perhaps elaborate and so far undetected structure. In particular, the third and fourth factors seem to hint at the existence within the two main parts of sections which are written in some special order. Since both 3.1–3.6 and 8.4–9.3 look forward to what is to be done in subsequent sections, and since both are roughly in the position where the two main parts of CN are traditionally said to begin, it would hardly be rash to start the examination of CN's structure from these two strangely parallel sections. Perhaps other sections, written, as it would seem from the first part of CN, in a special order, are parallel also. It will be convenient to label the two main parts of CN as A and B. Thus let 3.1–3.6 be A1, and let 8.4–9.3 be B1.

A1 (3.1–3.6) and B1 (8.4–9.3):
Two programmatic notes on the use of Scripture

Both A1 and B1 fall into two sub-sections: A1 into A1(a), 3.1–3.3, and
A1(b), 3.4–3.6; B1 into B1(a), 8.4–9.1, and B1(b), 9.2–9.3. This will be
clarified in the course of the following description of contents.[2]

Sub-section A1(a) begins with a complaint against the selective use made of
Scripture by heretics (3.1). Heretics deal only with individual verses of Scripture: they never attain the full truth in this way, and the Scriptures themselves,
which as a whole contain the truth, condemn heretics as ignorant.[3] Next, with
a forceful appeal to the indignation of the audience, there is instanced the
Patripassianist doctrine as an example of what can happen when Scripture is
wrongly interpreted (3.2); and this is followed by a flat denial of that doctrine
and a clear assertion that the Scriptures are the basis of what is orthodox
($\grave{o}\rho\theta\tilde{\omega}\varsigma$), whatever any private person such as Noetus might think the Scriptures say. It is not the Scriptures, but heretical thinking, that must be got rid
of (3.3). This first sub-section, A1(a), constitutes therefore a warning against
the misuse or deliberate disregard of what the Scriptures say.

Now sub-section B1(a) says the same thing, but in an interestingly different
way. The sub-section opens with an invitation to the Demonstration of that
Truth which is the downfall of each and every sect[4] (8.4). This invitation is

---

2   It will be helpful, throughout the exposition of the structure of CN, to keep an eye on
    the full analysis of the structure and contents of CN adjoining the translation.

3   The beginning of this section has caused some difficulty. $\kappa\alpha\grave{\iota}\,\tau\alpha\tilde{\upsilon}\tau\alpha\ldots\,\mu\upsilon\upsilon\acute{o}\kappa\omega\lambda\alpha$
    (3.1) has led some either to amend the text to $\mu\upsilon\upsilon\upsilon\kappa\acute{\omega}\lambda\omega\varsigma$ or to suppose that
    $\mu\upsilon\upsilon\acute{o}\kappa\omega\lambda\alpha$ is being used adverbially, with $\delta\iota\eta\gamma\epsilon\tilde{\iota}\sigma\theta\alpha\iota$. But there is an interesting
    passage in Irenaeus, AH 5.13.2 (Harvey II, 356) which may cast some light on what
    is actually meant by $\mu\upsilon\upsilon\acute{o}\kappa\omega\lambda\alpha$. Irenaeus speaks of the vanity and misery of heretics
    who flee the truth, blinding themselves like Oedipus. They are like people untrained
    in wrestling who fight others and hold on to one single part of their opponent's body,
    and thereby come to fall, but imagine that they have won because they keep up their
    grip on some extremity. Heretics do this with Scripture texts, $\psi\iota\lambda\grave{\alpha}\varsigma\,\delta\grave{\epsilon}\,\grave{\epsilon}\alpha\upsilon\tauo\tilde{\iota}\varsigma\,\mu\acute{o}\nu\upsilon\nu$
    $\tau\grave{\alpha}\varsigma\,\lambda\acute{\epsilon}\xi\epsilon\iota\varsigma\,\grave{\alpha}\pi\alpha\rho\tau\acute{\iota}\zeta\upsilon\nu\tau\epsilon\varsigma$ and thus overturn $\tau\grave{\eta}\nu\,\grave{\alpha}\pi\alpha\sigma\alpha\nu\,\upsilon\grave{\iota}\kappa\upsilono\nu\upsilon\mu\acute{\iota}\alpha\nu$ of God. It is pre-
    cisely this picture of the wrestlers that should be kept in mind to explain $\mu\upsilon\upsilon\acute{o}\kappa\omega\lambda\alpha$.
    The Noetians, like Theodotus, pick out single verses ('individual limbs'), cling tightly
    to them alone and find themselves in fact overthrown by the whole of Scripture.
    They will not come to grips with Scripture as a whole, only with $\mu\upsilon\upsilon\acute{o}\kappa\omega\lambda\alpha$.

4   This is surely the sense of $\pi\tilde{\alpha}\sigma\alpha\iota\,\tauo\sigma\alpha\tilde{\upsilon}\tau\alpha\iota\,\alpha\grave{\iota}\rho\acute{\epsilon}\sigma\epsilon\iota\varsigma$. The generalizing meaning of this
    phrase receives much support from the fact that it occurs at the very beginning of the
    introduction to the Demonstration of the Truth, i.e. the general Truth of the Christian
    religion which can silence all heretical sects. To take the phrase as necessarily referring
    to certain heresies or sects previously combatted in the now lost main part of a work
    to which CN may be thought to be the end-fragment, is both to fail to see at what
    precise juncture the phrase occurs, and to demand too much precision from what is,
    grammatically, a vague phrase. Certainly the insertion of $\alpha\grave{\iota}$, as by Nautin (*Contre les
    Hérésies*, p.249, 28; see p.89), is quite without justification.

followed immediately by an explanation of why the source of our knowledge of the one God and our practice of true piety must be the Holy Scriptures (9.1). The presence of the invitation can hardly be said to upset the parallelism which is obvious between A1(a) and B1(a). Indeed its presence is only natural considering that 8.4 marks the beginning of the second part of the whole work. The parallel interest of the two sub-sections remains. Both are concerned with the proper use of Scripture; but A1(a) deals with the proper use *negatively*: if you misuse Scripture, you will finish up in heresy – you cannot with impunity jettison the Scriptures. B1(a), however, deals *positively* with the proper use of Scripture: the truth about the one God, which is about to be demonstrated, can only come from the Holy Scriptures: the true religion from the utterances of God. Nor is this surprising: for 'the wisdom of this age' (1 Cor 2, 6) we would have to look to the teachings of the philosophers. This is not, like A1(a), a general warning against the misuse of Scripture: rather the Christian brethren are being invited to consider the truth and are being told why that truth is to be found in the Sacred Scriptures which are the utterances of God. Thus these two-sub-sections display likeness of theme, coupled with a contrast in approach and purpose. A1(a) tends to be negative and defensive: B1(a) to be positive and explanatory.

The two further sub-sections, A1(b) and B1(b), must now be examined. Both are programmatic in that they map out the plan and the purpose to be followed in the immediately subsequent sections. A1(b) begins with a rhetorical question which points the need to reconcile the unity of God with the undoubted fact of the 'economy' (3.4). To satisfy this need a refutation must be made of the wrong interpretation put on the passages of Scripture by the Noetians in the arguments of c.2, and their true meaning must be brought out in the light of the traditional truth (3.5). In this way a proper understanding of the Father-hood of God, as basis of the Christian faith, will be made possible (3.6).

B1(b), as sub-section, has the same programmatic function but shows a different approach to it. Here positive reasons are given why the correct interpretation of what the Sacred Scriptures proclaim and teach is important (9.2). It is from Scripture that we will learn to believe in the Father, to glorify the Son and receive the Holy Spirit in the way that has been willed by the Father. For our practice of true religion, which we can learn only from the Holy Scriptures, it is important that we receive God's revelation from the Scriptures in the way he intended to make it though them. To follow what we happen to think is to do violence to God's gifts (9.3). Thus in B1(b) there are accumulated positive reasons for complete obedience to the Scriptures as a whole in the search for truth and the practice of religion. The Scriptures enable us to discern God's will in the matter of religion and truth, and for this supreme reason we are to

scrutinize and learn to know them. There is no question here, as there is in
A1(b), of the refutation of wrong interpretations of Scripture: only positive
reasons are of interest.

So it may be said that as far as the contents of A1 and B1, in both their sub-
sections, are concerned, the two sections display a parallelism and a contrast
which are most striking. Both deal with the use of Scripture and are programmatic in purpose. But from contrasting viewpoints: A1 takes a negative,
defensive, apologetic line; whereas B1 makes a positive, explanatory, more
doctrinal approach.

If then in content and approach A1 and B1 are parallel yet contrasting sections
which stand at the head of the two main parts of the central body of CN, it is
reasonable to push the examination of possible subsequent sections further,
to see if there can be discovered similar parallelism and contrast in the rest of
the two main parts, A and B.

A2 (4.1–4.13) and B2 (10.1–12.4):
Two sections on the pre-incarnate Word

The section which follows immediately on A1 needs little defining. Its beginning is marked by a clearly resumptive ὡς εἶπον; its main purpose is simply to
develop and defend the correct interpretation of the passage from Isaiah 45
misused by the Noetians; and its end is signalled by a transition to the next
text to be discussed, from Baruch 3. A2, then, coincides exactly with the traditional c.4 of CN: 4.1–4.13. Within this section it is possible to distinguish three
roughly equal sub-sections: A2(a), 4.1–4.4, which consists of some opening
remarks on the importance of quoting Scripture passages in full. A2(b), 4.5–
4.8, in which it is shown how the correct interpretation of the passage in
question reveals the mystery of the 'economy', the pre-incarnate Word. A2(c),
4.9–4.13, where objections to the pre-incarnate state of the Word, arising
from the use of the title 'Son of Man', are answered.

A2(a) needs no long explanation. The programmatic outline of 3.5 is repeated
(4.1). There can be no doubting the polemical tone of this repetition and the
example of the selective mutilation of the passage from Isaiah 45 that follows.
Heretics employ deliberate trickery (4.2). Only if the passage is quoted in full
will it be possible to see the proper theological implications of it (4.3). By way
of good example the passage is then quoted in full (4.4). Here the fight is
carried to advantage into the camp of the heretical opposition.

A2(b) then can give an orthodox interpretation of the passage. The basic refutation of the Noetian position consists in showing that this passage clearly

indicates the existence of the Word of God, the mystery, in other words, of the 'economy' within the Godhead. Two phrases from Isaiah are singled out as especially significant: 'God is in thee', where 'thee' must be referred to Christ, the Word of the Father and mystery of the 'economy' (4.5); and 'I raised him up in justice . . .', which must refer to the incarnation of that Word as Son – and this is confirmed from St Paul (4.6). The main point of refutation is that 'God is in thee' points to the existence of the mystery of the 'economy', the Word of God: he who even when he became incarnate as Son was still united with the Father (4.7). God was still in him and he in God. The mystery of the 'economy' was this very Word, who from the Holy Spirit and the Virgin fashioned a single Son for God (4.8). It is important to note that the elements which refer to the incarnation of the Word are strictly secondary here: the main concern is to assert, against the Noetians, and on the basis of the very text they themselves have so selectively employed, the existence of the mystery of the 'economy', the Word. Not primarily the incarnation of that Word: but his pre-incarnate existence as the mystery of the 'economy' of the Godhead. That he also became incarnate as Son is important in that he was still, because he was Word, one with the Father; the Father in the Son and the Son in the Father. This incarnate state of the Word as Son has here the function of confirming the state in which the pre-incarnate Word was, when God was in him, as has been shown from the quotation, properly understood, from Isaiah. The actual overturning, the $\dot{\alpha}\nu\alpha\tau\rho o\pi\dot{\eta}$ proper, of the Noetian position consists at this stage in the assertion of the existence of the pre-incarnate Word, the primal mystery of the 'economy' of the Godhead. This is confirmed by what is known about the later incarnate Word.

Hence it comes about that the third sub-section, A2(c), must deal with a possible objection which takes its rise from the title, well-known from Daniel and used by John, of 'the Son of man'. First it is said that the assertion of the pre-incarnate existence of the Word has the support of Christ's own statement in John (3. 13) that the Son of man, who is in heaven, came down from heaven (4.9). Not that he was incarnate in heaven: the Word incarnate was in that self-sacrificial state assumed by the Word as perfect Son of the Father (4.10). In heaven the Word was without flesh – he was Spirit and Power (4.11). The 'Son of man' title was his from the beginning, as Daniel saw (4.13), because it enabled men to foresee and to comprehend his future incarnation (4.12). Thus this sub-section forestalls an objection against the pre-incarnate, fleshless state of the Word which it is the point of the whole section A2 to assert against the Noetian position. It is clear enough that the whole section has a polemical tone and a clearly apologetical purpose, opposing as it does the wrong-headed and even evil-intentioned interpretation of Scripture with balanced orthodox exegesis; and that the section is in effect a severely practical refutation of those who would deny the mystery of the 'economy' within the Godhead, which is in fact the Word in his pre-incarnate existence. There is an abundance of sharply rhetorical questions: 4.5; esp. 4.6 and 4.10; 4.11. A slightly trium-phalistic note appears: ἰδοὺ συνέστηκεν . . . (4.6); πρόδηλον οὖν ὅτι . . . (4.10); δικαίως οὖν . . . (4.13). And a note of challenge: ὁλοκλήρως δὲ εἰπάτω καὶ εὐρήσει . . . (4.3); τοῦτο δὲ οὐκ ἐγὼ λέγω, ἀλλ' αὐτός . . . (4.9); μήτι ἐρεῖ ὅτι . . . (4.10). Such positive and explanatory elements as appear, e.g., about the incarnation and the heavenly state of the Word, are here quite secondary and subordinate to the refutative purpose of the whole section. Objections, real or imaginary, are cleared from the path of the plain assertion of the exist-ence of the pre-incarnate Word in the mystery of the Godhead.

It would be only reasonable in view of the above description of the existence and contents of A2, as a definite section discernible in part A of CN, to look to part B to see if there is there a corresponding section, B2. In fact there is precisely such a section which deals with the pre-incarnate Logos, but, as might also be expected, from a different point of view and with a different purpose.

Section B2 runs from 10.1, which is an easily distinguishable beginning of a new theme, to 12.4, after which the interest shifts noticeably to the incarnate state of the Word. This long section B2, 10.1–12.4, may be divided, like A2, into three sub-sections, but on quite different lines:

B2(a), 10.1–11.3, deals with the role of the pre-incarnate Word in creation.

B2(b), 11.4–12.2, shows how the pre-incarnate Word functioned in the prophets.

B2(c), 12.3–12.4, gives a Scriptural summary of these two activities of the pre-incarnate Word.

The first long sub-section, B2(a), is concerned with the existence of the Word as it emerges from the Word's function within the highly complex process of creation. Creation depends on the will of the sole Creator God (10.1), who is, though alone the All, internally complex (10.2). In God the processes of willing creation and of actually creating required both Word and Wisdom (10.3), and in fact revealed the presence of the previously invisible Word visibly in the world (10.4). In this way it can be seen that the Word is other than, but not different from, God. He is the one power of the Father (11.1), the Mind, alone directly from the Father, his offspring (11.2). There can be no question of positing a whole series of Gods: as even well-known heretics confess, everything comes down in the end to the one God, the ultimate cause of everything, who created in accordance with his will (11.3). Even though certain heretics are named, mainly, one would suspect, to add colour and interest at the end of a difficult passage (11.3), this sub-section is in no way merely a counter-assertion of the existence of the pre-incarnate Word. Rather it is intended as a theological explanation of the function or role of the Word before and in the process of creation, i.e., during what might be called the 'first' stages of his pre-incarnate existence.

The second, short sub-section, B2(b), explains the role of the Word in the next stage of that pre-incarnate existence, the period known now as that of the Old Testament. The inspired prophets proclaimed the mind and will of the Father (11.4). In them, unrecognized, the Word was heralding his own coming (12.1) to reveal the Father's authority to men (12.2).

The third sub-section, B2(c), quotes passages from John (12.3) and from the Psalms (12.4) to show that the Word active in the prophets is the same Word through whom God made all things. This sub-section is no more than a summary of the whole section, B2: one and the same Word functions in creation and the prophets while still pre-incarnate. If A2 used Scripture, misused by heretics, to uphold the existence of the pre-incarnate Word, B2 elaborates a theology of creation and prophecy to show how that pre-incarnate stage of the Word's existence must be postulated in order to explain how the processes of creation and prophecy could be expressions of the Father's will. The difficult theology which lies behind this whole section can be examined later. For the present it is sufficient to note that A2 and B2 are both concerned with the existence of the pre-incarnate Word. But where A2 defends it against heretical denial and bad exegesis, B2 explains it as necessary in view of the way in which God has expressed his will through creation and the prophets. The parallelism suspected between A and B is clearly maintained in these two corresponding sections, A2 and B2; and the contrast in points of view and purpose remains the same as in A1 and B1. Part A remains defensive and apologetical; part B is expository and more doctrinal.

A3 (5.1–5.5) and B3 (12.5–13.4):
Two sections on the incarnate Word

Two short sections, A3 and B3, now follow on the sections which concern, as has been shown, the existence and functions of the pre-incarnate Word. It is the incarnation of the Word, as a further and final stage in the expression of the mind and will of the Father in Jesus Christ, that is the theme common to these two sections.

A3 coincides with the traditional c.5 of CN (5.1–5), and it consists in an orthodox interpretation of the passage quoted by the Noetians from Baruch 3 (cf. 2.5). In answer to a hostile question from a Noetian adversary about the apparently clear statement of Baruch 3 that no other will be reckoned alongside God, it is shown first that the implications of the very word λογισθήσεται and the whole text in fact indicate another to whom knowledge is given – Jacob his offspring, Israel his beloved (5.1). This then must be the Beloved Son of the Gospels (5.2). He it was, the perfect Israel, the real Jacob, to whom the types of the Old Testament looked forward, who was endowed with all knowledge by the Father and appeared on earth among men (5.3). Indeed the derivation of the word 'Israel' is shown to confirm this: there is only one 'man-who-sees-God', and he is the offspring of God, the perfect man who alone reveals the mind of the Father (5.4). As we know from St John, this is the only-begotten Son who came down from heaven to testify on earth what he had learnt from the Father, as a man among men (5.5). This interpretation of the Baruch passage is in effect yet another refutation of the Noetian position. It justifies the plain assertion that it was not in fact the Father, but the offspring of the Father, as expression of the Father's mind, who became incarnate to reveal that mind to men. Thus, following on A2 which concerns the pre-incarnate Word, A3 moves on to the incarnate offspring of the Father, the final reality of his prefiguration in Jacob-Israel, who came to live as perfect man among men and so revealed the will of his Father. As in A2, the tone of A3 remains refutative: the whole section in fact is a correction of the false interpretation of Baruch by the Noetians. The vigorous counter-questions of 5.2 and 5.4 mark the fact that the point of the section is to return the opening question of the Noetian adversary with interest.

B3, the corresponding section of part B on the incarnate Word, runs from 12.5 to 13.4. Its opening is signalled by a question which switches the attention of the reader from the pre-incarnate Word of B2, to the ἔνσαρκος Λόγος and his central role in our Christian religion (12.5). As can be seen from Jeremiah 23, it was a manifest and visible Word which was being announced even in the Old Testament (13.1). This visible Word of God was made visible to men, was sent (13.2) in Jesus Christ, as we know from the New Testament (13.3). This makes Jesus Christ the will of the Father (13.4), made incarnate and visible for us.

It is not difficult to demonstrate how much the two sections A3 and B3 have in common. Apart from the reference of the contents to the incarnate state of the Word, there is a wealth of corresponding expression, mostly of a scriptural kind. As only-begotten Son, the Word was originally hidden in God: εἰς τὸν κόλπον τοῦ Πατρός (5.5); ἐν ὑποστήματι κυρίου (13.1). While there, the Word came to possess the knowledge of the mind of the Father (5.3, 5). Later he became visible (5.3, 5; 13.1, 2), in that he was sent (13.2, 3, 4) down from heaven (5.5) and became incarnate (5.3, 5; 13.3), the perfect man (5.4), Jesus Christ (13.3, 4), who reveals what he as Word has heard and seen (5.5) of the Father's mind (5.4, 5) in his message (διηγησάμενος 5.4; διὰ κηρύγματος 13.3). He sees God (5.4) and is the Father's Beloved Son (5.2); in fact the very will of the Father (13.4), in whom the Father is well pleased (5.2), and revealed as a man among men.

The common theme, however, does not exclude a difference of approach and purpose. In A3 the text of Baruch is turned to advantage in scoring off an opponent. A rival interpretation is proposed, and is made to fit the wording of the text through the use of pun and sharp questions, as further texts are introduced to strengthen the desired interpretation of the original. In B3 the polemical note is quite absent. The text from Jeremiah is explained. The concern is now with the basis of our Christian faith (12.5); and faith (13.2) is what controls the interpretation of Scripture in B3, whereas in A3 it was the need to overthrow an adversary which controlled it. The tone of B3 is one of quiet exposition, even if this at times seems to be rather elliptical. Thus once again A3 is apologetical and anti-heretical in its purpose: it aims at proving the *fact* that it was the pre-incarnate Word that became incarnate. B3 is, however, expository and attempts to explain the *function* of the incarnate Word.

Before pushing this examination further into parts A and B of the main nucleus of CN, we may note that it is now possible to explain the curious displacement of the Isaiah and Baruch texts to which attention was called at the beginning of this chapter. Isaiah 45 has been used in A2 as the basis for an anti-heretical assertion of the existence of the pre-incarnate Word. In A3 Baruch 3 has served a similar purpose with regard to the fact of the incarnation of this Word. These two texts, clearly, could only be dealt with by a writer who held the orthodox faith and whose mind was to some extent formed by a clear idea of the course of salvation-history, in the order in which they have been dealt with in A2 and A3. The pre-incarnate Word logically and theologically must precede the incarnate Word. The order in which the texts were first mentioned, Baruch 3 in 2.5 and then Isaiah 45 in 2.6, was useless for a writer who desired to explain the orthodox faith and counter heresy in an ordered manner. This same consideration has also dictated, as we have seen, the order of contents in B2 and B3. So it came about that the two texts were taken in the opposite order to that in which they were first introduced. This is already valuable evidence that the writer of CN was working to a plan, the full extent of which has still to be discovered and appreciated.

A4 (6.1–7.7) and B4 (14.1–16.7):
Two sections on unity and distinction in God

The two sections A3 and B3, which have dealt with the incarnation of the Word, are remarkably short. Both of them are quickly followed by a section much longer in extent and more technical in matter, which is bounded, in both cases, only by a short section which is obviously the intended conclusion to the four sections which have preceded it. The long sections A4 and B4 must now be analysed and described. Like A2 and B2, but quite unlike the much shorter A3 and B3, both A4 and B4 fall neatly enough into three sub-sections. It will not be necessary to point out how the traditional chapter-divisions of CN, especially in part A, both coincide with and depart from these new divisions. To begin with A4: the three sub-sections are as follows:

A4(a), 6.1–6.6, stresses the fact that Christ and the Father are one God.

A4(b), 7.1–7.3, shows how Christ, as Son, is yet distinct from the Father.

A4(c), 7.4–7.7, answers a fundamental objection to this latter statement.

A4(a) begins by tackling the text from Rom 9 that had been thrown into the Noetian arguments for patripassianism at 2.8 as a makeweight to the two pairs of texts adduced to show that God is one, and that the one God became man. Here the text from Paul is claimed as an excellent support of the orthodox truth that Christ, who is indeed 'God over all', became man, and remains God for ever (6.1). John, too, virtually quoting Christ himself, attests the fact of Christ's almighty divinity (6.2), and Paul says so elsewhere in 1 Cor 15 (6.3). Of course, Christ is ultimately subject to the Father (6.4), and calls the Father his God (6.5). The unobjectionable gospel truth is that, although Christ is God, Christ is not the Father (6.6). In this way the description of Christ as 'God over all' in Romans 9 is shown to give an essential trait of the orthodox picture of Christ. Once again a text quoted by the adversary is turned to advantage, and the hostile and clever question of 6.6 concludes the sub-section with a direct confrontation between orthodoxy and the Noetian nonsense.

A4(b) turns to establishing the distinction between Father and Son. A further text, Jn 10, 30, not in fact previously quoted but seemingly favouring the Noetian position, is introduced. The very grammatical form of the Johannine Christ's statement that 'I and the Father *are* one' is now used to point, not to the unity of God, as Noetus and many Catholic theologians have used the text, but to the distinction between two Persons in the one Godhead (7.1). And then this distinction is confirmed with another Johannine text (7.2). Again this leaves the Noetians floundering.[5] They have no idea that the distinction between Father and Son is to be conceived as that between Father and his single Mind. This approach brings out the distinction of the Father and his offspring, while saving the unity of the Godhead (7.3). As in 6.6, so also in 7.3 a note of ridicule is allowed to sharpen the refutation of the Noetian position.

A4(c) imagines and answers a Noetian objection to the distinction between Christ and the Father, based on Christ's statement to Philip that he is in the Father and the Father is in him (Jn 14, 8–10). But little do the Noetians realize that once again they are fated to trip over their own text (7.4). Like Philip, they simply do not see that Christ, in all he said and did, was the Son of the Father (7.5), the very Image of the Father, through whom the Father can be known (7.6), as other statements in the same part of the Gospel confirm (7.7).

All three sub-sections of A4 are markedly opposed to the heretical interpretations of the scripture passages quoted. A hostile tone is maintained in each sub-section, as has been pointed out, by the use of ironical questions (6.6; 7.3; 7.6). Scripture itself provides all that is needed for the refutation of the Noetian heresy (6.6; 7.4; 7.7). Heretics do not have the νοῦς to understand about the Νοῦς of the Father (7.3, cf. 7.1). Even their grammar is defective and the subject of a joke (7.1; 7.3). They put down obstacles to trip themselves up (7.4) and cannot comprehend the power of the Godhead (7.5). So against the undoubted fact of God's unity and inner distinction, the heretics fail to make good their case. The Scripture they quote, or even might quote, can only turn into a weapon against them.

B4 has the same theme as A4, the unity and distinction of the Godhead. There are also three sub-sections, along the lines of the three sub-sections of A4.

B4(a), 14.1–14.8, declares how the three Persons of the Trinity are one God.

B4(b), 15.1–16.2, probes the distinction of the Father and the Word who became man and suffered as Son.

---

5   Precisely for this reason it is important to leave the ms-reading of 7.3 untouched. πάντες ἕν σῶμά ἐστιν has worried all the editors. The point, surely, of the strictly ungrammatical ἐστιν is to be found by referring it back to the Noetian inability to grasp the purport of the ἐσμεν of Jn 10, 30 in 7.1. Now they are portrayed as being themselves grossly – and amusingly – ungrammatical, since they apparently show no regard for grammar.

B4(c), 16.3−16.7, answers an obvious objection by trying to state why we cannot understand how the distinction between the Father and the Son arose.

B4(a), with an appeal to the brethren of the audience, goes straight to the point that the 'economy' in the Godhead is attested in the first chapter of John (14.1). The main interest of the sub-section is in the unity of the Godhead. The words of John are not evidence that there are two gods, but one God with two Persons, and, of course, the Holy Spirit as well (14.2, 3). Father and Son have correlative functions, but remain harmoniously one (14.4): just as in the Trinity as a whole all three Persons have correlative functions (14.5). There is in fact no other way of achieving a proper notion of the one God than by believing in the Trinity of Persons. Other approaches have always failed (14.6), as could be expected, considering the clear command of Christ that his followers should baptize in the names of the full Trinity (14.7). The Father is glorified in and through the Trinity, and all the Scriptures testify to this (14.8).

Certainly the most notable element in B4(a) is the repeated mention of the Holy Spirit as the third principle within the Trinity of the Godhead. CN as a whole has, naturally enough, little to do with the Holy Spirit. As has been seen in Chapter 1 of this present study, there have been some scholars who have accounted all mentions of the Holy Spirit as interpolations in the text. When, however, our author feels it his duty to give orthodox exposition, as opposed to the mere refutation of the Noetian heresy − and this, it is argued, is what he is doing with regard to the unity and distinction of the Godhead in B4 − then quite spontaneously, and therefore perhaps also rather surprisingly, the Holy Spirit takes his place alongside the other two Persons of the Trinity. Far from being interpolations, the mentions of the Holy Spirit in B4(a) can only reinforce the structural analysis of the text of CN which is being advocated. Those mentions are carefully localized: and the very localization of them argues for their being elements in an orthodox exposition of the Trinitarian faith. In B4(a) it is the unity of the Godhead that is being pressed; a unity which must take account of all three Persons of the Trinity.

B4(b) centres rather on the distinction between the Father and the Word who became man and suffered as Son. This sub-section contains an exposition of the direct answer to the doctrine of patripassianism supported by the Noetian sect. Against a suggestion that the Johannine Word was not in fact the Son who suffered (15.1), it is shown, from the Apocalypse of John, that John identified the Word and the suffering Son of the Father (15.2). The Word who could not suffer did suffer, as Son in the flesh (15.3), as Micah foretold (15.4), and as Paul said (15.5). This Son who suffered in the flesh must be the Word,

called Son in order to express God's love for mankind (15.6). Without flesh
the Word is not the perfect Son of God, and without the Word the flesh of
the Son has no subsistence (15.7). All the texts adduced show that it was not
the Father who became man (16.1), but the Word who came out of the Father
became man (16.2). Thus B4(b), on a basis of Scripture texts, exposes the key
truth that it was the Word of the Father who suffered as man. It is true that
this exposition is not without certain rhetorical devices which seem more fitted
perhaps to part A than to part B of CN. There is an introductory question from
an imaginary adversary (15.1); fairly sharp rhetorical questions (15.6; 16.2
[twice]). But in the main it is the exposition of the central truth against which
the Noetians have offended that holds the field. The address is to the brethren
(15.3; 16.1), not to an adversary.

B4(c) answers an objection which could be levelled at the foregoing exposition
of the unity (B4(a)) and distinction (B4(b)) of the Godhead. How does the
distinction arise within the unity? The answer is that you cannot explain your
own origin even though human birth is a daily phenomenon (16.3): you simply have to believe that God's handiwork goes into the production of a man.
And yet you want to know how the Word is produced (16.4). You must be
satisfied to know that God created the world, never mind whence he did it
(16.5). And so you must be satisfied to know that the Son of God was revealed
to save us, never mind how. This will be revealed in God's good time to the
saints (16.6). 'That which is born of Spirit, is Spirit' (Jn 3, 6) – the mystery
of his origin has not yet been revealed (16.7). With this final assertion of the
mystery of the origin of the distinction between Father and Word within the
Godhead, the third sub-section of B4 closes. Like A4, B4 consists of two sub-
sections devoted to the unity and distinction of the Godhead, followed in both
cases by a third sub-section in which an objection was posed and answered.
Other likenesses are not especially striking. It may be worth noting that τολμᾶν
and πρόσωπον occur almost exclusively in these two sections (τολμᾶν: 6.6;
16.5, 6 – elsewhere only at 8.3. πρόσωπον: 7.1; 14.2, 3; 16.6 – elsewhere non-
technically at 17.1). προκειμένος occurs only at 7.7 and 16.1; ποῖος only at
6.6 and 15.6. But the main argument for the parallelism and contrast of A4
and B4 must rest, as in the case also of the previous sections, on an analysis
of the contents and general approach.

A5 (8.1–8.3) and B5 (17.1–17.2):
Two sections which conclude parts A and B respectively

It remains to describe the two short sections which function, it would seem, as conclusions to the two parts of the main body of CN.

A5 (8.1–8.3) closes down the argument with the Noetians by first pointing out that the whole of Scripture so testifies to the orthodox truth that one is forced to admit the distinction, denied of course by the Noetians, between the Son and the Father – with the Holy Spirit to make a third (8.1). There is one God, a single power triply displayed, as will be shown in part B (8.2). And against this one God, the God of orthodox truth, Noetus, who has no notion of that truth, can bring no valid objection: so the section ends with a defiant and punning challenge to Noetus (8.3). The sudden appearance, at this stage, of a three-fold distinction within the Godhead is quite in order, precisely because A5 is the conclusion of part A and serves naturally enough to connect part A with part B which follows immediately afterwards, beginning at 8.4. A5, and especially 8.2, is in fact incipiently expository insofar as it points forward to the fuller exposition of the οἰκονομία to be given in part B. But there can still be no doubt, even from this short conclusion, concerning the hostile tone and approach, noticeable, as has been claimed, throughout part A, to the Noetian heresy. *Every* passage of Scripture refutes the Noetians with the truth, and *forces* acceptance of the orthodox truth even on the *unwilling* (8.1); a *challenge* is thrown down for Noetus to face the truth (8.2, 3).

B5 (17.1–17.2) is addressed, not to an adversary, but to those of the faithful who live the truth: for them the all-holy Spirit stimulates the faith of those who hear the unambiguous witness of Scripture (17.1). As brethren, all should believe in what the tradition of the apostles teaches about the incarnate divine Word, who became man to save fallen mankind and to give immortality to those who believe in his name (17.2). There is no need to emphasize that the appeal of this concluding section of part B is to the brethren of the faith who have heard the preceding exposition of the witness of Scripture to the orthodox truth concerning the incarnate Word of the Father. The tone is, if anything, paraenetic; certainly quite different from the challenge of A5.

Thus has been described the structure, as it reveals itself to an analysis of contents and approach, of the central block of CN. This main block contains two parts, A and B. Both these parts contain five sections: A1 to A5, B1 to B5. In content and interest these parts are parallel one to another as they are numbered; but in tone and approach they contrast obviously with one another. Sections A1 to A5 concern the refutation of the chosen heresy and its arguments, and they display lively hostility and a certain defensiveness. The aim is apologetic. Sections B1 to B5, on the contrary, expose the orthodox truth to a sympathetic audience: they display an elaborate, but only occasionally expanded, theology. The aim is positive and doctrinal. It is further noted that even where a section splits into discernible sub-sections, this happens also in the parallel section, as in the cases of A2 and B2, A4 and B4, i.e. in alternate sections of parts A and B.

All this will appear with greater clarity if the fruits of this analysis are now drawn up shortly and schematically. The following pattern is revealed:

PART A		PART B
Tone: hostile		**Tone:** friendly
Aim: anti-heretical apologetic		**Aim:** expository and doctrinal
A1, 3.1–3.6	Introductory programmatic note about the use of Scripture	B1, 8.4–9.3
A2, 4.1–4.13 (in three sub-sections)	On the pre-incarnate Word	B2, 10.1–12.4 (in three sub-sections)
A3, 5.1–5.5	On the incarnate Word	B3, 12.5–13.4
A4, 6.1–7.7 (in three sub-sections)	On Unity and Distinction in God	B4, 14.1–16.7 (in three sub-sections)
A5, 8.1–8.3	Conclusion	B5, 17.1–17.2

But before any attempt is made to point out the implications of the firm pattern thus discovered for the first time in the main body of CN, it must be remembered that there remain three chapters and more – two in front of part A and one-and-a-half after part B, which have yet to be accounted for. So attention must be turned to the first two chapters of CN.

1.1–2.8 The first two chapters: their structure and function

The first two chapters of CN reveal, when subjected to close analysis, remarkable features. They have a careful and purposeful structure and a polished ease with which they present an excellent setting of the single problem, the patripassianist heresy, that the author has determined to tackle in his work. Hence, it will be argued, these first two chapters, far from being awkward linking passages between the main parts of CN and the lost anti-heretical work of which CN has been thought to be the concluding fragment, form a dramatically satisfying introduction to the whole discourse. The parts and details of this introduction are rigorously subordinated to the main task in hand – the refutation of the basic tenets of patripassianism (part A) and the presentation of further relevant theological reflections (part B). Hence the main emphasis is not on historical details as such, which are of strikingly little interest to the writer, but on the origin and arguments of the patripassianist position. Schwartz was surely right in noting that for the writer Noetus was 'not much more than a name'. Whatever may be made of Schwartz's attendant opinion that the purpose of CN was not so much to deal with the Noetians as to attack Callistus and his community and to offer some defence against their charges of ditheism,[6] it is true that most of the writer's interest, both in the Introduction and indeed in part A, is in the sect of the Noetians and their doctrine rather than in the person of Noetus. An explanation of the rough changes in number from singular to plural – changes which occur throughout the work and to which Schwartz has called attention[7] – will be offered in the following chapter.

A general title for the Introduction formed by chapters 1 and 2, would be: *The Patripassianist Heresy*. This is clearly the main topic, and best expresses the real scope of the contents of the first two chapters. These two chapters represent the two halves of the Introduction – further evidence of the serviceability of the traditional chapter-divisions. Whereas chapter 1 deals with the Origins of the heresy, chapter 2 deals with the typical Arguments used by the heretics. The Arguments can be further divided into two sub-sections, as will be shown.

Chapter 1 (1.1–1.8) on Origins contains orderly information about the doctrine, the decline and the final fall of Noetus. Although Noetus necessarily moves in the foreground of this chapter, he is not really the main focus of attention. He is mentioned by name once only (1.1). A couple of details concerning him are thrown in – his place of origin and a rough idea of his period. The interest in him is not so much personal or even historical, but rather dramatic. From Noetus stems the patripassianist heresy which is to be refuted. It is his disciples, with their strange doctrine, who catch the eye from the beginning. With neat, bold strokes the cause of their perversion and his dreadful downfall are sketched. It would be wrong to expend too much effort on the historical, and even the textual, worries raised by this chapter. To do so would be to misread the real purpose of the chapter as an introductory and

---

6   E. Schwartz, *Zwei Predigten Hippolyts*, p.30f; see p.27.
7   Loc. cit., p.31.

therefore relatively subordinate section as regards the work as a whole. It serves as a mere curtain-raiser, consciously stylized as such, to the main theological drama between developing orthodoxy and the rigid views of an over-conservative and perhaps judaizing monotheism.

A consideration of the details of chapter 1 will reinforce this first impression. From the start (1.1) attention is focussed on Noetus' sect and the false doctrine they received from him. At 1.2 the stylized picture of Noetus' downfall begins. The first stage of decline is seen in the vanity and bloated pride which is behind his false teaching on the identity of Christ with the Father who was born, who suffered and died. The doctrine, against which the whole work is to be directed, is thus put in a prominent place at the beginning of the work. Details about Noetus and his mentality are secondary to this, and even seem fairly commonplace. St Paul's frequent use of φυσιοῦσθαι and cognates[8] will serve as an example of how the description of Noetus' condition is drawn from elements which had become classical in descriptions of heretics; and this fact points to the dramatic rather than strictly historical intention of this chapter on Noetus. Ways of delineating the heretical character seem to have been taken from a common stock. Similarly, other elements in this first chapter may be mainly echoes of NT terminology. Thus, for example, the ἑτέραν διδασκαλίαν παρεισάγουσιν of 1.1 probably recalls both the ἑτεροδιδασκαλεῖν of 1 Tim 1, 3 and the παρεισάγειν of 2 Pet 2, 1 (of ruinous heresy); and the blasphemy against the Holy Spirit of 1.3 is at least an allusion to Lk 12, 10. But 1.2, as a part of the whole chapter, points to Noetus' personal defects as the opening stage in his decline towards open rebellion, excommunication and final independence of the Church.

The tale of his public downfall (1.4–8) is introduced by 1.3, which brings up 'the rest of his doings' which led first to his expulsion from office and later from the Church. The outrageously ambitious claims of 1.4 occasion his first public examination before the 'blessed presbyters'.[9] It would seem that the charge of ambition was the first that official orthodoxy was able to make. There may have been some attempt on Noetus' part to establish his private authority and with it his doctrine within the Church. Possibly it was easier to bring a charge of ambition than one of heresy. Perhaps it is more likely that on the principle that 'pride goes before a fall', the ambition represents the ultimate stage of pride which we are to think that Noetus reached. At any rate, in spite of denials, Noetus was apparently deposed from whatever dignity it

---

8   E.g., 1 Cor 4, 6, 18; 5, 2; 8, 1; 13, 4; 2 Cor 12, 20; esp. Col 2, 18 . . .
9   On the status of the 'presbyters' see C.H. Turner, JTS 23 (1921), p.28ff.

was that he held – a bishopric according to Schwartz.[10] No more is heard of the Moses-Aaron claim. Once this ambitious plan was scotched, the next step, the secret formation of a sect, was inevitable (1.5). Again it appears that the primary concern of the writer is to describe the emergence of the doctrine, against the background of the decline of Noetus.

The second summons and refutation (1.6) led to a condemnation of his doctrinal views and resulted in open defiance, a further step in Noetus' decline and fall. He claimed that he was doing no wrong because he was in fact giving glory to Christ by identifying him with the Father. Within the dramatic framework of this first chapter it is not necessary, as has been argued on textual grounds at the beginning of chapter 2, to supplement Noetus' perfectly intelligible question with some sort of statement concerning his beliefs. It can be readily inferred from 1.2 what precisely he means by his clever rhetorical question. He means simply that his patripassianist doctrine, far from detracting from the glory of Christ, only enhances that glory, because Christ is the Father in person, who became man, suffered and died. The long reply of the presbyters in 1.7, couched as it is in well-established credal formulae,[11] demands no fuller statement on Noetus' part. It is an official reply in the formulae of the Church's creed and need not correspond to any long statement of Noetus' beliefs. Not only do Noetus' question and the orthodox reaction make perfectly sound sense as they stand, but it must also be borne in mind how 1.6 and 1.7 are to be related to the whole chapter of which they are a part, and to the mainly dramatic purpose of that chapter. Noetus appears to be the stylized starting-point in a dramatic account of the rise of a hated heresy. It is then unlikely that time would be spent on allowing Noetus to elaborate his views, which are known from the beginning to be only too clearly wrong. Indeed the end of 1.7 makes it clear that it would be idle to suppose, particularly on the basis of a lacuna which can be textually shown to be false, that the presbyters' reply is meant to be a point-for-point answer to Noetus. They precisely do not make this sort of reply: rather ταῦτα λέγομεν ἃ ἐμάθομεν. The real reply to Noetus' specious claim to be glorifying Christ lies in the sheer statement of the Church's traditional faith as found in the credal formulae here, and in the

---

10 E. Schwartz, loc. cit., p.27. The argument is based on the fact that Noetus had a deacon, Epigonus, see Hippolytus, Elench. 9.7.1 (GCS Hippolytus III, ed. Wendland, p.240, 17f).

11 J.N.D. Kelly, *Early Christian Creeds*[3], London 1972, p.81f. Unfortunately Dr Kelly uses the Nautin version of the 'creed' of CN 7.1. Enough has been said in the present study, and see also the following note, to show that it is at least inadvisable, if not simply wrong, to import foreign elements into the perfectly intelligible text of CN 1.6–7.

exposition of that faith which is to follow in the second half of the discourse. Care must be taken not to distort the first chapter so that it no longer fulfils the precise purpose of the writer with regard to the work as a whole. An imported wrangle between Noetus and the presbyters would be a quite unjustified distortion.[12]

1.8 marks the climax of the whole chapter. Not only is Noetus condemned and excommunicated at the end of 1.7; he now goes to the ultimate lengths of setting up a school of doctrine independent of the Church. Further than this his heresy could not go. Thus is concluded a carefully staged picture of Noetus' decline and fall and the emergence of the doctrine of patripassianism. From pride and doctrinal obtuseness (1.2) flows first demotion (1.3) for ambition (1.4), then the deceitful inauguration of a sect (1.5), followed by an open stand for false doctrine (1.6), resulting in the official rebuttal at the hands of orthodoxy (1.7), and the setting up of a doctrinal school by an excommunicate (1.8). The economy, and even artistry, displayed in the description of this dramatic decline are surely indication enough of the purpose of chapter 1 as the first part of an appealing Introduction to the whole discourse. The difficult opening words, which have led so many to think that CN must be a fragment of another work, can in fact be well explained; and this will be done in the treatment of the style of CN. But from the structure alone it is plain to see that here is no fragmentary, mainly historical account of Noetus' career taken from a source or sources which it would be helpful to be able to reconstruct. Chapter 1 is a quick sketch of a heretic's downfall for the purpose of providing an attractive explanation of the origins of the doctrine whose main position and arguments are then equally sketchily listed in chapter 2.

This second chapter (2.1–2.8), the second half of the Introduction, contains samples to show how the patripassianist position maintained by Noetus' disciples (2.1) is said to derive from Scripture. The texts adduced in support may be placed in two pairs, both with a patripassianist argument based on them. Hence there are two sub-sections in chapter 2. The first pair of texts and

---

12 Normally the longer account of Epiphanius is employed to show that Noetus' question needs extending. But it is dangerous and unwarranted, especially in the light of the essentially dramatic function and interest of the whole of the first chapter of CN, to put much trust in Epiphanius' account of the interchanges (*Panarion haer.* 57.1.8 [GCS Epiphanius II, ed. Holl, p.344, 14–17]). This account differs in so many respects from the account in CN, on which, however, it is probably based, that great allowance must be made for the strong possibility that it is largely an elaboration by Epiphanius of an interchange which he, like a later scribe of Vat. graec. 1431, did not quite grasp. Epiphanius' account smacks of rewriting and the gratuitous supplying of additional detail.

argument aim at establishing the oneness of God (2.1–3). These constitute a general argument for patripassianism and from a source which is always plural. Interestingly, the texts quoted in this first sub-section are not dealt with in the subsequent ἀνατροπή of part A, nor are ever mentioned again. Possibly their connection with patripassianism is too general and too indirect, and this may render them in the writer's mind too innocuous to merit close attention. At any rate they are dismissed once and for all with a scornfully brief comment (2.4).

The second pair of texts and argument (2.5–7), along with the appended witness of St Paul (2.8), are clearly more relevant, in that they seek to establish the basis of the patripassianist position, namely that it was the one God – therefore the Father – who became man and suffered and died. It is with the correct exegesis of this second pair of texts, and of Rom 9, that the actual refutation of patripassianism is concerned; and in an order which, as has been shown above, is significantly altered in the interests of the structure of the main body of CN. The source of the second pair of texts and the argument based on them changes violently from plural (2.5) to singular (2.5, 6, 7) and then back again to plural (2.7). An explanation of such changes will be given in the treatment of the style of CN. A change to the singular is no indication that Noetus himself argued in this way. The main interest, enlivened by the use of the singular, remains with the teaching of the members of the διδασκαλεῖον of 1.8. The texts themselves are quoted more at length than is the case with the first pair of texts, and forcefully appealing comment is attached to both of them before the argument based on both of them is developed (2.7). The presentation of this second sub-section of chapter 2 is more urgent and more dramatized than that of the first sub-section. It may be that the texts in fact represent an actual patripassianist argument used by Noetus' followers; and it is they, along with their use of Rom 9, that are carefully refuted in part A of what follows.

According to this analysis of chapters 1 and 2 of CN, it is clear that the discourse has an elaborate and purposeful Introduction to its subsequent parts. The discussion of the precise heresy with which the whole work is uniformly concerned is admirably initiated in these chapters. The Introduction is elaborate in its structure, and consciously so; and this makes it entirely fitted to the purpose which it is seen to serve – to sketch in an attractive and memorable way the Origins of patripassianism in the decline and fall of the unfortunate Noetus (chapter 1), and to provide a rapid and clear summary of both the general and the actual arguments and position of the patripassianist heretics apparently contemporary with the writer (chapter 2). It must be remembered that it is only the phrase ἕτεροί τινες ἑτέραν διδασκαλίαν, at the very beginning of the work (1.1) which has distracted scholars from the interior structure of CN in general and the structure of the Introduction in particular. It will be argued that there is a perfectly good explanation of these words which does not require the hypothesis that CN must be the fragment of a larger work now lost. Granted this, and supposing that the purposeful structure of the Introduction is not the invention of the over-eager literary analyst, but that the analysis of the structure is supported by the text, it seems to follow that the first two chapters of CN furnish the discourse with an Introduction the structuration of which would seem to be confirmed by the consideration above of the purposeful structures which can be detected within the two parts of the main body of the work.

Thus, then, a new picture of CN begins to be built up. So far it has been discovered that there is a central main block of two carefully corresponding and contrasting five-fold parts, the first of which refutes heresy, the second of which expounds the relevant orthodox truth. And this central block is prefaced by a pair of chapters which together form an Introduction admirably suited to explain the Origins and Arguments of the heresy which is under attack in CN. The first two chapters of CN are thus a dramatic opening to the struggle between heresy and orthodoxy in the main parts of CN: a struggle which is concluded in the triumph of orthodoxy in the only section of CN that remains to be considered, the Peroration.

17.3–18.10 The Peroration: A Meditation on 1.7

The remarkable Peroration, with which CN is concluded, could be approached from a number of points of view. The elevated, even hymnodic style need not concern us at this point. It will be sufficient for present purposes to indicate a fact concerning the structure of this final part which has not, it would appear, caught the attention of those who have studied CN as a whole.

While allowance must be made in dealing with this part for what might be thought a certain lack of neatness in the structure – and clearly the kind of writing in question here is not the same as in the rest of CN – it remains true that there is a detectable structure to the section, and one which closely follows the progression of the credal formulae whose presence in the reaction of traditional orthodoxy of 1.7 has already been pointed out. Thus there can be distinguished six sub-sections in the Peroration (a–f), in parallel with the six major assertions of 1.7, and apart from the obvious, and indeed famous, doxology of 18.10 (g).

a. 17.3. Here the Peroration begins with a re-assertion, now in the developed terms of a full orthodoxy, of the first statement of the 'creed' of 1.7 that 'we too acknowledge one God in accordance with the truth'. It is precisely that truth which demands the belief in the Son whom the Father sent to save mankind which is explicitated here.

b. 17.4–17.5, explains the implication of asserting in 1.7 that 'we acknowledge Christ'. This sub-section gives a short account of the promise and fully incarnate presence of Christ in the world as perfect man.

c. 18.1–18.3, takes the next part of 1.7, 'we acknowledge that it was the Son who suffered as in fact he suffered', and describes in heavily scriptural detail the full range of the human suffering of Christ, not only in his passion (18.2, 3), but also in the course of his public life (18.1).

d. 18.4, considers the reality of Christ's death, in accordance with the next step in the creed of 1.7, 'who died as in fact he died'.

e. 18.5, takes a further step, 'who rose again on the third day', and concludes, on a basis of Isaiah 53, 4, that Christ underwent all this – suffering, death and resurrection – for sinful mankind.

f. 18.6–18.9, now turns to a meditative consideration of the divinity of Christ, prompted by the final step of 1.7, 'and is at the right hand of the Father, and is coming to judge the living and the dead'. The divinity of Christ apparent in his final, heavenly state is acknowledged by his faithful followers from the very start of his human life, up to and including his baptism (18.6). Similarly that divinity is displayed in the miracles of his public life and death (18.7). It is confirmed by the natural phenomena attendant on his death (18.8), and in his post-resurrection appearances and ascension into heaven, whence he is to return as judge (18.9).

g. 18.10, the Doxology, is to the glory of Christ, made man for us, made Lord of all by his Father.

This striking Peroration thus has strong links not merely in general with the whole argument of CN that it was not the Father but Christ the incarnate Word who suffered and died as Son on behalf of mankind, but also in particular with the traditional expression of orthodox faith quoted against Noetus at the beginning of the work. So it may be said that what have been called the Introduction and the Peroration of CN, are justifiably so called: if 1.1–2.8, as has been argued, introduces the heresy to be refuted, then 17.3–18.10 concludes the refutation and subsequent explanation of the true doctrine in a way that leaves no doubt of the triumph of the traditional faith, expressed formulaically in 1.7, over the heresy of patripassianism. As an expanded, *pari passu* treatment of 1.7, taking into consideration the poetic style, 17.3–18.10 may be called a Peroration which is a 'meditation' on 1.7.

If any conclusions concerning CN can be drawn from this lengthy analysis of what are revealed as its constituent parts, there is surely one that must be drawn. It is that CN thus gives every appearance of being a work, not torn from some larger block, but possessing a literary unity, indeed a very strict literary integrity, of its own. Not only is the main body of the work in two intimately connected parts, such that one can hardly be fully explained without reference to the other, but there is also an obviously introductory section at the beginning and a concluding section, which picks up its theme from the Introduction, at the end. It would be difficult to amass, from a consideration of mere structure, more powerful indications than these that CN is no concluding fragment of an otherwise lost work. CN stands well on its own: a carefully, even elaborately, structured literary unit with a beginning, a diptychal middle, and an end. And this conclusion not only seems to flow from the evidence adduced above: it is also consonant both with the fact that no one has ever been able to explain how and why CN could ever have become a fragment anyway, and with the sole primitive title of CN as 'A Discourse of Hippolytus . . . against the heresy of a certain Noetus'.

The description we have undertaken to give is necessary in a study of CN because there are definite advantages in knowing precisely how the work is structured. Thus, for instance, it could enable us to explain why references to the Holy Spirit – not strictly relevant to the theme of CN – should occur at such and such a juncture, and not elsewhere. There would be no need to suppose that such references were interpolations. Again, in the question of the suspected interpolation of other phrases and passages, the meticulous structuration of the whole work leads us to treat the text of CN as it stands with much greater respect. While the presence of interpolations cannot, of course, be entirely ruled out, a knowledge of the structure of the whole enables us to evaluate certain phrases and passages in their proper context. Lastly, the structure we have discovered and displayed helps us towards the defining of the literary genre to which CN belongs. And this in turn should help us to assess rightly the kind of theology contained in CN, and the level of understanding at which it is directed. But the question of literary genre must be fully resolved in the next chapter.

4
THE STYLE OF CN

It is perhaps surprising that the distinctive style of CN has not attracted the attention and invited the researches of more scholars. But that connoisseur of Greek prose style, Eduard Norden, showed an interest in CN that is happily exceptional. In his discussion of the style of the Greek sermon in the second and third centuries,[1] he notes that the Gnostics were not averse to the employment of the techniques of Greek rhetoric; indeed their over-hasty blending of Christian with Hellenistic modes of thought might be unfavourably compared with the more enduring results more cautiously achieved by the Church.[2] In the Church the first writers who can be said to favour the 'kunstmässige Predigt' are Hippolytus and Origen. Of the former's works the λόγος εἰς τὰ ἅγια θεοφάνεια,[3] if it can be said to be authentic and not better ascribed at the earliest to the middle of the fourth century, would make Hippolytus rank, as a speaker, with Gregory of Nazianzus. Norden then continues:

> Of Hippolytus' other speeches we possess only a ὁμιλία against the Noetians. We can clearly sense, in the passages that are not purely doctrinal, a heightening of tone effected by means of the artifices of rhetoric; e.g. in the παραίνεσις [here Norden quotes CN 9.2] . . ., or in the hymn-like 'Lobpreisung' [represented by 18.7−8]. In this latter passage which is more effective? − the fine expression of the panegyrist, or the simple word of the Gospel which underlies his treatment? . . . Hippolytus attacked the heretics

---

1 Ed. Norden, *Die antike Kunstprosa vom VI. Jahrhundert v. Chr. bis in die Zeit der Renaissance,* II, Leipzig−Berlin 1915, pp.545−550. It is encouraging to see that Norden seems never to have imagined that CN was anything but a work complete in itself, and with its own distinctive style.

2 Ibid., II, pp.545−547, and p.547, n.2.

3 Cf. GCS Hippolytus I/2, ed. Achelis, pp.257−263. Achelis remarks, p.[256], that the authenticity of the work is disputed; and on p.VI he admits that there is serious opinion against him.

for the content of their teaching. In the choice of literary form *(Formgebung)* he did not hesitate to employ, as they did, the effective techniques of Hellenistic rhetoric, and in a generous fashion.[4]

From what Norden says in a later section,[5] it appears that a source of certain techniques for didactic homilies of the third century, but already of importance for certain passages of the New Testament, is the kind of popular speech known as 'Diatribe'. Origen's sermons, in addition to other evidence from Tatian and Clement, show that the use of elements from diatribe was by that time quite normal. If one particular element of diatribe may be instanced, it is is the use of $\varphi\eta\sigma\iota(\nu)$ to introduce the view of an imaginary opponent.[6] Indeed the presence of $\varphi\eta\sigma\iota(\nu)$ is taken as in some way typical of the diatribe manner by those who have attempted to list the characteristics which diatribe possesses.[7] Hence in beginning to study the style of CN, it will be interesting to see how the work reacts to the rather simple test of the occurrence of $\varphi\eta\sigma\iota(\nu)$. If Norden is right in implying that diatribe was a source of stylistic techniques in CN, CN should contain at least this element.

$\varphi\eta\sigma\iota(\nu)$, introducing a 'direct' quotation of the opinion of an unnamed opponent occurs at least eight times in CN: 2.5; 2.6 (twice); 2.7 (twice); 4.2; 4.5; 5.1. In 2.2 it presumably means that God is the speaker of the statement quoted from Isaiah 44, 6. But even here diatribe may not have been without its influence. As Thyen points out in his reconstruction of the style of the synagogue homily in the Hellenistic diaspora, subject-less $\varphi\eta\sigma\iota(\nu)$, placed mainly inside the quotation as here in CN 2.2, is a normal way of introducing Scriptural quotations. Although the synagogue homily used quotations (mainly, of course, from the Septuagint) more for the purposes of proof than did the profane diatribe, where quotations from the poets and so forth were often

---

4 Op. cit., II, pp.547–548. On p.548, n.1 Norden notes certain rhetorical techniques which are to be found in Hippolytus' *De Christo et de Antichristo*. Very little work has been done on the lively style of Hippolytus. Occasional percipient remarks on the style of his works are to be found – such as those made by G. Bardy in his introduction to *Hippolyte, Commentaire sur Daniel*, ed. M. Lefèvre (SC 14), Paris 1947, pp.17–18.

5 Op. cit., II, pp.556–558.

6 Ibid, II, p.557, and see n.1.

7 For example: R. Bultmann, *Der Stil der paulinischen Predigt und die kynisch-stoische Diatribe*, (Forschungen zur Religion und Literatur des Alten und Neuen Testaments, 13. Heft) Göttingen 1910, p.10; J.H. Ropes, *A Critical and Exegetical Commentary on the Epistle of St James*, (International Critical Commentary), Edinburgh 1916, p.12; A. Oltramare, *Les origines de la diatribe romaine*, Geneva 1926, p.11; H. Thyen, *Der Stil der jüdisch-hellenistischen Homilie*, (Forschungen zur Religion und Literatur des Alten und Neuen Testaments, N.F. 47[= 65 der ganzen Reihe]), Göttingen 1955, p.69, with p.72; W. Capelle, s.v. *Diatribe*, in RAC III, Stuttgart 1957, col.992. References to these basic works will be given by name of author and page-number only.

confirmatory or even just decorative, the way of introducing quotations in the synagogue homily owes much to the influence of diatribe.[8] More could be said about the interesting coincidences which can be detected in CN and in the ways of introducing Scripture quotations listed by Thyen as typical of synagogue homilies;[9] but since the latter usages owe so much to diatribe, it would be foolish to conclude that CN owes more in this matter to the homily than to the diatribe as such. For the present it is enough to note that in CN at least one important diatribe feature, φησί(ν), occurs sufficiently often, and in part A of CN, where precisely the heretical views of opponents are under attack, to stimulate further enquiry along the same lines.

After all, φησί(ν) is no more than a single, but constant, element which forms part, by introducing supposedly *ipsissima verba* of a representative of the opposing view, of an overall characteristic of diatribe, lively familiarity.[10] This familiarity is essential to diatribe as a style; for above all else diatribe is directed towards an audience and demands a measure of artificial audience participation. As Norden states expressly of CN:

> The [sermon!] of Hippolytus against the Noetians ... is quite outstanding for its familiar tone. To a certain extent he conducts his investigation in union *(gemeinschaftlich)* with his audience, whom in the normal way he addresses as ἀδελφοί, and from whom he imagines objections coming, with ἐρεῖ μοί τις [15.1], ἐρεῖς μοι [16.3].[11]

Such familiarity is engendered and maintained in diatribe by a wide range of generally admitted techniques, of which the best analysis is still that made more than half a century ago by Rudolf Bultmann as preface to his investigation of St Paul's preaching style.[12] With this analysis of Bultmann as some

---

8 Thyen, pp.69–73, esp. pp.72–73; cf. also pp.56–58.
9 Thyen, p.73: 'Diese Ähnlichkeit in der Zitationsweise [beruht] ... auf einer Abhängigkeit von der griechischen Predigern'. See also pp.69; 72.
10 Bultmann, pp.10f; 58; 61; Oltramare, p.13; Thyen, p.62; Capelle, col.993, cf. col.998 (by H.-I. Marrou).
11 Norden, op. cit., II, p.542. And see n.1 for a suggestive note on Irenaeus' homilies, based on Photius' phrase, ὁμιλοῦντος Εἰρηναίου *(Bibliotheca,* Cod.121: PG 103: 401CD–403B).
12 Bultmann, pp.10–62. Many others have also been attracted by the presence of diatribe elements in the New Testament, and have enumerated them: C.F.G. Heinrici, *Der litterarische Charakter der neutestamentlichen Schriften,* Leipzig 1908, pp.11–12; 66; P. Wendland, *Philo und die kynisch-stoische Diatribe* (in P. Wendland and O. Kern, *Beiträge zur Geschichte der griechischen Philosophie und Religion,* Berlin 1895, pp.1–75); but esp. P. Wendland, *Die hellenistisch-römische Kultur in ihren Beziehungen zu Judentum und Christentum*[3], Handbuch zum Neuen Testament, I/2, Tübingen 1912, pp.75–96; M.-J. Lagrange, *Saint Paul, Epître aux Romains,* Paris 1916, pp.LIII–LX. See also Ropes, pp.10–18; and the whole of the excellent article on 'Diatribe' by W. Capelle and H.-I. Marrou, in RAC III, Stuttgart 1957, col.990–1009.

sort of basis, encouraged by Norden's spontaneous but undeveloped remarks on the style of CN, along with the positive results of the $\varphi\eta\sigma\iota(\nu)$-test, and following the advice and example of Thyen,[13] it may be permitted to enquire how the style of CN as a whole measures up to the known characteristics of the diatribe style.

But first it is necessary to mention the existence of a controversy which, while perhaps strictly irrelevant here, gives nonetheless a necessary warning against endowing diatribe with a hard and fast style which it seems never to have actually possessed. Briefly, the controversy is between those who would make diatribe into a firmly formed, more literary genre, and those who, more realistically, would prefer to leave its outlines clear but fluid. Wilamowitz-Moellendorff seems to have set the fashion of viewing diatribe as a development of the philosophical dialogue of a type familiar from Plato.[14] Hence an older school of thought, represented for example by Hirzel,[15] Bultmann himself,[16] Norden,[17] Colardeau,[18] Oltramare,[19] Ropes,[20] Lagrange,[21] and others, has tended to hold that diatribe developed quite simply out of philosophical dialogue; that it was a vulgarization or truncation of dialogue transformed into a set speech on a fixed topic of popular interest or importance; that it was declaimed by a single speaker who preserved, to maintain liveliness and hold the attention of the audience, certain techniques of literary dialogue. Thus there emerged a new form of set speech with easily detectable characteristics. More modern scholars have reacted against this rather shortsighted reconstruction. As Marrou says: 'modern erudition has worked hard on the diatribe, and not without running the risk of somewhat ossifying this form, which is of varying shape'.[22] Capelle's reaction is stronger: 'Die Diatribe ist von Hause aus durchaus keine Literaturgattung, sondern eine besondere Art mündlicher Propaganda . . .'; and he holds that what in diatribe look like elements drawn from dialogue, are in fact

---

13 Thyen, p.40, says that Bultmann gives 'ein gut übersichtliches Bild der Diatribe . . . An diesem Massstab sollen unsere Schriften nun gemessen werden'.

14 U. von Wilamowitz-Moellendorff, *Antigonos von Karystos,* = *Philologische Untersuchungen,* ed. A. Kiessling and U. von Wilamowitz-Moellendorff, Heft 4, Berlin 1881, Excurs 3 (*Der kynische prediger Teles*), esp. pp.307–314.

15 R. Hirzel, *Der Dialog, ein literarhistorischer Versuch,* Leipzig 1895 [photo. Hildesheim 1963], I, p.369, n.2; II, pp.12; 116f.

16 Bultmann, p.10. But see pp.46–54 for certain reservations concerning diatribe as a fixed form.

17 Op. cit., I, p.129 and n.1.

18 Th. Colardeau, *Etude sur Epictète,* Paris 1903, pp.294–304.

19 Oltramare, p.9.

20 Ropes, p.12.

21 Lagrange, p.LIII.

22 H.-I. Marrou, *Histoire de l'éducation dans l'antiquité,* Paris 1948, p.533, n.43.

favourite techniques of older Greek rhetoric which had been taken into pre-Platonic Greek prose.[23] But whatever the truth about the origins of diatribe, whether from Platonic dialogue alone or from earlier sources used also by Plato, there is sufficient general agreement about the leading features of diatribe as it is recoverable from the fragments and works of antiquity. While Bultmann's analysis of the features of diatribe style is thorough in its listing, a different order of treatment has been adopted here in order to simplify the task of showing how CN possesses these very features. Not to talk of 'the speaker' and 'the audience' would be impossible when describing diatribe techniques; but the use of these terms is in no way meant to prejudge the unanswerable question whether CN was actually delivered orally or not. For present purposes it seems best to make a two-fold division: first it will be shown how in CN the speaker used features of the diatribe style to claim and then to hold the attention of the audience; secondly something will be said about the way in which CN is divided and the diatribe kind of arguments that are used in it.

CN and the diatribe style

It may be said that, since diatribe is directed towards an audience and invites audience participation, its style contains two sets of features: the first, those devised by the speaker to allow him to identify the audience with himself and so to build a bridge of mutual sympathy over which he can pass the views he is proposing; the second, those techniques designed to hold the attention of the audience once the essential contact between speaker and audience has been made. While these two sets of features are not, of course, neatly exclusive of one another, to classify them thus is helpful in trying to describe the features which occur in a particular work such as CN.

Identification of the audience with the speaker

Certain techniques show, as Bultmann has said, that 'der Redner sich nicht allein reden denkt, sondern dass er gleichsam in gemeinsamer Untersuchung mit seinen Hörern begriffen ist'.[24] More than this, it is in the nature of diatribe for the speaker to make a *personal* appeal to the audience.[25] The speaker must be accepted in order that his doctrine may be accepted. Many of those who

---

23 Capelle, col. 992; see also Thyen, p.62, n.184.
24 Bultmann, p.13.
25 Bultmann, p.61.

have studied the diatribe technique remark that in order to achieve the transference the speaker identifies himself with his audience by implying that he is one of them. He speaks of 'we', giving his words a warmth and immediacy which naturally increases their persuasiveness.[26]

CN contains many examples of this technique. Mostly it is a matter of the use of the first person plural verb, by which the speaker simply supposes his solidarity, and, more precisely, Christian solidarity, with his audience: 7.3; 9.1 (thrice); 12.5 (four times); 14.6 (twice); 17.1. On two occasions the speaker seems to use the plural of majesty: the first person plural pronoun in 8.2, and the first person plural verb in 17.3. But both of these cases may in fact contain overtones of simple identification. The use of the first person plural pronoun is common: 6.6; 8.3; 10.1; 14.1 (twice); 17.1; 17.3; 18.5 (five times); 18.10. The appearance of the pronoun in 18.3 is probably due to a scriptural echo; and in 3.6 to a variant of little authority for 1 Cor 8, 6.

On other occasions the first person plural verb has an exhortative function: 4.1 (twice); 8.4 (twice); 9.2 (five times); 9.3; 13.1; 16.1; 17.2. It is worth noting that in certain passages the identification of the speaker with his audience is highly intensified, and that these passages occur at important junctures in the structure of the whole: in 8.2–9.3 (the change from part A to part B); at 12.5 (the beginning of B3, on the Incarnate Word); and at 18.5 (in the Peroration).

But of course the most significant usage in the speaker's approach to his audience is the address ἀδελφοί, which is typical of the specifically Christian development of diatribe.[27] In CN this address occurs at 3.2; 4.8; 8.3; 9.1; 14.1; 15.3; 16.1. At 17.2, on its final appearance, in the conclusion to part B, it is μακάριοι ἀδελφοί.

In an important passage of part B (16.3–16.7 = B4(c)) there is posed an imaginary objection from a member of the audience who directly questions the speaker. The objection is answered with an *ad hominem* argument of some force, in which the speaker employs a number of counter-questions. Similar speaker-audience exchanges, but without the counter-questions, occur at 14.2 and 15.1. Once again, this is a favourite technique in diatribe.[28] The identification of the speaker with the audience in these cases is not at all lessened, but rather a difficulty felt in common by the speaker and his audience is aired

---

26 E.g., Ropes, p.13; Oltramare, p.13; Thyen, p.73; 87–88; Marrou, RAC III, col.1002.
27 Cf. Ropes, p.15; Thyen, pp.89–92; Marrou, col.998–1002.
28 Cf. Hirzel, op. cit., II, p.248f; Bultmann, pp.11; 13f; 58; Ropes, p.13; Thyen, p.42; Marrou, col. 998.

and tackled from the standpoint of their common faith. This technique is obviously useful in keeping alive, especially in the later stages of the work as a whole, the solidarity of speaker and audience forged in the way described above. Marrou notes that in Christian homily the lapse into the singular, involved in addressing a single member of the audience, is a sign that the speaker is using diatribe technique.[29]

A different way of maintaining solidarity between speaker and audience in diatribe is to employ the imagined presence of an opponent or an opposing party to raise objections from the point of view under attack, and so to answer them from the standpoint of orthodoxy.[30] The opponent or opponents can be anonymous, or more or less precisely defined; but they are there for the purposes of cross-talk or altercation, in which the speaker can raise real or factitious difficulties against the truth he is preaching, can defend it, and can thus make his proposal of it more clear and more forceful.[31] The supposition is, however, that speaker and audience together share a common standpoint against which opposing arguments can make no headway. The audience is put in a position where it can judge and refute the opposing arguments dramatically created or related by the speaker: in this way the speaker wins their sympathy and builds on the shared identity he has assumed through the use of other techniques.

It is to be expected that the imagined presence of opponents should loom large in part A of CN. There is, of course, nothing anonymous or imprecise about the party under attack. From the beginning the origins of the Noetians as follows of Noetus are clearly described (1.1–1.8), and at the end of part A it is considered that it is Noetus himself who has been refuted (8.4). Noetus is mentioned by name some six times in the text (1.1; 3.3 (twice); 6.6; 8.3; 8.4), and the Noetians once (7.3); but apart from these clear cases, it seems that the speaker used a series of puns which kept the opponents in the forefront of the audience's mind. Thus: 3.1 (νενοήκασιν); 3.5 (τὸν ἐκείνων νοῦν); 4.2 (οὐ νοῶν); 7.3 (τὸν νοῦν μὴ ἔχοντες), and in 3.3 and 8.3 Noetus is mentioned in punning connection with part of νοεῖν. To these instances might be added 7.1 (ἐπιστανέτω τὸν νοῦν) and even 9.3 (μηδὲ κατ᾽ ἴδιον νοῦν). Certainly such puns, as will be shown later, were a stock-in-trade of diatribe.

---

29 Marrou, col. 1002: 'wenn er seiner Homilie einen eigentlich diatribischen Charakter gibt, . . . er [vertauscht] den Ihr- oder Wir-Stil mit dem Du-Stil'.
30 Cf. Bultmann, p.10; Oltramare, p.11; Marrou, col. 998. Also Hirzel, op. cit., I, p.518, n.2; II, p.241, n.7; Lagrange, op. cit., pp.LII–LV; Colardeau, op. cit., pp.304–309.
31 Cf. Bultmann, pp.10–12; Ropes, p.12; Thyen, pp.41–42.

And as in diatribe there are rapid changes, for the sake of maintaining liveliness, from singular to plural and back again, when opponents are being refuted. So Noetus' followers are first a singular διδασκαλεῖον (1.8) which becomes plural (2.1), speaks in the singular (2.3; 2.5; 2.6; 2.7), switches to plural (2.7; 3.1; 3.2), returns to singular (Noetus, 3.3), then to plural (3.5), and again to singular (4.4; 4.2), is generalized in the plural (4.2), but then stays in the singular (4.3; 4.10; 5.1; 6.6; 7.1), appear as 'Noetians' (7.3) and remains plural (7.4; 7.5), then finally becomes singular again (8.1; 8.2) as Noetus (8.3; 8.4). By this use of singular and plural opponents there is engendered a sense both of the immediacy and the urgency of the threat of heresy in the minds of the audience; and the speaker is thus enabled to keep the audience involved in the argument and on his side.

The opposing party is allowed to put its position fully in 2.1–2.8, where Scripture arguments are interspersed with Noetian explanations and orthodox comments. The whole passage is substantially an extended objection to Christian orthodoxy dramatically presented. The opponent is allowed to use persuasive appeals (ὁρᾷς, 2.5; 2.6). Later on in part A even hypothetical objections are framed by the speaker from the standpoint of the opposition (6.6; 7.1; 7.4). An objection in the form of a question is raised by the opponents at 5.1: at 1.6 – Noetus' impertinent question – and at 2.3, questions are thrown out by the opposition as challenges to orthodoxy. The objection-question of 5.1 is met with a flurry of counter-questions from the speaker (5.1; 5.2; 5.4); and on other occasions counter-questions can be sarcastically rhetorical (4.10 (twice); 7.3 (twice)); or a reply to a hypothetical objection (6.6), an open challenge (7.3), and especially importantly, a rhetorical challenge-question at the end of a section (8.3 – end of part A).[32] Other challenges to opponents are of an imperative kind (4.3; 7.1; 7.4; 8.2). But more subtle ways of meeting the threat of opposing views are through the use of irony (καλῶς, twice, 5.1), or of more biting sarcasm (2.1; 2.4; 3.3; 4.2; 4.10; 7.4; 7.5), or of straight ridicule (3.1; 3.2; 4.10; 6.6; 7.4) in which bad grammar may be called on to play a part (7.3; cf. 7.1). Even plain insults are not disregarded (3.1 ἀμαθία; 3.2 ἀναισχύντως;

---

32 On objections, questions, counter-questions, and challenges in diatribe, see Bultmann, pp.10–11; 14–15; 32; Capelle, col.992; Thyen, pp.41–43; 53f. The rhetorical challenge-question at the end of part A (8.3) is a fine example of diatribe technique. On such questions, Thyen, p.52 f, has this to say: 'Häufig wird die Darlegung am Schlusse eines Abschnittes in einer rhetorischen Frage zusammengefasst, und darauf folgt dann die Paränese. Wie in der Diatribe, so erscheint die Frage gelegentlich auch als herbe Mahnung oder als Vorwurf am Ende der Erörterung, oder sie fasst noch einmal knapp das Ergebnis zusammen, um den Hörer zum Nachdenken zu zwingen'. These words might well have been written with CN in mind.

6.6 ἀφροσύνη, and cf. the φλυαρία of the other heretics mentioned in 11.3). All these ways of beating down opposition are to be found in diatribe.[33]

In these ways, then the speaker has made and used a feeling of identity between himself and his audience – by first identifying himself with them and then by exercising this solidarity against opponents dramatically presented in this first part of CN. But he uses as well a wide range of rhetorical and verbal techniques to keep constantly alive the contact he has made with his audience, and these must now be described and instanced.

Holding the attention of the audience

Most striking in this regard and hardly needing any detailed illustration is the simple sentence structure which is predominant throughout the whole work. Diatribe was a popular form of speech and used, for the most part, a simple λέξις εἰρομένη which could be followed by those not trained in the rhetorical schools.[34] Thus in CN there are many sentences in which a participle-construction or an uncomplicated subordinate clause is attached to a main verb. The order of words occasionally undergoes an obvious inversion; but, generally speaking, a fairly unambiguous sense is readily discernible. Most subordinate clauses are either of a relative type or 'ὅτι-, εἰ- or ὡς- clauses. Particles are unsophisticated: only connective καί, δέ (with occasional μέν - δέ), γάρ and οὖν are really common, although ἀλλά and ἀλλ' ἤ are fairly frequent. The speaker both needs or uses certain words often: emphatic and pronominal αὐτός, διά especially with the genitive, the reflexive ἑαυτόν, εἰς, εἷς, ἐκ, ἐν, Θεός, κατά with the accusative, λέγειν, Λόγος, many negatives, the relative ὅς and the demonstrative οὗτος, οὕτω(ς), πᾶς, Πατήρ, πνεῦμα, τίς, φάναι, ὤν. But beyond these homely words and a few others of fairly common occurrence, the vocabulary of CN, as is the case with the diatribe style, is wide and varied.[35]

The basic simplicity of the linkage of sentences is perhaps best illustrated by the very frequent use of the demonstrative pronoun in a connective function, at or near the beginning of a sentence: 1.2; 1.4 (twice); 1.7; 1.8; 2.7; 3.1; 3.5 (displaced); 4.9; 4.11; 5.5; 6.1; 6.2; 6.5; 7.3; 7.5; 7.7; 8.1; 8.3 (twice); 11.4; 12.1; 14.1; 17.4; 17.5; 18.5; 18.6 (delayed); 18.7 (double); 18.8; 18.9; 18.10. Sometimes the neuter pronoun occurs in an 'id est' capacity – 7.6; 15.4; 16.2;

---

33 Cf. Bultmann, p.51 (elements from 'Scheltrede'); Ropes, p.13; Thyen, p.44; Marrou, col.998. Also Lagrange, op. cit., p.LIV; Oltramare, op. cit., p.15.
34 Bultmann, p.14; Thyen, pp.41; 44; Capelle, col.993; Marrou, col.998; Norden, op. cit., I, p.130; Lagrange, p.LV.
35 Bultmann, p.17; Oltramare, p.13; Marrou, col.998.

at other times the demonstrative adjective is used – 11.2; 16.1. Less frequent, though still common, is the use of the relative for the same purpose: 1.1; 1.6; 1.7; 1.8; 2.1; 2.3; 4.12; 5.1; 5.5; 6.1; 7.4; 7.5; 10.1 (twice); 10.3; 10.4; 12.2; 14.4; 17.4. Linkage within a sentence is often achieved by the use of 'sign-posting' devices to simplify as much as possible the connection between main clause and subordinate clause or other elements: 1.3; 1.7; 1.8; 2.6; 2.7; 3.3; 4.4; 4.8; 4.12; 6.2; 7.4; 9.3 (elaborate use of τρόπον); 11.3; 17.4. These devices usually involve the demonstrative or ὃν τρόπον or both (17.4). But by means of the various linkages described here there is achieved an overall simplicity in the way that the predominantly short sentences are clearly delivered by the speaker to be easily assimilated by the audience.

Of course, elaborate sentences occur. In the section B1 (8.4–9.3), significantly the programmatic note with which part B opens, there are a number of clearly and elegantly structured sentences. Departures from the normal run of simple sentences are certainly in the manner of diatribe at key junctures in the course of a work.[36] In CN the passage mentioned is almost unique. A perhaps comparable sentence is to be found at 17.2; and this again is the last sentence in the concluding section B5 (17.1–17.2) of part B. In other attempts at complex sentences the speaker is not so successful. In 7.4 and in 11.3 long sentences appear to get out of hand: both attempts founder on an ill-controlled parenthesis of inordinate size. They contrast with 17.2, where the long sentence can carry the short parenthesis with ease. There are other 'failures' in CN: if other factors, such as word-play, are for the moment discounted, these seem to be due to the speaker's over-reaching his own rhetorical resources, and the result is contortion and unclearness rather than the desired elegance or impact. Thus an inversion in 1.3 produces what has been for some a difficult αὐτῶν; in 3.1 the connection between ταῦτα and μονόκωλα is obscured by a quaint order; in 3.5 διὰ ταῦτα, and in 4.8 οὗτος ὁ Λόγος, are badly displaced; in 4.13 the second sentence is dislocated, apparently in an attempt to conclude forcefully with 'the Word of God'; in 7.7 σημαίνοντα is too distant from the word which governs it. It is interesting that in all these cases 'editors' have tried to impose by textual emendation a cure for a malady which is not so much textual as simply rhetorical. The fact is that the speaker in CN, while aware of the power of striking word-order, is rarely at ease with an elegant sentence or with a word and clause order much removed from fairly simple λέξις εἰρομένη.

Especially clumsy are the genitive absolutes for which the speaker shows a fitful taste (e.g. 2.6; 2.7 (twice); 4.7 (twice); 7.4; 7.5); and even his attempts

---

36 Bultmann, p.14; Thyen, pp.41; 44.

at simple chiastic order cannot be said to be either successful or effective (e.g. 3.3; 3.5; 4.1; 10.2; 11.1; 11.2). A notable failure in this regard occurs at 3.5 and 3.6 (ὄντως ... πρότερον ... πρότερον ... ὄντως). But with repeated parallel phrases and clauses the speaker is much more at home (e.g. 4.11; 8.2; 8.3; 9.2; 10.1; 10.3; 11.1; 12.5; 14.4; 14.5; 14.8); and of course the great incantatory cadenza of the Peroration (18.1–18.9) is built on such parallelisms with outstanding effect. Not that the success of the whole work can be gauged by the seeming failure of a few tropes, or by constructions which sound clumsy to the modern ear; the overall effect of CN would have been powerful on an audience whose ear did not demand an Isocratean elegance and would not in any case have been much influenced by it.

The speaker in CN is an adept in the diatribe manner he has adopted. Another characteristic of that manner is the use of rhetorical questions.[37] Some instances of such questions have been given in the description of the ways in which the speaker deals with his imagined opponents. But there are also many others addressed to his audience. Thus short questions are thrown out at 3.4; 5.1; 11.3; 12.5 (the beginning of B3). Longer questions, using ἀλλ᾽ ἤ to exclude an alternative answer, are used in 4.11; 5.2; 5.4; 12.2; 15.6. In 7.6, Jn 14, 9–10 is redramatized for the benefit of the audience and the opponents, and a rhetorical question is used to give bite to the point of Christ's original question. On another occasion there is an accumulation of rhetorical questions aimed at the opposing view: 4.5–4.6 contains three such questions together with an expostulatory τί οὖν. The sarcastic questions of 4.10 (twice); 6.6. and 7.3 (thrice) have already been mentioned. Rhetorical questions are used also against the difficulty raised in B4(c): 16.2 (twice); 16.5–16.6 (four times). Again, the speaker occasionally appeals to his audience with a challenging imperative form: 1.2; 3.2; 15.3 all have ὁρᾶτε; 4.6 has ἰδού. This is another well-known way of holding the audience's attention in diatribe.[38]

Elliptical constructions are used to sharpen the effect of what is said on the audience.[39] Ellipse of the article is very frequent and needs no full detailing. But it occurs, or tends to occur, when the speaker is pressing for emphatic clarity. Thus, for example, in 11.1–11.2, the ellipse is almost total, but it seems meant to make clear the distinction the speaker has in mind between δύναμις, Πατήρ, Λόγος, νοῦς, παῖς. Indeed it is when the divine Persons are being discussed that the article is often dropped: 2.3; 4.8; 4.11; 8.1; 9.2–9.3; 14.3–14.6; 14.8; 15.1. In the Peroration, especially in 18.6–18.10, the article

---

37 Bultmann, pp.30–31; 55; Ropes, p.13; Thyen, pp.45; 52–53; Capelle, col.993.
38 Bultmann, pp.13; 15; 32–33; Ropes, p.13; Thyen, p.43; 53–54; Marrou, col.998.
39 Bultmann, p.17.

is frequently omitted as superfluous and perhaps inhibitive of the fine effect of the accumulated parallel phrases. Ellipse of part of εἶναι , is also fairly common: 4.5; 5.4; 9.1; 11.1–11.2; 13.2; 14.3; 14.5; 16.4; 17.1, may be given as examples. Apart from the instances of subjectless φησί(ν), the subject of the verb is omitted abruptly at 4.10; 7.1; 7.4; although it is clear enough from the context that either Noetus or his party are meant. Sometimes an object of the verb is omitted; e.g. in 1.4 (ἐξήταξον); 3.1 (χρώμενοι – perhaps); 8.3 (τολμήσει – but contrast 6.6; 16.5; 16.6); 9.1 (ἀσκήσομεν); ἐν ἑτέρῳ is also elliptical (2.2; 2.6; 5.1). Remarkable, too, is the phrase – important, as has been observed in Chapter 1, in the discussion of the integrity of CN – πᾶσαι τοσαῦται αἱρέσεις (8.4). In the elliptical manner of diatribe it is unwise to make this refer to a set of heresies dealt with previously in the supposed lost parts of an 'Against All the Heresies'. It seems more realistic to take it to be an elliptical form which should strictly be complemented with ὅσαι γεγένηνται or some equivalent expression. Later it will be shown that other considerations – those of alliteration – may also help to defend this interpretation of the troublesome phrase. τοσοῦτο is used with a strictly correlative construction in 1.8; but in 8.4 the taste for ellipse has led to the omission of the correlative clause.

Another phrase, ἕτεροί τινες ἑτέραν διδασκαλίαν παρεισάγουσιν (1.1), whose abruptness has led so many to think that CN must have been preceded by the rest of a whole work devoted to countering other heresies, may be mentioned here. Quite apart from considerations of word-repetition and pun which will be dealt with presently, abrupt openings are not at all unsuitable to the lively diatribe manner, and in fact occur elsewhere in CN: e.g. in 9.1, but more remarkably in 10.1, the beginning of B2(a). In general, sentence linkage is achieved, as has been said, by the use of simple particles and demonstrative and relative words, although liveliness at times appears to dictate their omission: 1.2 (οἰήσει πνεύματος . . .; ὁρᾶτε ὅσον . . .); 3.2 (ὅρατε . . . contrast 15.3); 5.1 5.1 (καλῶς εἶπεν cf. 6.2); 6.1 (ὁ ὤν . . . but quoting Rom 9, 5); 10.3 (ὅτε ἠθέλησεν . . .); 10.4 (προτέραν φωνήν . . .); 12.5 (Πατέρα δι' αὐτοῦ); 13.2 (ὅπου ὁρᾶν . . .); 14.4 (Πατὴρ ἐντέλλεται . . . οἰκονομία συμφωνίας . . .); 14.6 (μαθηταὶ ἐπέγνωσαν . . .); 16.7 (αὔταρκές σοι . . .). Asyndeton is certainly one of the features of diatribe.[40] Paralleled clauses are often without linkage: 4.11; 8.3; 10.3 init.; 12.5, although there is a single δέ; 14.4; 14.8. In 8.3 three adjectives in alpha-privative are in asyndeton; but what is of more interest here is that such adjectives grouped together are said to be common

---

40 Bultmann, p.14.

in diatribe.[41] There is a fine run of them in 10.2 (four examples), and other obviously alpha-privative words occur in 3.1; 3.2; 4.11; 6.6; 10.4 (twice); 15.3; 15.7; 16.4; 17.1 (twice); 17.2; 18.1; 18.2; 18.4.

Attractive emphasis is effected by the occasional use of paradox.[42] Of course, the God-man 'paradox' itself, basic as it is to orthodox faith, is an obvious source of this: thus, for example, in 5.4 the derivation of the name Is-ra-el produces a paradoxical definition 'man-seeing-God'. Again, similar God-man contrasts are expressed in 6.1; 8.1; 17.5; 18.1; and especially in 18.10. Some further examples of paradoxical expression may be found in 10.2 (μόνος . . . πολύς . . .); 10.4 (ἀόρατος . . . ὀρατός . . . twice); and 15.3 (ὑπὸ πάθος . . . ὁ ἀπαθής).

Pun-like modes of expression, too, are to be found in CN. The most obvious has been already mentioned above – the use of νοῦς and νοεῖν in connection with Noetus and the Noetians. The thrice-repeated λογισθήσεται in the context of 5.1 surely contains a broad hint at the Logos; and the complicated πάντων κρατεῖ – παντοκράτωρ play in 6.2 looks like another attempt at a pun. It is worth noting that it is only in these two places (5.1 and 6.1–6.2) that καλῶς occurs, almost as a wink at the audience. And etymological plays of the kind 'Is-ra-el' and πάντων κρατεῖ had their place in diatribe.[43] A curious kind of pun stands near the beginning of CN: τὸ μὲν γένος – γενόμενος (1.1), if taken to be a phrase with some mildly punning purpose, is more easily explained than by trying to endow μέν with any particular significance. Σμυρναῖος (ibid.) is, of course, capable of bearing more than one meaning, and and μὴ καθαρῷ – καθαρῶς (1.3; 1.5), which avoids the perhaps more obvious ἀκάθαρος, looks like a sarcastic pun. Other examples may be found in: λόγος – Λόγος (17.3); ἐνανθρωπήσαντος – ἐν ἀνθρώποις (4.7); ἐντέλλεται – ἀποτελεῖ (14.4); and even, more obscurely, in ὁμοφρονία and εἰς νοῦς (7.3).

But while puns are of the stock-in-trade of diatribe, they are only a special example of a much more general tendency that the diatribe manner has to play with words.[44] In CN this tendency shows itself in at least three ways: the repetition of the identical word or words, the repetition of identical and common-rooted words in varying forms, and the alliterative repetition of the same or similar vowels or consonants. The complete listing of these three kinds

---

41 Bultmann, p.18: 'Häufig finden sich aneinander gereihte Attribute mit α-privativum'. Cf. CN 10.2; and esp. 8.3.
42 Bultmann, p.27; Thyen, p.50; Colardeau, op. cit., pp.343–331.
43 Thyen, p.84.
44 Bultmann, p.21; Thyen, pp.47–50; Marrou, col. 998.

of word play in CN would be tedious as well as unnecessary; so some brief account of them must be given in order to show the surprising extent to which this diatribe feature is to be found in CN.

First, then, there is the simple repetition of an identical word or phrase within a relatively short space. The twenty instances of ὑπό in the body of the Peroration (18.2—18.9) are clearly for a special rhetorical purpose and hardly count. But more strictly in the manner of diatribe are the five-fold repetitions in 3.2; 10.1—10.2; 10.3; 14.3—14.5; the four-fold repetitions in 4.10—4.11; 10.2; 11.1; 11.3; 11.4; the three-fold repetitions in 1.7; 3.6; 4.6; 4.12—4.13; 6.2; 8.3; 9.1—9.3 cf. 17.4; 9.2; 11.1; 11.3; 15.7; 16.5—16.7. Twice-repeated words and phrases are so common as not to require listing, but the doublings of words and phrases in 1.5; 5.4; 7.3 (where the articles and connective drop out in repetition); 11.3; 15.1—15.2 (with special alliterative effect); 16.5—16.6; 17.4: 17.5, are especially noteworthy.

Next, and slightly more subtle, there are to be found in CN a great number of repetitions of the same and common-rooted words in differing forms. So many instances of this particular mannerism could be given that it must suffice to exemplify it with a few cases. Thus the changes rung on the 'root' παντ- in 3.6; 6.2; 6.4; 10.2—10.3; 11.1—11.3; 14.5, would serve as a good example: or on αὐτ- in 3.1—3.2; 7.2—7.3; 7.4—7.5; 10.2—10.3; 11.2. It is easy to miss this mannerism in the course of a silent reading of CN; but once the relevant sentences are read aloud a strong impression of the repetitiousness of certain 'roots' is quickly obtained. There are occasions on which this common trick could be of the greatest importance in determining whether to accept certain phrases in the text of CN as genuine. For instance, throughout CN great play is made with the 'roots' λογ- and/or λεγ-. This occurs in 2.8; 5.1; 7.4; 11.1; 13.1—13.4; 14.1—14.2; 15.1; 15.7. In the light of the known frequency of such play the phrase λογικὴν δὲ λέγω in 17.2, suspected by some as an interpolation, takes on a much more authentic air. Similarly with the suspect κατὰ φαντασίαν of 17.5. It must be noted that it occurs shortly after ἐφανερώθη. And it is important to note the comparable play in 12.1—12.2 on φαίνεσθαι — ἐμφανής. Again the 'roots' γιν-/γεν-/γενν- obviously lend themselves to just this form of word-play: see 6.1; 10.4; but especially 16.2—16.7. Clearly, in the light of such play, the temptation to make textual changes in CN which simply reduce legitimate word-play to monotony, especially in CN 16, should be firmly resisted.

But sometimes it is the addition or change of a prepositional prefix which makes the word-play. Thus in 7.7 different prefixes are attached to κειμεν-; in 11.3 to τρεχ-; in 8.2 to δεικ-. In 9.1 τυχ- is first without, then with a prefix;

and the same is true of ζητ- in 16.4–16.6, and of μαρτυρ- in 17.1. But this order is reversed for γνω- in 14.6–14.7; for πηγ- in 18.3; and for τιθ- in 18.4–18.5.

In view of the foregoing evidence concerning the repetition of 'roots' in varying forms, it is important to give special consideration to the case of the repetition of ἑτερ- in 1.1. As has been said, the statement ἕτεροί τινες ἑτέραν διδασκαλίαν παρεισάγουσιν was one reason, if not the major reason, behind the view that CN should be considered as a fragment of a larger work. Now, in the first place, it has been : 1own above that abrupt beginnings are neither out of place in diatribe, nor in fact absent from other parts of CN. In the second place, we are now in a position to appreciate the ἕτεροι – ἑτέραν type of word-play. Indeed there are two other examples of ἑτερ- play in CN: 5.1 and 11.1. And in the third place, due account must be taken of the obvious ambiguity of ἕτερος itself, on which it may now be reasonably suspected that the speaker is basing yet another pun. The Noetian doctrine is not just *another* doctrine in a series of already refuted heretical doctrines, but rather a *hetero-*doxy which 'strangers', not just 'others', were in fact importing. All things thus considered, it seems fair to say that argument based on ἕτεροι – ἑτέραν for CN as a fragment, has no validity in the light of the style and the known word-play techniques in the whole work. It might be added at this point that the ὑποστῆναι – σύστασιν phrase of 15.7, which like the phrases from 17.2 and 17.5 mentioned above has been suspected of being interpolated, should also be reconsidered and surely approved in the light of the known stylistic tricks of CN. This is not to say that it can thus be proved that the places where these words occur could not be interpolated. But the stylistic data detailed here do make it easier to see that words sometimes questioned are at least not stylistically misplaced, and that in fact from considerations of the style of the whole of CN those words fit very well indeed.

The final sort of word-play that needs to be considered consists in the alliterative repetition of the same or similar consonants or, less often, vowels. By far the most common alliteration in CN, and a very apt one in view of the character of the work as a whole, is of the consonant π. Indeed once the attention has been caught by this device, used both at the beginning and in the middle of words, π-play can be detected in almost every section of CN. For the more obvious instances, see in 1.4; 1.6; 2.7; 3.2; 3.6; 4.2; 4.7; 4.10; 5.1; 5.2; 5.3; 6.1–6.4; 6.6; 7.2; 7.3; 7.4; 7.7; 8.1; 9.2; 10.1; 10.3; 11.1; 12.5; 15.3; 16.5–16.6; 17.1–17.2; 17.3; 18.1; 18.2; 18.3; 18.6 and 18.10. In some cases, it will be noted, ρ is alliterated at the same time, and β appears occasionally. This π-play is particularly common in the livelier part A of CN, although it recurs with renewed intensity in the exchange with a member of the audience in

16.5–16.6. It would be interesting to discover to what extent the penchant for π-play affects the order and even the choice of words at various points in CN. The odd order of words in 7.4, Φίλιππον – λέγειν, may result from π-play; and παρέξ (6.4) and παρεκτός (8.1) are strange variants for the scriptural ἐκτός (1 Cor 15, 27: cf. CN 6.3). But both variants occur in π-play. Forms of ὅσπερ are rare; but the two instances (6.1 and 16.4) occur in sections where π-play is strong.

τ is another letter which appears in alliteration: 1.8; 3.1; 8.1; 8.3 fin.; 8.4; 11.2–11.3; 12.2; 14.2; 14.7; 14.8; 16.6; 18.2. Other single alliterated letters are θ, κ, φ. The alliteration of σ needs a special mention, since it plays its part in the famous phrase πᾶσαι τοσαῦται αἱρέσεις in 8.4. Here it may well have been used for the derogatory hissing effect it has in repetition. Some letters are alliterated in combinations: for example, ε – κ – λ (1.4; 1.8; 18.4); ἀλ – λ 13.2–13.3; 15.1; 17.5); ω – ς (10.4; 11.1); ε – υ – ρ (18.7); β – λ (1.3). Opening syllables, sometimes prepositional prefixes, also recur: δει- (4.3); αὐτ- (17.1); ἀπ- (8.2; 11.3); συ- (1.5; 14.4; 14.5); παρ- (18.2). And rhyming jingles are common: in -ο(υ)μεν (1.7; 12.5); -ῆναι (3.5; 10.4); -ανέτω (7.1); -ντος (7.5); -ροις (17.3); -σαν (14.6); -σεν (14.8); -ειν (16.4). Certain kinds of rhyme, while found in the main body of CN, are especially intensified in the Peroration: -μενος/-μενον/-μενα (7.7; but nine times in 18.6); -ται (14.4; but six times in 18.3, five times in 18.8, four times in 18.9); -ξεται (10.3; but three times in 18.8); -ων/-ον (14.5; but nine times both in 18.7 and 18.9). Bolder jingles are made of ἀγίοις – ἀξίοις (16.6), and of δυνάμει – διαθέσει (7.3). Vowels are sometimes used repetitiously. The diphthong -ου- is the outstanding favourite: see in 2.4; 2.6–2.7; 3.1; 4.9; 4.11; 7.4; and in the οὐ πολλοῦ χρόνου phrase of 1.1, where the scholarly insertion of πρό might spoil the jingle effect (cf. the simple genitive of 16.3). The vowel η occurs often in 3.3, and if ει was similarly pronounced, the effect would be quite striking. But so much must suffice to show how general is the tendency in CN to play with words and letters. From this tendency, as from the other techniques described and instanced so far, it can be seen that the debt of CN to the techniques of diatribe is very considerable.

A further feature in the style of CN, and one which comes from the attempt to be brightly emphatic, is the use of strong καί. There appear to be some thirty-three uses of this καί in CN. Twenty-one mean more or less 'also'; six mean rather 'even'; but on the remaining six occasions the point of the usage is difficult to discern: cf. 2.7; 3.3; 6.2; 8.4; 16.1; 18.1. It certainly seems that the speaker was too free with strong καί. At any rate the scribe becomes muddled by them, and has to erase καί twice: in 6.4 (through a memory of a similar phrase in 6.2), and in 6.6. The most important usage of strong καί for the purposes of this present study is, of course, the καὶ ὁ Νοητός of 8.4. As has been explained in Chapter 1, great weight has been laid on this καί. But it should be noted that strong καί is used with proper names on no less than nine occasions in CN, and sometimes very little positive sense seems to be attached to the usage. A comparison should be made with the καὶ Νοητός of 3.3 before it is decided that the καί of 8.4 must mean 'also'. Although in the majority of instances strong καί does mean 'also', on more than a third of its appearances it does not seem to do so: it is merely used for necessary, and even unnecessary, emphasis. It seems possible, and indeed better, to translate the καί of 8.4 by 'even', almost in the sense of 'at long last', considering that it occurs at the very point where the transition between part A and part B of CN is being made.

So much for the main ways in the which the speaker in CN tries to hold the attention of his audience. No doubt closer research would reveal even more tricks of his trade, but it may be reasonably claimed that the main point of this present chapter so far has been made. CN is a work with a distinctive style which contains many of the features found in diatribe. If the work is at times somewhat odd in its grammar and its syntax, this is perhaps not to be wondered at, and certainly need not be a sign that textual 'emendation' is called for. The order of words can be very contorted (3.1; 3.5; 7.4); genitive absolutes can be rough (2.6–2.7; 4.7; 7.4; 7.5; 18.9); grammatical agreement can be lacking (4.10; 9.1; 16.1); the Greek can fall short of what might be expected (3.5; 8.1; 4.6; 15.3; 16.6; 16.5); at certain places rules seem to have been forgotten (6.1; 10.1; 11.3; 14.2). Like diatribe, CN is a popular work, aimed at attracting and holding the attention of an audience by the use of the techniques we have enumerated. Certain inconcinnities are surely to be expected in a work of this kind, and, especially where other ms authority is totally lacking, it would be wrong to seek to improve on the undoubtedly able presentation of the speaker.

CN and the diatribe method

When we turn our attention from the stylistic features of diatribe which are so common, not only in the non-doctrinal passages of CN, as Norden thought,[45] but in fact throughout the whole of the work, and turn to the method of the speaker and the kinds of argument that he uses, we find that in this respect too CN owes much to diatribe technique. It is agreed by those who have studied this technique that diatribe is not primarily a matter of rational

---

45 See n.4 above.

arguments. Its appeal to the audience, as one might have guessed from the consideration we have given to its stylistic features, is not an intellectual appeal, as would be the case with a philosophical work.[46] It is true that there are to be found in diatribe occasional attempts at rational argument; but these arguments are not of an especially elevated kind, and tend to be based ultimately on common sense – a level of appeal which would be understood by a popular audience. The kinds of argument used are said to be either *a fortiori*, or *a maiore ad minus*, or *a minore ad maius*:[47] in other words, forceful and easily intelligible forms of reasoning with a strong *ad hominem* coloration. In CN there are undoubted attempts at this kind of argumentation. In 16.3– 16.4 and in 16.5–16.7 the impossibility of knowing how the Word was born of the Father is urged on the basis that we do not even know how man is born from man, or how the world was made – let alone how he through whom the world was made is born of God. It is noteworthy that the ultimate refuge of the speaker in this passage is in the statements of Scripture (16.7), and in the traditional faith of the hearers (17.1). There is no serious attempt at intellectual argument as such. A further indication of the level at which the speaker is aiming is to be seen in the absence of difficult speculative or theological explanations. The 'explanation' of how the Word is differentiated from the Father in the process of creation (10.1–11.2) contains nothing that would not impress – even if it did little to enlighten – an audience which was not interested primarily in intellectual depth or exactitude. The same could be said of the account of the inner arrangements of the Trinity somewhat later (14.1– 14.5). In both passages it is more the heat of convinced belief that is generated than the light of reasoned explanation. Clearly an appreciation of this fact could be of great importance in the assessment of the 'theology' contained in those passages.

In fact, diatribe was much more a matter of persuasiveness than of rational or intellectual argument. In its secular usage it had a predominantly ethical purpose: to persuade people that a certain mode of behaviour was wrong, whereas another mode of behaviour was right. Its aim was to win people over to certain courses of action; to make them see the rightness of the point of view maintained by the speaker, over the wrongness of opposed views. Thus diatribe had to be popular, and it had to entertain an audience it sought to win. It was a work of moral propaganda, not of moral philosophy. So it depended for its

---

46 Bultmann, pp.54–55; Ropes, p.15; Thyen, p.60.
47 See esp. Thyen, p.60 and n.163.

effect largely on the personal appeal of the speaker to the audience.[48] We have seen how this appeal was made through the use of a large number of stylistic tricks. Similarly the kinds of argument the speaker both avoided and used heightened the appeal. He avoided, as we have seen, arguments of a too intellectual kind. The stock arguments he used consisted much more in a few popular and appealing approaches. Thus, for instance, simple comparisons or analogies are common in diatribe, especially those based on familiar areas of experience.[49] They are not lacking in CN; in a passage of relatively difficult and brief 'explanation', there are references to sound (10.4), light (10.4; 11.1), running water and the sun (11.1), breath (11.4). The fact that these comparisons are, in most cases, traditional ways of trying to clarify what is expressed does not alter the fact that they are also easily grasped by ordinary minds.

A more blatant way of appealing to the audience in the attempt to win them over is to be found in the dramatic and colourful presentation of the opponent or the opposing view.[50] There is certainly no lack of such presentation in CN, whether of the opponents (1.1–1.8), or of their arguments (2.1–2.3; 2.5–2.8), or of their methods in the interpretation of Scripture (3.1; 4.2–4.3), or of their lamentable shortcomings in the matter of understanding the Scriptures (2.3; 2.7; 3.1; 3.3; 7.1; 7.4; 8.1). A development of this kind of lively presentation is to be seen in the use of insulting ridicule against the opponents or their view.[51] In CN insulting remarks are made about the Noetians (3.3; 4.2; 6.6), and they are insultingly associated with other known heretics (3.1, with Theodotus; 11.3 (by implication) with certain Gnostics). The views of the Noetians are ridiculed freely: 1.4 (Noetus as Moses *and* Aaron); 3.2 (Father = Son, and raised himself up); 4.10 (the idea of the Word as flesh in heaven); 6.6 (what Father is there for Noetus' Christ to go up to?); 7.3 (the incongruous ἐστιν); 7.4 (the Noetians as their own worst enemies). The speaker does not fail to make the most of the more absurd aspects of the Noetian position, and in so doing is employing a well-known diatribe technique.

While methods such as those just described are helpful in breaking down the case which opposes the speaker's own, it may still be asked what sort of positive

---

48 Bultmann, pp.54–55; 61; Thyen, p.60; Capelle, col.992f; Marrou, col. 998. Ropes, p.13f, puts the point well: 'In general the Greek preachers were well aware that in their diatribes they were awakening sinners and inculcating familiar but neglected principles, not engaged in investigating truth or in carrying thought further to the conquest of the unknown. Not originality but impressiveness was what they aimed at. The argument is from what the readers already know and ought to feel.'
49 Bultmann, pp.14; 35–39; 55–56; Ropes, p.14; Thyen, pp.45; 49; 55f; Capelle, col. 992f; Marrou, col.998.
50 Bultmann, pp.58–59.
51 Bultmann, pp.57–58; 60; Thyen, p.61f; Oltramare, p.15.

support, apart from a few simple arguments and popular analogies, he can give his own view. In diatribe the weight of positive support for the speaker's case came from authority;[52] and especially from the quotation of an authoritative source, often a poet, such as Homer.[53] Of course, it is true that often quotations were made largely for the purpose of display; but more often than not, and more in the case of the Hellenistic diaspora sermon than in the case of diatribe as such, quotations were made for the purpose of proof.[54] It is worth examining CN rather closely on this point.

The weight of authority is thrown against the Noetian case right from the very start of CN, in the credal reply of the elders to Noetus' captious question (1.7). But it is the authority of the Scriptures which, more precisely, is brought to bear against the arguments of the heretical sect. Throughout CN the presumption is that it is the truth expressed in the Scriptures which is the basic cause of the downfall of heresy. It is to this Scriptural truth, and to the accepted explanation of it, that appeal is constantly made against the Noetians: 2.4; 3.1; 3.3; 3.5; 4.9; 7.4 fin.; 7.7; 8.1; 9.1–9.3 (especially); 13.1; 14.1; 14.8; 15.3; 16.1. And it is Scriptural truth which lies at the root of the counter-arguments and explanations. Here the method of CN is a very simple one. In the first part (A) of the work, a text, either adduced by the opponents or at any rate apparently suiting their book, is shown to have an obviously orthodox sense both by the explanation given to it and by the confirmatory accretion of other texts. Thus, for instance, the text in 4.4 has its real sense brought out (4.5), and this sense is then confirmed by the quotation of other texts in 4.6, 4.9, 4.13. Similarly the text in 5.1 is confirmed by further texts in 5.2 and 5.5: the text in 6.1 is confirmed by further texts in 6.1, 6.2, 6.3, 6.5: and the text in 7.1 by further texts in 7.2 and 7.4. This alone would be enough to show how dominant in the anti-heretical argument is the authority of the quotation from Scripture. But even in the more positive second part (B) of CN, the method in which the work proceeds is largely through the compilation of Scriptural quotations. Thus a quotation in 12.1 is supported by more quotations in 12.3 and 12.4: the quotation in 13.1 by another in 13.3: and the quotation in 14.1 by many others in 14.5, 14.7, 15.2, 15.4, 15.5, and 16.2. To a very large extent, then, argument in CN is not of the rational or intellectual kind, but has all its probative force in the authority of the word of God, transmitted by the Holy Spirit through the Apostles (17.1).

---

52 Bultmann, pp.56–57.
53 Bultmann, pp.42–46; Thyen, p.72; Capelle, col.993; Marrou, col.1006.
54 Thyen, pp.56–58; 71; also Bultmann, pp.56–57.

It is worth adding here a couple of further points in which CN appears to be using the known techniques of diatribe in the making of authoritative quotations. As Bultmann remarks, a quotation in diatribe is often described by the speaker as nicely or aptly put.[55] The most common adverb used in diatribe for this purpose – καλῶς – has this precise function on no less than four occasions in CN: 5.1 (twice); 6.1; 6.2. Again, Lagrange makes the valuable point that it must be remembered that quotations in diatribe are made largely from memory, and that therefore it is not surprising that they are not always accurately reproduced or repeated.[56] In view of the similarity we have discovered between CN and diatribe in other respects, this point too should be kept in mind when it is found that Scriptural quotations are not always as accurate as we might prefer them to be. To see in slight inaccuracies in quotations an excuse for textual emendation or for speculation on a new or different tradition of the text of Scripture would be to endow inaccuracies with too much significance. In diatribe they are almost to be expected, and so it is not surprising that they occur in CN. As was the case with the consideration of the stylistic techniques to be found in CN, so also the methods and the kinds of argument used in the work display a dependence on the popular form of diatribe.

CN and the diatribe structure

There is one final respect in which it is reasonable to suppose that diatribe has had its influence on CN, and that is in the elaborate structuration of the work which has been examined and detailed in the foregoing chapter. It certainly cannot be maintained that there is any other work, whether diatribe or Hellenistic homily, which is known to have as carefully balanced and arranged a structure as CN. Indeed it is commonly acknowledged to be difficult to find any fixed or firm association of parts (*Gliederung*) in diatribe,[57] although the homily-like works examined by Thyen show a tendency to be more structured than profane diatribe.[58] It is however possible, with Bultmann, to say that in diatribe 'there are to be found a number of "moments" which do not always appear in the same order'.[59] From Bultmann's analysis it appears that the basic

---

55 Bultmann, pp.45–46: 'Manchmal wird das Angeführte als καλῶς oder εἰκότως Gesagtes und ähnlich charakterisiert.' Cf. Thyen, p.58, for a similar use of ὀρθῶς (see CN 3.3!) and ἀληθῶς. Thyen, p.69, mentions the more common formulae for the introduction of Scriptural quotation into the homily-form which he is studying. Many of these formulae appear in CN.
56 Lagrange, op. cit., pp.LVIII–LIX.
57 Bultmann, pp.48–49; Ropes, p.14.
58 Thyen, pp.58–59.
59 Bultmann, p.50.

'moments' in diatribe consist of a part which is taken up with the positive presentation of the problem, normally followed by a part in which the falsity of the position presented is criticized in a severe and lively manner (the so-called *Scheltrede*); which in turn is usually followed by a warmer, protreptic final section, 'in which the listener is called upon to give up evil ways and proceed along the right path'.[60] This analysis is so close to what in fact happens in CN – of course, in a much more elaborate and organized way than is the case with any known diatribe – that it is difficult not to believe that once again CN is indebted to the structural technique of diatribe.

As with diatribe, CN gets its unity from the discussion of a single problem or theme.[61] It has been shown in the foregoing chapter how this single problem is expounded in the first two introductory chapters of the work. What in diatribe was often a concrete occasion or a particular action, set out at the beginning to catch the attention of the audience, in the Hellenistic synagogue homily became an Old Testament text, or the pericope to be read on a particular sabbath.[62] The two introductory chapters of CN are neither of these; but the opening-technique of diatribe has been cleverly adapted in the abrupt description of the heretical sect and its baleful doctrine. In fact, as several scholars have remarked,[63] diatribe provided an almost perfectly prepared tool for the combatting of heresy. As with the moral failings against which profane diatribe was employed, so the same techniques could easily be turned against doctrinal failings. And not merely in the adaptation of diatribe's lively opening presentation of the facts: it was to an even greater degree the 'two-sidedness' of the main body of diatribe that gave the defender of the faith the chance to do battle with and conquer heresy and to present and enlarge on the opposing truths of the apostolic faith.

It is surely in the light of the 'two-sidedness' of diatribe structure that we are to see the division into Part A and part B in CN. Part A contains that ἐλέγχειν of falsehood which Bultmann would make the main part of profane diatribe.[64] Sharp though the examination and criticism of the Noetian position in part A is, it falls short of the roughness and liveliness to be found in the ordinary kind of *Scheltrede*. But this development towards a more serious and staider treatment of whatever subject has been chosen is one of the acknowledged marks

---

60 Bultmann, p.51.
61 Bultmann, pp.46–48.
62 Thyen, p.59.
63 Notably Lagrange, op. cit., p.LIV; Capelle, col.994; Marrou, col.998–1001.
64 Bultmann, p.62: 'Sein Hauptbestandteil ist das ἐλέγχειν, die Überführung von der Schlechtigkeit der allgemeinen Anschauung und Moral, die Polemik gegen die vorgefassten Meinungen, die falschen δόγματα . . .'

of the Christian adaptation of the diatribe.[65] In the synagogue homily, of course, there was no place for a negative or critical part.[66] Part B of CN is close to the νουθετεῖν of the audience which, according to Bultmann, generally followed the ἐλέγχειν of the false doctrine.[67] There can be no doubt of the encouraging warmth of the speaker's tone in part B. Flashes of solidarity with the audience appear: 12.5; 14.6; 16.1. But it is particularly in the opening and concluding sections of part B that this warmth is at its most intense: 8.4–9.3 (B1) and 17.1–17.2 (B5). The long Peroration also contains a note of personal appeal: 18.3; 18.5; 18.10. This Peroration contains a great deal of antithetical construction, and Bultmann notes that antithesis was often to be found in the end-part of diatribe.[68] More interestingly still, Thyen remarks that final doxologies, of the kind that is so striking in CN 18.10, are a feature in the homilies he studies. They stem from the traditional practice of the Palestinian synagogues.[69] But obviously they have nothing to do with diatribe.

The way in which the structure is manipulated in CN has also much in common with the practice in diatribe. Linkage between sections was achieved by the introduction of an objection, to be answered in the following section: or by the interposition of a question or a command to the audience.[70] It is clear that something like this technique was used by the speaker in CN. His favourite way of passing from one section to another is by closing the prior section with a Scriptural quotation. Thus in the case of the transition from the Introduction to section A1 (2.8); from A1 to A2 (3.6); from A3 to A4 (5.5); from B4 to B5 (16.7). At other times an odd or emphatic order of words in the concluding sentence of one section calls for a new beginning in the next section. So with the transition from A2 to A3 (4.13); from A4 to A5 (7.7 fin.); from B3 to B4 (13.4). Again a summarizing or elegantly turned sentence can be used to mark the transition – from B1 to B2 (9.3); from B2 to B3 (11.3); from B5 to the Peroration (17.2). And of course there is the striking case, already mentioned, of the challenging rhetorical question which marks the link between A5, the conclusion of part A, and B1, the opening of part B. These findings not only show, once again, a certain indebtedness to diatribe technique, but also confirm the analysis we have made of CN into two main parts with sections. It would be difficult to deny that the speaker was not conscious of the parts and sections of his work when he takes such care to mark the transitions in such forceful ways.

---

65 Thyen, pp.62; 117.
66 Thyen, p.59.
67 Bultmann, p.62.
68 Bultmann, pp.52–53.
69 Thyen, p.53.
70 Bultmann, pp.53–54.

Conclusion

We may say then that CN, in its very structuration as well as in its style and its methods, seems certainly to owe much to the contemporary profane diatribe manner – a more or less literary genre which also exercized influence on the synagogue homily of the same period, and one which played its part – a part perhaps not sufficiently acknowledged – in certain Christian writings of the second and subsequent century.[71] In view of the large amount of evidence we have adduced in this chapter, it can scarcely be doubted that diatribe played its part in the composition of CN. Coupled with the analysis of the structure of CN, made in the previous chapter, this evidence of diatribe technique and manner in CN makes a much more precise appreciation of the whole possible. It would be wrong to say that CN is a diatribe, but it certainly appears to be an outstanding and – except by Norden – a hitherto unacknowledged example of the Christian adaptation of profane diatribe for anti-heretical and teaching purposes. To know the source both of the structure and the style of CN enables us to know not only what sort of literary entity we are dealing with, but also, more importantly, to assess and appreciate with much more accuracy than has been previously possible the true *theological* value of the work. If CN is not a fragment of a longer heresiological treatise, but a short and popular sort of discourse – or homily, as its title states – on a single topic, the destruction of the Noetian sect, then the theology which it contains must be seen in the light of this important fact. It would be wrong to put too much reliance on the apparently technical parts of CN as fully developed and expressed accounts of what the writer's theological position really is – although of course those parts of CN should furnish a fair guide to the thought of the writer.

---

71 See, e.g., Norden, op. cit., II, pp.557 and n.1; 558.

142

BIBLIOGRAPHY
of works consulted and quoted in this study

The Contra Noetum (editions in chronological order)

Vaticanus graecus 1431

G. **Vossius,** *Sancti Gregorii Episcopi Neo-Caesariensis, cognomento Thaumaturgi, Opera Omnia,* quotquot in insignioribus, praecipue Romanis bibliothecis reperiri potuerunt . . . [to which are added] *Miscellanea Sanctorum aliquot Patrum Graecorum et Latinorum ante hac non edita.* . . Auctore et Collectore Doct. Gerardo Vossio, praeposito Tungrensi, Mainz 1604. [For the Latin translation of CN by Torres]

J.A. Fabricius, *S. Hippolyti, Episcopi et Martyris Opera,* curante Jo. Alberto Fabricio, Hamburg 1716. [For Torres' translation of CN with chapter-divisions and notes]

idem, *S.Hippolyti Episcopi et Martyris Operum Volumen II,* Hamburg 1718. [For the first edition of the Greek text of CN, with translation, chapter-divisions and notes]

A. **Gallandi,** *Bibliotheca Veterum Patrum antiquorumque scriptorum ecclesiasticorum.* . . Cura & Studio Andreae Gallandii Presbyteri Congregationis Oratorii, Tome II, Venice 1766. [For Fabricius' edition, plus more notes]

M.J. Routh, *Scriptorum Ecclesiasticorum Opuscula praecipua quaedam,* I, Oxford 1832. [For Fabricius' text, with some excellent suggestions, Torres' translation and additional notes]

P.A. de Lagarde, *Hippolyti Romani quae feruntur omnia graece,* e recognitione Pauli Antonii de Lagarde, Leipzig-London 1858. [CN is taken largely from Routh's edition]

E. **Schwartz,** *Zwei Predigten Hippolyts,* in Sitzungsberichte der Bayrischen Akademie der Wissenschaften, Philosophisch-historische Abteilung, Jahrgang 1936, Heft 3, Munich 1936. [For a good but not quite perfect text of CN]

P. **Nautin,** *Hippolyte: Contre les Hérésies, Fragment.* Etude et Edition critique par Pierre Nautin, (Etudes et Textes pour l'histoire du dogme de la Trinité, 2), Paris 1949. [The current but deficient edition of CN]

Patristic writings

Chronicon Paschale, CHSB, I, ed. L. Dindorf, Bonn 1832.

Epiphanius, *Panarion haer.*, GCS Epiphanius, ed. K. Holl, I, Leipzig, 1915; II, Leipzig 1922.

Eusebius, Hist. eccl., GCS Eusebius, ed. E. Schwartz and T. Mommsen, II/1–3, Leipzig 1903–1909.

Gelasius, *De Duabus Naturis*, in A. Thiel, *Epistolae Romanorum Pontificum genuinae*, I, Braunsberg 1868.

Georgius Syncellus, *Chronographia*, CSHB, I, ed. W. Dindorf, Bonn 1829.

Hippolytus Romanus, *In Danielem etc.*,GCS Hippolytus, ed. G.N. Bonwetsch and H. Achelis, I/1–2, Leipzig 1897.

also: *Hippolyte: Commentaire sur Daniel*, Introduction de G. Bardy, texte établi et traduit par Maurice Lefèvre, (SC 14), Paris 1947.

Elenchus, GCS Hippolytus, ed. P. Wendland, III, Leipzig, 1916.

Irenaeus, *Adversus Haereses, Sancti Irenaei episcopi Lugdunensis libros quinque adversus Haereses. . .* edidit W.W. Harvey, 2 vols., Cambridge 1857.

Jerome, *De viris inlustribus*, TU XIV, 1, ed. E.C. Richardson, Leipzig 1896.

Nicephorus Callistus, Eccl. hist., PG 145.

Photius, *Bibliotheca*, PG 103.

Theodoret, *Eranistes*, PG 83.

Other writings

H. Achelis, *Hippolytstudien*, in TU XVI, 4, Leipzig 1897.

A. d'Alès, *La théologie de saint Hippolyte*, Paris 1906.

O. Bardenhewer, *Geschichte der altkirchlichen Literatur*[2], II, Freiburg im Breisgau 1914.

G. Bardy, *L'enigme d'Hippolyte*, in MélSR 5(1948) pp.63–88.

idem, *Le souvenir de Josèphe chez les Pères*, in RHE 43 (1948) pp. 179–191.

idem, [review of Nautin's *Hippolyte et Josipe*] in RHE 43 (1948) pp.197–200.

P. Batiffol, *L'abbaye de Rossano: Contribution à l'histoire de la Vaticane*, Paris 1891.

B. Botte, *Note sur l'auteur du 'De Universo' attribué à saint Hippolyte*, in RTAM 18 (1951) pp.5–18.

G. Bovini, *Sant'Ippolito, dottore e martire del III secolo*, Rome 1943.

R. Bultmann, *Der Stil der paulinischen Predigt und die kynisch-stoische Diatribe*, in Forschungen zur Religion und Literatur des Alten und Neuen Testaments, 13, Göttingen 1910.

C.C.J. Bunsen, *Hippolytus und seine Zeit*, I, Leipzig 1852.

B. Capelle, *Le cas du pape Zéphyrin*, in RBén 38 (1926) pp.321–330.

idem, *Hippolyte de Rome*, in RTAM 17 (1950) pp.145–174.

idem, *A propos d'Hippolyte de Rome*, in RTAM 19 (1952) pp.193–202.

W. Capelle and H.-I. Marrou, art. *Diatribe*, in RAC III, col. 990–1009.

C.P. Caspari, *Ungedruckte, unbeachtete und wenig beachtete Quellen zur Geschichte des Taufsymbols und der Glaubensregel*, III, Christiania [Oslo]1875.

Th. Colardeau, *Etude sur Epictète*, Paris 1903.

G. da **Bra,** *I Filosofumeni sono di Ippolito?,* Rome 1942.

J. **Daniélou,** [review of Nautin's *Hippolyte et Josipe*] in RechSR 35 (1948) pp.596–598.

R. **Devreesse,** *Les premières années du monophysisme: une collection antichalcédonienne,* in RSPT 19 (1930) pp.251–265.

idem, *Introduction à l'étude des manuscrits grecs,* Paris 1954.

idem, *Les manuscrits grecs de l'Italie méridionale,* (Studi e Testi 183), Città del Vaticano 1955.

I. **von Döllinger,** *Hippolytus und Kallistus, oder Die römische Kirche in der ersten Hälfte des dritten Jahrhunderts,* Regensburg 1853.

R. **Draguet,** *Le florilège antichalcédonien du Vatic. Graec. 1431,* in RHE 24 (1928) pp.51–62.

J. **Dräseke,** *Zum Syntagma des Hippolytos,* in Zeitschrift für wissenschaftliche Theologie, 46 (1903) pp.58–90.

H. **Elfers,** *Die Kirchenordnung Hippolyts von Rom,* Paderborn 1938.

idem, *Neue Untersuchungen über die Kirchenordnung Hippolyts von Rom,* in Abhandlungen über Theologie und Kirche, Festschrift für Karl Adam, ed. M. Reding, Düsseldorf 1952.

G. **Ficker,** *Studien zur Hippolytfrage,* (Habilitationsschrift), Leipzig 1893.

P. **Franchi de' Cavalieri** and J. **Lietzmann,** *Specimina Codicum Graecorum Vaticanorum*[2], Berlin-Leipzig 1929.

S. **Giet,** *Le texte du fragment contre Noët,* in RevSR 24 (1950) pp.315–322.

J.-M. **Hanssens,** *La liturgie d'Hippolyte: ses documents, son titulaire, ses origines et son caractère,* (Orientalia Christiana Analecta, 155), Rome 1959.

A. **von Harnack,** *Geschichte der altchristlichen Litteratur bis Eusebius,* 2/II, *Die Chronologie der Litteratur von Irenaeus bis Eusebius,* Leipzig 1904.

C.F.G. **Heinrici,** *Der litterarische Charakter der neutestamentlichen Schriften,* Leipzig 1908.

A. **Hilgenfeld,** *Die Ketzergeschichte des Urchristentums, urkundlich dargestellt,* Leipzig 1884.

R. **Hirzel,** *Der Dialog, ein literarhistorischer Versuch,* Leipzig 1895, (photo. Hildesheim 1963).

W. **Holtzmann,** *Die ältesten Urkunden des Klosters S. Maria del Patir,* in Byzantinische Zeitschrift 26 (1926) pp.328–351.

J.N.D. **Kelly,** *Early Christian Creeds*[3], London 1972.

M.-J. **Lagrange,** *Saint Paul, Epître aux Romains,* Paris 1916.

L.S. **Le Nain de Tillemont,** *Mémoires pour servir à l'histoire ecclésiastique des six premiers siècles justifiez par les citations des auteurs originaux,* III, Paris 1695.

H. **Lietzmann,** *Apollinaris von Laodicea und seine Schule,* (Texte und Untersuchungen von Hans Lietzmann, I), Tübingen 1904.

J.B. **Lightfoot,** *The Apostolic Fathers,* Part I, vol. II, London 1890.

R.A. **Lipsius,** *Zur Quellenkritik des Epiphanios,* Vienna 1865.

idem, *Die Quellen der ältesten Ketzergeschichte neu untersucht,* Leipzig 1875.

P. **Maas,** *Textual Criticism,* Oxford 1958.

H.-I. **Marrou,** *Histoire de l'éducation dans l'antiquité,* Paris 1948.

Ch. Martin, Le 'Contra Noetum' de saint Hippolyte: fragment d'homélie ou finale du Syntagma? in RHE 37 (1941) pp.5–23.

P. Nautin, Notes sur le catalogue des oeuvres d'Hippolyte, in RechSR 34 (1947) pp.99–107; 347–359.

idem, Hippolyte et Josipe: Contribution à l'histoire de la littérature chrétienne du troisième siècle, (Etudes et Textes pour l'histoire du dogme de la Trinité, 1), Paris 1947.

idem, La controverse sur l'auteur de l' 'Elenchos', in RHE 47 (1952) pp.5–43.

idem, Le dossier d'Hippolyte et de Méliton dans les florilèges dogmatiques et chez les historiens modernes, Paris 1953.

idem, Encore le problème d'Hippolyte, in MélSR 11 (1954), pp.215–218.

idem, L'auteur du Comput Pascal de 222 et de la Chronique anonyme de 235, in RechSR 42 (1954) pp.226–257.

Ed. Norden, Die antike Kunstprosa vom VI. Jahrhundert v.Chr. bis in die Zeit der Renaissance, Leipzig-Berlin 1915.

G. Oggioni, La questione di Ippolito, in La Scuola Cattolica 78 (1950) pp.126–143.

idem, Ancora sulla questione di Ippolito, in La Scuola Cattolica 80 (1952) pp.513–525.

A. Oltramare, Les origines de la diatribe romaine, Geneva 1926.

R. Puchulu, Sur le Contre Noet d'Hippolyte – les attaches littéraires et doctrinales de la doxologie finale, (Thèse de Doctorat presentée à la Faculté de Théologie de Lyon, Année académique 1959–1960).

B. Reynders, Lexique comparé du texte grec et des versions latine, arménienne et syriaque de l' 'Adversus Haereses' de saint Irénée, (CSCO Subsidia, vols. 5–6), Louvain 1954.

M. Richard, Saint Hippolyte, in MélSR 5 (1948) pp.294–308.

idem, Comput et chronographie chez Saint Hippolyte, in MélSR 7 (1950) pp.237–268; 8 (1951) pp.19–50.

idem, Les florilège diphysites du Ve et du VIe siècle, in Das Konzil von Chalkedon, ed. A. Grillmeier and H. Bacht, I, Würzburg 1951.

idem, Encore le problème d'Hippolyte, in MélSR 10 (1953) pp.13–52; 145–180.

idem, Dernières remarques sur S. Hippolyte et le soi-disant Josipe, in RechSR 43 (1955) pp.379–394.

H. de Riedmatten, [review of Nautin's Hippolyte et Josipe] in Dominican Studies 1 (1948) pp.168–173.

E. Rolffs, Urkunden aus dem antimontanistischen Kampfe des Abendlandes, in TU XII, 4, Leipzig 1895.

J.H. Ropes, A Critical and Exegetical Commentary on the Epistle of St James, (International Critical Commentary), Edinburgh 1916.

L. Saltet, Les sources de l'Eranistes de Théodoret, in RHE 6 (1905) pp.289–303; 513–536; 741–754.

E. Schwartz, Codex Vaticanus gr. 1431: eine antichalkedonische Sammlung aus der Zeit Kaiser Zenos, in Abhandlungen der Bayrischen Akademie der Wissenschaften, Philosophisch-philologische und historische Klasse, XXXII, 6, Munich 1927.

C. Sommervogel, Bibliothèque de la Compagnie de Jésus, Bibliographie, tome VIII, Brussels-Paris 1898.

146

H. **Thyen,** *Der Stil der jüdisch-hellenistischen Homilie,* in Forschungen zur Religion und
Literatur des Alten und Neuen Testaments, N.F. 47 (=65 der ganzen Reihe),
Göttingen 1955.

C.H. **Turner,** *The 'Blessed Presbyters' who condemned Noetus,* JTS 23 (1921–22)
pp.28–35.

G. **Volkmar,** *Die Quellen der Ketzergeschichte bis zum Nicänum,* I, *Hippolytus und die
römischen Zeitgenossen,* Zurich 1855.

P. **Wendland,** *Philo und die kynisch-stoische Diatribe,* in *Beiträge zur Geschichte der
griechischen Philosophie und Religion,* ed. P. Wendland and O. Kern, Berlin 1895.

idem, *Die hellenistisch-römische Kultur in ihren Beziehungen zu Judentum und
Christentum*[3], in *Handbuch zum Neuen Testament,* I/2, Tübingen 1912.

U. **von Wilamowitz-Moellendorff,** *Antigonos von Karystos,* in *Philologische Untersuchungen,* ed. A. Kiessling and U. von Wilamowitz-Moellendorff, Heft 4, Berlin 1881.

INDEX OF BIBLICAL QUOTATIONS
AND ALLUSIONS IN CN

*(The references are to sections of the text, **not** to pages)*

Old Testament

Exodus	3:6	2.1
	20:3	2.1
Psalms	32(33):6	12.4
	109(110):3	16.7
	134(135):6	8.3, 11.3
Proverbs	8:22	10.4
Isaiah	40:13	10.4
	40:22	18.3
	44:6	2.2
	45:11−15	4.4
	45:13	4.6
	45:14−15	2.6
	45:14	4.2, 4.5, 4.7
	45:15	4.2
	53:1	17.1
	53:4	18.5
	65:1	12.1
Jeremiah	23:18	13.1
Baruch	3:36−38	2.5
	3:36−37	5.1
	3:37	5.5
	3:38	5.3, 5.5
Daniel	7:10	18.3
	7:13	4.10, 4.13
Micah	2:7−8	15.4

New Testament

Matthew	2:1−2	18.6
	2:9	18.6
	3:17	18.6
	4:2	18.1
	4:10−11	18.7
	4:24	18.7

New Testament (continued)

Matthew (continued)	8:17	18.5
	8:26	18.7
	9:2	18.7
	11:27	6.1, 6.2
	14:25	18.7
	17:5	5.2
	21:18	18.1
	26:14−16	18.3
	26:36−37	18.1
	26:39	18.2
	26:65−66	18.3
	26:71	18.7
	27:22	18.3
	27:28−31	18.3
	27:51	18.8
	27:52	18.8
	27:54	18.8
	27:59−60	18.5
	28:19	14.7
Mark	4:38	18.1
	16:19	18.9
Luke	1:35	4.11
	2:13	18.6
	2:17	18.6
	2:25	18.6
	2:38	18.6
	2:46.49	18.6
	12:10	1.3
	22:43	18.2
	22:44	18.2
	23:11	18.3
	23:44−45	18.8
	23:46	18.4

148

New Testament (continued)

John	1:1	14.1
	1:1.3	12.3
	1:3	11.2
	1:6	7.7
	1:10–11	12.3
	1:10	7.3
	1:12	17.2
	1:15.29	18.6
	1:18	5.5
	2:1–2	18.7
	2:9	18.7
	3:6	16.7
	3:13	4.9, 5.5
	3:32	5.5
	4:1–3	18.1
	4:6	18.1
	4:7	18.1
	4:23	12.5
	5:36	7.7
	6:15	18.1
	6:70	18.3
	9:1.6–7	18.7
	10:18	18.4
	10:30	7.1
	11:25	18.5
	11:26	18.4
	11:43–44	18.7
	11:49–52	18.3
	12:27	18.2
	14:8	7.4
	14:9–10	7.4
	14:9	7.5
	14:10	4.7
	14:12	7.7
	16:27–28	16.2

New Testament (continued)

John (continued)	17:22–23	7.2
	19:1	18.3
	19:30	18.4, 18.8
	19:34	18.4, 18.7
	20:17	6.5
	20:19	18.9
	20:22	18.9
	20:23	18.7
Acts	1:9	18.9
	3:15	10.4
	5:29	6.6
	10:36	13.3
	10:40	18.5
	10:42	18.9
	17:31	18.3
Romans	1:21	14.6
	3:2	9.1
	3:25	7.7
	8:3–4	15.5
	8:11	4.6
	9:5	2.8, 6.1
1 Corinthians	2:6	9.1
	8:6	3.6
	15:23–28	6.3, 6.4
	15:27	8.1, 18.10
Ephesians	2:15	17.4
	3:15	3.6
	3:21	18.10
	4:6	14.5
1 Timothy	1:3	1.1
Hebrews	4:15	17.2
2 Peter	2:1	1.1
1 John	5:12	7.3
Apocalypse	1:8	6.2
	19:11–13	15.2

INDEX OF GREEK WORDS
OF GENERAL THEOLOGICAL INTEREST IN CN
*(The references are to sections of the text, **not** to pages)*

This selective index does not include words from biblical quotations, and confines itself to those words and names which seem likely to be important for the general study of patristic theology.

Ἀαρών   1.4
ἀβούλευτος   10.2
ἀγένητος   8.3
ἅγιος   1.3(2), 4.8, 8.1, 9.1, 9.2, 9.3, 11.4, 12.5, 14.2, 14.3, 14.5(2), 14.6(2), 16.6, 17.2, 17.4, 18.7, 18.10(2)
Ἀδάμ   17.2, 17.4
ἀδελφός   1.4, 3.2, 4.8, 8.3, 9.1, 14.1, 15.3, 16.1, 17.2
ἀδύνατος   10.2
ἀθάνατος   8.3
αἵρεσις   tit., 8.4
αἴτιος   11.3
ἀκουστός   13.2
ἀκτίς   11.1
ἀλήθεια   3.1, 3.5, 4.1, 6.1, 8.1, 8.2, 8.3, 8.4(2), 11.3, 17.1, 17.3
ἀληθής   3.1
ἀληθινός   5.3
ἀληθῶς   1.7, 17.5
ἀλληγορεῖν   15.1, 15.2
ἀλλότριος   1.2(2)
ἄλογος   10.2
ἁμαρτία   17.2, 18.7
ἀνακεφαλαιοῦσθαι   12.3
ἀνάστασις   18.5

ἀνατρέπειν   3.5, 8.4
ἀνατροπή   4.1
ἀνεκδιήγητος   16.4
ἀνθρώπειος   17.2
ἀνθρώπινος   18.1
ἄνθρωπος
   (manhood)   3.1, 4.12, 5.4, 6.1, 8.1, 17.2, 17.4, 17.5(2), 18.10
   (mankind)   4.7, 4.12, 5.4, 12.1, 12.2, 13.2, 15.6, 16.3, 16.4, 17.2, 17.3
ἀνιστᾶν   1.7, 14.7, 18.5, 18.7
ἀόρατος   10.4(2)
ἀπεργάζεσθαι   4.8
ἄπιστος   17.1(2)
ἀποδείκνυσθαι   4.10, 8.2, 17.3
ἀπόδειξις   8.4
ἀποθνῄσκειν   1.2, 1.7(2)
ἀποκαλύπτειν   16.6, 16.7
Ἀποκάλυψις   15.2
ἀπόπνοια   11.4
ἀποστέλλειν   4.11, 7.7, 12.2, 13.2(2), 13.3, 13.4, 15.2, 17.3
ἀπόστολος   2.8, 4.6, 6.1, 17.1, 17.2
ἀποτελειν   14.4, 18.7
ἀρνεῖσθαι   1.4, 7.3, 14.6

150

ἀρχή	1.4, 4.3, 4.4, 4.12, 4.13(2), 15.2	δύο	7.1, 11.1, 14.2(3), 14.3, 16.6
ἀρχηγός	10.4	δωρεῖσθαι	9.2
ἄσαρκος	4.11, 15.7	δῶρον	4.10
ἄσοφος	10.2	ἐγείρειν	3.2, 4.6, 18.5, 18.8
ἄυπνος	18.1	εἰδέναι	1.7(3), 10.1
ἀφθαρσία	17.2	εἰκών	7.6(2)
ἀχώριστος	18.4	εἰς etc.	1.7, 2.3, 2.6, 2.7,
βούλεσθαι			2.8, 3.4, 4.8, 6.4,
(God)	9.3, 10.1, 14.7, 16.4		7.1(4), 7.3(3), 8.2(3),
(man)	1.5, 2.1, 3.1(2), 7.4,		8.3, 9.1, 11.3(4),
	8.2, 9.1(2)		14.2, 14.3, 14.4, 14.5,
βουλή			14.6, 15.7, 17.3
(divine)	5.4, 11.4	ἔκβλητος	1.3, 3.3
γενέσθαι		ἐκκλησία	1.4, 1.7, 18.10
(incarnation)	6.1, 8.1, 12.2(2),	ἐλέγχειν	1.6, 1.7, 3.1, 7.4
	15.6, 17.2, 17.4, 17.5,	ἔλεγχος	1.3
	18.5, 18.10	ἔμπειρος	16.4
γένεσις	16.4	ἐμφανής	2.6, 12.2(2), 12.4,
γεννᾶν			13.1
(God)	10.4(2), 16.2, 16.3,	ἐνανθρωπεῖν	4.7
	16.4, 16.6, 16.7	ἐνδείκνυσθαι	18.1
(man)	1.2, 3.2, 6.1, 16.3	ἐνθυμεῖσθαι	10.3
γέννησις	16.6, 16.7	ἐννοεῖσθαι	10.1
γῆ	4.11, 18.3, 18.7,	ἐνπολιτεύεσθαι	4.7
	18.8	ἔνσαρκος	12.5
γραφαί	2.4, 2.6, 3.1, 3.3(2),	ἐνσώματος	17.5
	4.2, 9.1, 9.2, 9.3,	ἐντέλλεσθαι	14.4
	14.1, 14.8	ἐξουσία	12.2, 18.7
Δανιήλ	4.13	ἐπίγειος	17.4
δεικνύειν		ἐπιγιγνώσκειν	7.5, 9.1, 9.2, 14.6(2)
(God)	2.6, 4.11, 7.5, 9.3,	ἐπίδειξις	8.2
	10.3(2), 11.2, 12.1,	ἐπιζητεῖν	16.5, 16.6
	12.2, 12.4, 14.4, 14.7	ἐργάτης	10.4
(man)	2.1, 3.5, 4.3, 4.6, 4.7,	ἔργον	16.4, 18.2
	6.3, 7.1, 8.3, 12.3,	ἔτερος	1.1(2), 1.3, 2.1, 2.5,
	15.1		2.6, 5.1, 8.1, 11.1(2),
δεξιά	1.7, 18.9		16.1
δημιουργεῖν	16.4	εὐαγγελικός	6.6
διάθεσις	7.3(2)	εὐαγγέλιον	6.5, 6.6, 14.1
διαμαρτυρεῖσθαι	17.1	εὔγνωστος	7.6
διδασκαλεῖον	1.8	εὐχαριστεῖν	14.6
διδασκαλία	1.1	ζητεῖν	4.10, 16.4, 18.6
διηγεῖσθαι	2.4, 3.1, 3.6, 4.1, 5.4,	ζωή	18.4(2), 18.5
	6.1, 15.3, 16.6	ἥλιος	11.1, 18.8
διήγησις	16.3, 16.6	Ἡσαίας	18.5
δόγμα	1.5, 2.1, 3.2, 7.4,	θάνατος	18.4
	9.1	θεῖος	9.2
δόξα	18.8, 18.10	θέλειν	
δοξάζειν	1.6, 9.2(2), 14.6,	(God)	8.3(3), 9.2(3), 10.1(3),
	14.7(2), 14.8		10.3(4), 11.3, 14.8,
δύναμις	4.11, 7.1, 7.3(2), 7.5,		16.4
	8.2(2), 11.1(2), 11.4,	(man)	4.2, 7.4, 7.6, 8.1,
	16.1		11.3

θέλημα 11.4, 13.4, 14.7
Θεόδοτος 3.1
Θεός 1.7, 2.3(4), 2.5, 2.6,
2.7, 2.8, 3.4, 4.5,
4.8, 4.10, 4.13, 5.4(2),
6.1(2), 6.4, 6.5,
8.1(3), 8.2(2), 8.3,
9.1(2), 9.3, 10.1, 10.3,
11.1, 11.2, 11.3, 13.2,
14.1, 14.2(4), 14.4,
14.5, 14.6, 14.7, 15.2,
15.3, 15.6, 16.4(2),
16.5, 16.6, 17.2, 17.5,
18.1(2), 18.3, 18.10
θεωρεῖν 12.5, 18.6
Ἰακώβ 5.2, 5.3
Ἰερεμίας 13.1
Ἰησοῦς 18.7
Ἰησοῦς Χριστός 13.4(2)
Ἰουδαῖοι 14.6
Ἰσραήλ 5.2, 5.3, 5.4
Ἰωάννης 5.5, 6.2, 12.3, 14.1,
15.1
(Baptist) 18.6
καθαρός 1.3
καθαρῶς 1.5
καινός 17.4
καιρός 10.3, 11.3, 16.7,
17.3
Κανά 18.7
κελεύειν 14.5
Κήρινθος 11.3
κῆρυξ 12.1
κηρύσσειν 2.6, 9.2, 13.1, 14.8,
17.4(2)
κλῆρος 1.3
κοινός 4.12, 15.6
Κορνήλιος 13.3
κοσμεῖν 10.3
κοσμήτωρ 18.8
κόσμος 7.3, 10.1(2), 10.4(3),
11.2, 16.5, 17.4, 17.5,
18.2
κρατεῖν 6.2, 6.4
κράτος 18.10
κρατύνεσθαι 7.4
κρίνειν 1.7, 18.3
κριτής 18.9
κτίζειν 10.1, 10.3, 10.4
κτίσις 10.4, 18.8
κυριεύεσθαι 18.4
κύριος 7.4, 7.5, 10.4
Λάζαρος 18.7
λόγια 9.1

λογικός 17.2
Λόγος 4.5, 4.7, 4.8, 4.10,
4.11(2), 4.13, 10.3(3),
10.4(2), 11.1, 12.1(2),
12.2(2), 12.3, 12.4,
12.5, 13.1, 13.2(3),
13.4, 14.1, 14.2,
14.4, 14.7, 15.1(2),
15.2, 15.3, 15.6,
15.7(4), 16.1(2),
16.2(2), 16.4, 16.7,
17.2, 17.3, 17.4
λόγος 8.2, 17.3
μαθητής 1.1, 7.2, 14.6, 14.7,
18.7, 18.9(2)
μακάριος 1.4, 1.6, 12.3, 14.1,
15.4, 15.5, 17.2
μανθάνειν 1.7, 7.1, 8.2, 16.5,
16.6
Μαρία 17.2
Μαρκίων 11.3
μαρτυρεῖν 2.7, 3.1, 4.6(2),
4.9, 4.13, 6.2(2),
8.1, 13.3, 14.1,
15.3, 18.6(2)
μαρτυρία 2.5, 16.1, 17.1
μέλλειν 4.12, 12.1, 15.6,
16.6, 16.7, 18.3
Μιχαίας 15.4
μονογενής 15.7
μονόκωλος 3.1
μόνος 2.5, 5.4(2), 10.1,
10.2, 10.4, 11.2,
13.2
μυστήριον 4.5, 4.7, 4.8, 6.1
Μωυσῆς 1.4
Ναζωραῖος 18.7
νοεῖν 3.1, 3.3(2), 4.2, 8.3,
12.5, 14.6, 16.4
Νοητιανοί 7.3
Νοητός tit., 1.1, 3.3(2), 6.6,
8.3, 8.4
νόμος 2.1, 11.4, 17.4
νοῦς
(divine) 7.3(2), 10.4, 11.2
(human) 3.5, 7.1, 7.3, 9.3
οἰκονομία 3.4, 4.5, 4.7, 4.8,
8.2, 14.1, 14.2, 14.4,
14.7, 16.3
ὁμολογεῖν 2.3, 2.7, 2.8, 6.5,
7.3, 7.4, 8.1, 11.3,
14.1
ὁμοφρονία 7.3

152

ὄνομα	4.12, 4.13, 15.6, 17.2		πιστός	17.1
ὄντως	3.5, 3.6, 4.8, 8.1, 14.6, 16.1		πλάσσειν	10.3
			πληθύς	11.3
ὁρατός	10.4(3), 13.2(2)		πνεῦμα	1.2(2), 1.3, 18.4, 18.8
Οὐαλεντῖνος	11.3		(divine)	4.11, 14.8, 16.2, 16.6(2), 18.9
οὐράνιος	17.4			
οὐρανός	4.10, 4.11(3), 4.13, 16.1, 17.2, 18.3		(Holy)	1.3, 4.8, 4.10, 8.1, 9.2, 11.4, 12.5,
οὐσία	7.3			14.2, 14.3, 14.5(2),
πάθος	2.7, 15.3, 18.2			14.6(2), 17.1, 17.4,
παῖς	5.2, 5.4, 7.3(2), 11.2			18.10
παλαιός	17.4		ποιεῖν	
πᾶν	10.2, 11.1(2), 11.3, 18.8		(God)	8.3, 10.1, 10.3(3), 10.4(2), 11.3, 14.8,
πανάγιος	17.1			16.5(2), 17.3, 18.7
πάντα			πολιτεύεσθαι	12.1, 18.6
(universe)	6.1, 6.2, 6.3, 6.4(5), 7.5, 8.1, 8.3, 10.2,		πολύς (God)	10.2
	10.3(2), 11.2, 11.3(2),		πρεσβύτεροι	1.4, 1.6, 1.7
	12.3, 14.5(3), 17.3,		προαίρεσις	9.3
	18.10		προβαίνειν	11.2
παντοκράτωρ	6.2(2), 8.1		προελθεῖν	17.5(2)
παραβάλλεσθαι	11.3		προιέναι	10.4
παράδοσις	17.2		προσκυνεῖν	12.5
παρθένος	4.8, 4.10, 17.2, 17.4(2)		προσφέρειν	4.10(2)
			πρόσωπον	7.1, 14.2, 14.3, 16.6, 17.1
πάσχειν	1.2, 1.7(2), 2.3(2), 2.7, 3.2, 15.4		προφήτης	4.6, 11.4, 12.3, 12.4, 15.3, 16.7, 17.4,
Πατήρ	1.2(2), 1.7, 2.3(3), 2.7, 3.2, 4.6(3),			18.5
	4.7(2), 4.10, 5.1,		σαρκοῦσθαι	4.7, 17.2, 17.4
	5.3, 5.4, 5.5, 6.2,		σάρκωσις	16.1
	6.4(2), 6.5, 6.6(2),		σάρξ	4.6, 4.10(2), 4.11,
	7.2, 7.3(3), 7.4(2),			15.3, 15.4, 15.6,
	7.5, 7.6(3), 7.7(2),			15.7, 16.6
	8.1(2), 9.2, 11.1,		σημαίνειν	4.6, 4.8, 7.7, 14.1,
	11.2, 11.4, 12.2(2),			16.7, 18.6
	12.5, 13.4, 14.3,		Σμυρναῖος	1.1
	14.4(2), 14.5(2),		σοφία	9.1, 10.3(2)
	14.6(2), 14.7(2),		σοφίζεσθαι (God)	10.3
	14.8(2), 16.1, 16.4,		σύμβολον	15.3
	16.6, 17.3(2), 18.4(2),		σύμβουλος	10.4
	18.5, 18.6(2), 18.9,		συμφωνία	14.4
	18.10(2)		συμφώνως	8.3
πατρῷος	4.5, 4.10, 11.4, 14.7, 16.1, 17.4		συνάγεσθαι	14.4
			συνετίζειν	14.5
Παῦλος	4.6, 6.3, 15.5		συνιστᾶν	1.8, 2.3, 3.1, 4.6, 8.4
Πέτρος	13.3		σύγχρονος	10.1(2)
πηγή	11.1		σύστασις	2.1, 15.7
πίπτειν	17.2		σώζειν	2.7, 10.4, 17.2
πιστεύειν	6.6, 7.3, 8.3, 9.2(2), 12.5, 13.2, 14.4,		σῶμα	7.3
	14.6, 16.4, 16.6(2),		σωτηρία	16.6, 17.3
	17.1, 17.2(2), 18.2		τελεῖν	10.1, 10.3, 17.1
			τέλειος	4.10, 5.3, 5.4, 15.7(3), 17.5

τελείως 14.7
τεχνάξεσθαι 10.3
τέχνη 16.4
τρία 8.1
τριάς 14.8
τριήμερος 18.5
τρίτος 1.7, 14.2, 14.3
τριχής (?) 8.2
τροπή 17.5
ὕδωρ 11.1
Υἱός 1.7, 3.2, 4.6(2),
4.7(3), 4.8, 4.10,
4.12, 7.3, 7.5, 7.6,
7.7, 8.1, 9.2, 12.5,
14.3, 14.4, 14.5(2),
14.6(3), 14.8, 15.1,
15.6(3), 15.7(2),
16.6
ὑπακούειν 14.5
ὑποστῆναι 15.7
φαίνεσθαι 6.4, 10.4, 12.1

φανεροῦν 14.8, 15.7, 16.6,
17.4, 17.5
φαντασία 17.5
φθέγγεσθαι
(God) 10.1, 10.3, 10.4, 12.1
Φίλιππος 7.4, 7.5
φιλοστοργία 15.6
φύσις 18.1
φωνή 6.6, 10.4
φῶς 10.4(2), 11.1(2)
χαρίζεσθαι 18.4
χάρις 14.2
Χριστός 1.2, 1.6, 1.7, 2.3(2),
2.7, 3.2, 6.2(4),
6.4, 6.5, 6.6, 7.5,
16.7
Χριστὸς Ἰησοῦς 4.5, 8.1
χωρεῖν 7.5, 18.8
χωρητός 4.12
ψιλός 3.1
ψυχή 17.2

INDEX OF MODERN AUTHORS
(The references are to pages)

Achelis, H.	17, 18n
d'Alès, A.	18
Bardenhewer, O.	18
Bardy, G.	23f, 119n
Batiffol, P.	2n, 3, 4n, 5n, 6
Botte, B.	27–29
Bovini, G.	8n
Bultmann, R.	119n, 120–122, 123n, 124n, 125n, 126n, 127n, 128n, 129n, 130n, 135n, 136n, 137n, 138–140
Bunsen, C.C.J.	13, 18
Cadiou, R.	28
Capelle, B.	26, 28f, 37
Capelle, W.	119n, 120n, 121, 122n, 125n, 126n, 128n, 136n, 137n, 139n
Caspari, C.P.	16
Colardeau, Th.	121, 124n, 130n
da Bra, G.	23
Daniélou, J.	24
Devreesse, R.	1n, 2n, 3, 5n, 6n
von Döllinger, I.	14
Draguet, R.	1n
Dräseke, J.	17, 18
Elfers, H.	28
Fabricius, J.A.	11–13, 16f, 19, 38f, 94
Ficker, G.	36, 39
Franchi de' Cavalieri, P.	3n
Gallandi, A.	12f
Hanssens, J.-M.	8n
von Harnack, A.	14–18, 19n
Heinrici, C.F.G.	120n
Hilgenfeld, A.	16
Hirzel, R.	121, 123n, 124n
Holtzmann, W.	2n
Kelly, J.N.D.	112n
de Lagarde, P.A.	13, 39
Lagrange, M.-J.	120n, 121, 124n, 126n, 138, 139n
Le Nain de Tillemont, L.S.	10f
Lietzmann, H.	2n, 3, 4n
Lightfoot, J.B.	16, 17n
Maas, P.	34f
Marrou, H.-I.	120n, 121, 123n, 124, 126n, 128n, 130n, 136n, 137n, 139n
Martin, Ch.	20f
Nautin, P.	1n, 3n, 6n, 9n, 10n, 12n, 21–31, 35n, 37, 39, 94, 96n
Norden, Ed.	118–121, 126n, 134, 141
Oggioni, G.	21n
Oltramare, A.	119n, 120n, 121, 123n, 124n, 126n, 136n
Puchulu, R.	10n, 31f, 37
Reynders, B.	39
Richard, M.	1n, 21n, 24f, 27, 29, 30f
de Riedmatten, H.	24
Rolffs, E.	17
Ropes, J.H.	119n, 120n, 121, 123n, 124n, 126n, 128n, 135n, 136n, 138n

Routh, M.J. 13
Saltet, L. 10n
Schwartz, E. 1n, 2–5, 6n, 19–21, 32, 110, 112
Sommervogel, C. 5n, 6n
Thiel, A. 9n, 10n
Thyen, H. 119–121, 122n, 123n, 124n, 125n, 126n, 127n, 128n, 130n, 135n, 136n, 137n, 138, 139n, 140

Torres, F. 5–7, 11–13, 19, 94
Turner, C.H. 111n
Volkmar, G. 14–18
Vossius, G. 6f, 11
Wendland, P. 120n
von Wilamowitz-Moellendorff, U. 121

175

THE CONCEPT OF SPIRIT
A Study of Pneuma in Hellenistic Judaism
and its Bearing on the New Testament
by Marie E. Isaacs

'This study deserves a warm welcome from several points of view. First it asks an interesting question, how the Church came to give so central a place to the doctrine of Spirit when the idea seems so marginal in the world from which the Church came. Then Dr Isaacs is familiar with the large literature on the subject, and gives us confidence in the solidity of her judgement: she sums up the views of many who have written before her, and criticises them convincingly. Her own arguments are well supported, and set out with clear sub-divisions and without the wordiness that so often makes for tedium. The result is an authoritative statement at a very reasonable price, which deserves to be widely used.'

Michael D. Goulder in
Scripture Bulletin

x, 186 pages $8.50 USA and Canada
£3.50 (£3.75 including postage)   (postage included)